WARTIME
LMS

L.G. Warburton

NOODLE N.B. BOOKS

WARTIME LMS

L.G. Warburton

© L G Warburton and Noodle Books 2012

ISBN 978-1-906419-95-0

First published in 2012 by Kevin Robertson
under the **NOODLE BOOKS** imprint
PO Box 279
Corhampton
SOUTHAMPTON
SO32 3ZX

www.noodlebooks.co.uk

Printed in England by Berforts Information Press Ltd., Oxford.

Front cover / Title Page - Preparations for Attack'. Gas Mask training at Blackpool in 1938.
Corbis Images HU048497

Frontispiece - A roof spotter keeps watch, courtesy "The LMS at War", G. C. Nash.

CONTENTS

INTRODUCTION

World War Two and The LMS Management

The Second World War was declared on 3rd September 1939 when Britain declared war against Germany. The war in Europe was concluded on the 8th May 1945 following the surrender of all German troops the previous day. On 10th August, following the dropping of atomic bombs on Hiroshima and Nagasaki, the Japanese expressed their willingness to surrender, and on 14th August it was announced that Japan had surrendered. This then is an attempt to consider the implications of the war as far as the LMS Railway was concerned, and whilst it would be possible to detail every instance of bomb damage, stoppages, special trains, problems caused by weather etc together with a great many statistics, the result would not be very readable. Therefore before the story begins we need to consider how the LMS Railway was managed.

The 1921 Railways Act that formulated the LMS called for 27 directors, the first Chairman being Sir Guy Granet, ex Midland Railway, the Secretary was Sir Arthur Watson of the LYR. Watson was soon to retire, being replaced by H. G. Burgess. In 1926 Josiah Stamp was brought in as President, and in 1927 four Vice Presidents were appointed each being responsible for certain of the Company's activities, at which time Burgess retired. At the end of 1927 the Chairman, Guy Granet retired and Josiah Stamp became the new Chairman as well as President. Vice President Robert Reid died in 1929 when the number of Vice presidents was reduced to three. This is how things remained until the night of 16th April 1941 when Sir Josiah Stamp was killed, aged 60, together with his wife Olive Jessie and his son Wilfred Carlyle Stamp when their home in Beckenham (Kent) received a direct hit. Also killed earlier in an air raid was Director William Lionel Hitchens who died on 14th October 1940 in Church House Westminster. On Lord Stamp's death, Sir Thomas Royden, Bart. took over the chair until he retired in 1946 when Sir Robert Burrows became Chairman until Nationalisation on 1st January 1948.

So what was the LMS Railway all about? The principle function of a railway company is the movement of passengers and freight and to do this, in 1939, the LMS had 19,000 miles of track and 250,000 staff, 7,500 engines and 303,000 items of rolling stock. It carried 434,000,000 passengers representing 7,500,000,000 miles of travel, and 125,000,000 tons of freight representing 6,750,000,000 ton miles. The Company owned 25 docks, harbours and piers, 66 steamships, 4,000 motor vehicles and 3,000 trailers, 8,000 horses, 28 hotels, 25,000 dwelling houses, aeroplanes and 535 miles of canals, all of which came under Government control on September 1st 1939. Of interest is that the Operating Department of the LMS Railway had more personnel than the peacetime Royal Navy. Whilst the railway companies constantly sought to encourage people to travel, the declaration of war led to its discouragement.

L.G. Warburton. Summer 2012.

1

THE PRE-WAR SITUATION ON THE LMS RAILWAY

There can be no better means of describing the LMS pre-war situation than that written by the Chief Operating Manager, T. W. Royle in his Wartime Report (TNA Rail 418/197) that is reproduced here in full.

The year 1923 witnessed the amalgamation of the railways of Great Britain into four Group Companies, and on the LMS there ensued years of arduous work in the standardisation of the organisation, procedure, and equipment, and the welding of the concern into a corporate whole. This task having been completed, there followed a decade of rationalisation and modernisation, during the course of which, by means of close study and analysis on scientific lines of all methods and practices, the efficiency of the railway increased almost beyond measure, all forms of waste, be it of effort or material being eliminated. During the process of rationalisation and modernisation, obsolete and inefficient types of apparatus and equipment were superseded by the most modern and sometimes novel types of mechanised appliances, and were reduced in quantity to economic levels, so that whilst the units may have been reduced in number, their total capacity and efficiency was greater.

There is no better illustration of this than the reduction effected in the locomotive stock that, at the close of 1929, consisted of 9,797 steam locomotives, which by the outbreak of the war had been reduced by 2,243 or 23%. The number of different types had been reduced from 267 to 148, or by nearly half, in the same period. Whilst in the matter of progress it can never be said that finality had been reached, and many other developments were envisaged, the Operating Department was at no time more efficient than when war broke out.

The LMS was planned for the conveyance of passengers and freight under peacetime conditions, and although it possessed a sufficient margin of reserve for any demands likely to be made upon it under normal circumstances, it would have been guilty of carrying surplus assets had this reserve been greater than that justified by the tasks it was required to perform. No investment policy had been embarked upon by the Government in the way of equipping the railways, whether in track, locomotives, or rolling stock, to meet wartime conditions, as was done in other directions, e.g. the erection of shadow factories for the production of aeroplanes

Thomas Wright Royle MBE, M. Inst. T entered the service of the LYR in August 1898 in the Trains Section of the Passenger Superintendent's Office, being transferred to the personal staff of the Passenger Superintendent in 1900 where he remained until October 1914 when he was appointed Confidential Assistant to the then Superintendent of the Line (Arthur Watson), in connection with the work of the Railway Executive Committee in London. In February 1919 he was appointed Assistant Superintendent of the Line and on the amalgamation of the LYR with the LNWR on 1st January 1922, Assistant Divisional Superintendent (Northern Division) on £2000 pa, and in 1923 Assistant General Superintendent (Western Division) on £2500 pa. In the 1924 re-organisation he became Divisional Superintendent, Manchester on the same salary before eventually succeeding C. R. Byrom as Chief Operating Manager on 1st June 1938 with a salary of £4000 pa that rose to £4500. On 1st September 1944, after six years as Chief Operating Manager, Mr. Royle was appointed an LMS Vice President on £6000pa later increased to 7000, being succeeded by S. H. Fisher. He was a prodigious worker and a great leader who by his example and powerful personality inspired his staff to great achievements in the face of every difficulty. He received his MBE for services rendered during the 1914/18 Great War. On Nationalisation in January 1948 he became Chief Regional Officer London Midland Region, retiring on 30th September 1948.

Photo. TNA Rail 1156/22

and the railways were under no obligation to do so, being in this respect no different from any other business concern in the country. That the railways were not lacking in foresight is evident from the warnings given in many ways before the war, one such being by Lord Stamp at the LMS Annual General Meeting in February 1937, when he said - "Now a stiff price can properly be paid for war preparation in time of peace. But that price ought to be paid by the right people"----- "It is clear to me that the framework of the country's transport must be formed by the railways, if economy and efficiency are the tests, and to me it is also clear that this is of even greater importance in times of war than in times of peace. A policy of sapping the railways in times of peace, whether by legislative or administrative action, will be to the Nation's detriment in times of war".

The amount of work done during the war broke records in all directions, but when additional equipment was needed, difficulty was experienced in obtaining what was required owing to the demands on the available manpower and materials for the manufacture of munitions. The principal function of a railway is the movement of passengers and goods, all other interests being ancillary. Nothing can be moved without motive power, yet the LMS Railway was not even able to maintain normal replacements of its locomotives, let alone expand the stock, owing to the pre-occupation of its workshops with munitions at the request of the Government. The situation was aggravated by the heavy calls made upon it for locomotive power for overseas and at Government establishments, the Service Departments having made no provision to meet their own needs until the war was well advanced. Similar conditions applied to a greater or lesser degree to other types of equipment, and the position arose that the Operating Department had to perform a greater task than in peacetime with fewer tools, having previously brought the number down to economic levels; in other words, the department had to live on its fat after having already "reduced".

The Railways vis-à-vis Industry.

To view the Railways in their right perspective it is necessary to compare in peace and war vis-à-vis industry under like conditions. In peace time the railways always worked a 24 hour day, whereas industry, on average, only used its resources 50% of the time, but in the worst months of winter it was necessary for the railways to work a seven-day week to carry the industrial output of a single shift working a five-and-a-half day week. To put the matter another way, under adverse conditions in winter the railway had to go full out to cope with peacetime output. The war brought a black-out, that, together with air raid warnings and damage caused by enemy action, seriously slowed down the operations of the railways; the effect of these conditions on the scheduled workings upon which railway operation depends is explained in subsequent chapters, but let it be said here that they reduced the capacity of the railways to a material degree.

Large numbers of additional private siding connections to works and factories were laid in during the war. Of a total of 1,185 additional sidings, 542 were on the LMS that required extra staff/locos/wagons but most remained after the war gifting a lot of facilities the LMS would not have afforded in peacetime. On the other hand, industry had plenty of slack to take up, three shift (24-hour) working and Sunday duty were introduced on a considerable scale, and vast new factories for the manufacture of munitions of war of various kinds were erected and brought into production. In fact, the whole production capacity of the nation was eventually mobilised for war purposes. So a greatly intensified industrial manufacturing machine was producing twenty-four hours of the day, seven days a week, whereas the railway machine, with reduced resources, was, through no fault of its own, considerably slowed down.

Planning of operation

All well-ordered industrial concerns compile long-range programmes of their requirements of men, materials, and machines based upon known and probable commitments, and the railways were no exception to this rule. In peace-time, planning by the railways to meet anticipated traffic requirements reached a high degree of precision as passengers and goods moved in well defined flows, and variations in volume according to the season could be forecast within reasonable limits, and the disposition and complement of men and rolling stock was gauged with comparative accuracy. Nevertheless, preparations had to be made well in advance for the construction of locomotives, wagons and carriages of suitable types, for other classes of equipment, and for the recruitment and training of men.

During the period of the most rapid expansion of war industry, the railways laboured under the serious handicap of lack of information as to the requirements of the Government departments for transport and the needs of the production programmes. The large production departments, i.e. The Ministry of Supply, the Ministry of Aircraft Production, and Admiralty Establishments, were working independently, their requirements were frequently in direct conflict and wasteful from a railway point of view, and no information was forthcoming as to the output to be expected from the factories, the mines, and the Government Depots of various kinds. The last thing which seemed to be thought of was prior advice to the railways of what should be expected of them so that the necessary provision could be made, and the attitude seemed to be – if indeed thought were given to the matter – that the railways had unlimited resources, and would have available in the right places and at the right times all the equipment in the way of lifting machinery, wagons, locomotives, and other appliances – even though they be of special types to move any class of goods in any quantity, of any size, to any destination at almost a moments notice, and with the right to require prompt delivery regardless of the ability of the consignee to accept. It might be regarded as flattering to the railways that such confidence should be placed in their aptitude to meet any circumstances that might arise, but these were far from ordinary times, and the rapidly increasing output, and the shape and size of articles to be conveyed, e.g. tanks and aircraft in cases, could not be encompassed by the peace-time resources of the railways.

Only slowly did the transport implications gain ground, and realisation dawn of the necessity for the aggregation and co-ordination of transport requirements, but at no stage were forecasts of the probable requirements of the Fighting Services and Government Departments, of the volume of imports or the output of industry generally, sufficiently reliable to materially assist the railways. The operating machine is a sensitive instrument, the movement of train crews, locomotives, carriages and wagons being scientifically planned and dovetailed to secure the most efficient user, the ideal being to pre-determine and schedule the highest possible percentage of the workings of men. and machines. The scheduled movements usually cover about 95% of the work in peace-time, but these pre-arrangements are only practicable by reason of prior knowledge of the task to be performed. There is always the unknown and unexpected, representing the remaining 5%, and this is catered for under the Control organisation. The conditions described, together with the necessity for affording priorities, reduced the amount of work that could be planned well ahead and increased the percentage that needed specialised treatment, circumstances that were accentuated under the stress of enemy air activity and bad weather. There were also other features which will be mentioned briefly, which contributed to the disturbance of peacetime standards.

The Lancashire town of Blackpool receives its first evacuees, from St. James School, Stafford, in September 1939.
Hulton Getty Archive 81001033

Altered war-time traffic.

At the outbreak of the war, the Government decided upon a policy of decentralisation, and munitions factories, warehouses, and storage grounds were spread in widely separated parts of the country. Concurrently, the war demanded an immense increase in the fighting forces, and camps and airfields were established in far-flung and often remote districts. Immediately war broke out there was a transfer of shipping from the East to the West coast ports, and following the German occupation of Norway, the Low Countries and France, nearly all the shipping was dealt with on the west side of Britain, and the cutting off of supplies from Europe involved imports on an enormous scale from the American Continent.

The convoy system involved surges of traffic into the ports that had to be cleared with the utmost expedition to reduce the turn around time of ships, which were so vital to the war effort. Much of the coastwise traffic was discontinued, thus further increasing the burden on the railways. Road services for the transportation of passengers and freight were severely curtailed and the traffic diverted to rail - a process that was accentuated when the need for the conservation of petrol and

rubber became more pronounced in 1942, in which year motoring other than for authorised business purposes was discontinued. To a considerable extent, movements of Services personnel and equipment were required to be made at short notice and in directions differing so vastly from peace-time travel, that, for the most part, they precluded the possibility of balancing the workings.

In the 1914-1918 war the major portion of the fighting forces was on the Continent and in other theatres of war, and in the early days it was expected that a similar state of affairs would prevail in this latest war. It could never have been anticipated that our armies would be driven out of France and that Britain was destined to become the equivalent of a fortress manned by vast armies, and later a bastion for striking at the enemy, at the same time filling the roll of an arsenal. During this time the population of Britain which had to be fed and maintained, must have greatly exceeded anything known in the past, a large part of it, both forces and workers, were located in unaccustomed places, involving an exceptional amount of internal distribution and travel. These variations in character, quantity and flows of traffic, both passenger and freight, represented a revolutionary change-

Euston during 'rat week', 7 November 1939. The LMS had instigated an intensive campaign in the vicinity of the station. The terrier was a crucial part of the 'armoury' although one may wonder how it coped with the electrified lines.

Hulton Getty Archive 81002502

over from peace-time conditions resulting in traffic passing by routes for which they were not designed, and greatly increased the intensity of movement over many sections of the railway.

The operating grades were skilled men and needed considerable training and experience to carry out their work satisfactorily, but the war-time task of the railway had to be performed with a labour force seriously depleted by the calls of the services, that involved the introduction of a large number of inexperienced male and female staff, many of whom did not possess the physical attributes demanded by certain types of work. These, and other phases are referred to later but are mentioned here to give an appreciation of the situation experienced by the various departments. Summing up, in every section of the transport system the war added to the burden, and reduced the means by which it could be borne.

Government Control.

In ordinary times there are always large numbers of people who, by their actions, give the impression that they are more conversant with the way in which a railway should be run than those who have made a life long study. Government Control added to the numbers of those who probably felt some responsibility for the management of the railways, and subjected them to the idiosyncrasies of 615 Members of Parliament and an array of would-be Managers in the guise of the Civil Servants. Whilst such questioning arose over everyday business that could be better left to the railways to perform in their own way, the greatest difficulty was experienced in obtaining essential materials, and in securing action on matters affecting the public or trades that needed a Government pronouncement or regulation for their enforcement. Delays of a year or more were not uncommon when a month should have sufficed to bring about a reform required by the railways to enable them to do their wartime job. In the meantime the railways were between two fires, e.g. on the one hand they were criticised for happenings for which they knew, and wished to apply the remedy, and on the other hand, encountered a bureaucratic tardiness that frequently placed them in a most invidious position. A railway is not in the happy position of a business concern, that, when its orders for all the work it can undertake, may refuse to accept further work. It is expected to convey any number of passengers who present themselves, or any quantity of goods offered, at any place or time, and disappointment is expressed should there be any hitch in the process.

In common with other forms of Government policy during the war, far too much reliance was placed upon appeals for a particular course of action or line of conduct, which left the decision to the individual and the way open to the complacent to gain an unfair advantage. It is admitted that the United Nations were fighting dictatorships, and anything in the nature of dictatorial action might be regarded as inconsistent, but democracy does not preclude strong leadership. The temper of the nation generally, especially as the war progressed was in favour of firm direction and a strong lead by the Government on anything that would contribute to the successful prosecution of the war, and the task of the railways would have been easier had more resolute and speedy action been taken on the recommendation of the Railway Companies.

Consistency of policy in Ministerial circles was not helped by the frequency with which the office of Minister of Transport was changed. In the first stages of the war this office maintained its pre-war reputation for brief occupancy, and no sooner had a Minister gained some familiarity with railway problems than he was moved to other fields. In April 1939, Dr. Leslie Burgin, the Minister during much of the period of preparation for war, vacated the post and was succeeded by Captain Euan Wallace, who occupied it for thirteen months. During the next twelve months, two other Ministers, viz., Sir John Reith (five months), and Lt. Col. J. T. C. Moore-Brabazon (seven months), had come and gone. On 9th May, 1941, the Ministries of Shipping (only created on the outbreak of war) and Transport were amalgamated and by their fusion the Ministry of War Transport was borne, the first Minister being The Lord Leathers. It may be said that the needs of the War demanded sterner action, but in any event the new Ministry achieved more success than its predecessors as it relied less on exhortation and more on action to secure the desired ends. It later transpired from documents coming out of Germany that problems very similar to our own, such as regulation of passenger travel, overcrowding of trains, prompt loading and release of railway wagons, shortage of locomotives and of labour and the like were also encountered, but indications are that they were dealt with in a more forcible manner.

The part played by the railways.

The most successful nation is the one with the most efficient form of transportation, and this is particularly so in the case of a nation at war. Great Generals, from Julius Caesar down to the present day, realised that transport was the key to war, with the Boer war being an excellent example.. In this war, when so much depended upon the production of weapons, the British railway system may be regarded as having been in the front line. A modern army requires a vast amount of equipment, and when the war began, 600 men had the firepower of 20,000 in the 1914-1918 war.

Transport played a vital role in every phase of the war, and on occasions was referred to as the "Fourth Arm". It carried raw materials from the ports or mines to the factories, as well as the workers and conveyed component parts from one place to another for assembly into complete weapons and it delivered the finished arms to the storage grounds, or to the men who required to use them. It transported the men and their equipment during training; it carried them to the ports for shipment to the theatres or war and subsequently supported them by regular supplies of food, clothing, and the variety of stores and equipment needed for their maintenance and to enable them to defeat the enemy. At the same time it was the means by which the foodstuffs and commodities necessary to maintain the life of the nation were distributed.

The railways were the blood stream of the nation, and, as in the case of the human body, anything that restricts circulation results in the general loss of vigour, as any failure of rail transport could have crippled the war effort. However the railways did not fail, they brought vast powers of resourcefulness, enterprise and resiliency to bear upon the problems that confronted them, and despite tremendous odds, achieved a success, the measure of which, so far as the LMS Railway is concerned, will be gleaned from the pages that follow. All the railways collaborated and co-operated to the maximum extent in the performance of this huge task, but the LMS Railway, by reason of its geographical position, was called upon to bear the heaviest burden. The war brought a moving picture of events and problems in rapid succession, dominated at times by the military situation and aerial activity, but with an ever present background of the necessity of moving men, war materials and munitions essential to the prosecution of the war and the supplies necessary for the maintenance of the life of the nation. Most of the problems were capable of solution and the remedy applied, but others, such as the shortage of engine power, excessive passenger travel, the existence of bottle necks – to name but a few – were like a malady which reached a crisis from time to time and could not be completely cured, the best that could be done in these cases was to apply a palliative. In a record of this description it is impossible to deal with matters strictly in chronological order, so it has been necessary to compromise in this respect, but the war could be broken down into clearly

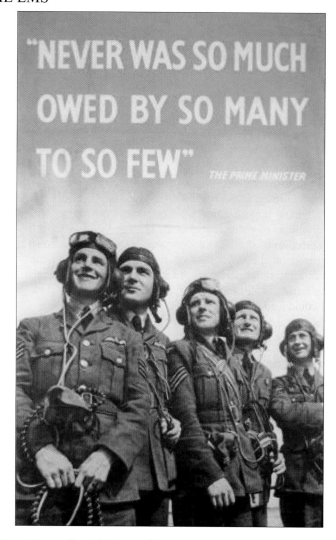

defined portions as follows:-

September 1939 to summer 1940.- a period of preparation during which record traffics were worked under conditions free from enemy air activity, including the evacuation of children and terminating with the evacuation of the British Forces from France.

From the summer of 1940 to summer 1941 – a period embracing the intensification of defensive measures, the Battle of Britain, and widespread and devastating enemy air attacks that involved severe dislocation of railway operating.

From the summer of 1941 to September 1942 – an interval when there was comparatively little enemy air activity, and the output of munitions was rising to the peak in preparation for the time when the great forces assembled in the country could strike back at the enemy.

From September 1942 to spring 1944 - when there was again reduced enemy air activity but a tremendous build up of forces following the American entry into the war with the massive movement of these forces to the south of England in preparation for "D" Day.

From the spring of 1944 to the end of 1945 – a period when enemy air attacks resumed with flying bombs and rockets replacing attacks by conventional aircraft. The "D" Day landings took place in June 1944, and following victory, the return of troops/ prisoners etc.

Each phase of the work of the complex machine that constituted the Operating Department - the movement of troops and stores, the working of passenger and freight trains, goods terminals and cartage operations – and whilst each is independent, all are so inter-dependent that they form an indivisible entity.

2

PRE-WAR PREPARATIONS BY THE CIVIL ENGINEER'S DEPARTMENT

The amalgamation of the railways in 1923 presented the railway Civil Engineers with two major problems; the need to create a uniform organisation and the establishment of a uniform standard of maintenance. The former provided obvious opportunities economically, not only with the abolition of redundant and duplicated staff, but also by the selection of the most economical methods of administration based on the experience of the constituent Companies. A uniform standard of maintenance was required to raise the general standard to that of the best-maintained railway that would lead to decreased expenditure.

By the end of the nineteen twenties the re-organisation had been largely completed and good progress had been made in achieving a uniform standard of maintenance, particularly with regard to permanent way. In 1923 the mileage of track

renewed was 345 at a cost of £3,555 per mile. In 1930 555 miles were renewed at a cost of £2,548. The cost of permanent way maintenance for the same period fell from £548 per route mile to £437 and the total expenditure on permanent way and structures from £1,295 per route mile to £1,038.

Further economical progress continued right up to the war, but the financial depression of the nineteen thirties did not help. The first calls for reduction in expenditure were minimal and largely absorbed in the continuous process of improving the methods of working and the organisation. However, as the financial situation worsened, the 'cuts' became more and more drastic and the problem was not how to maintain and improve the railway, but to decide what work could be temporarily left undone without serious consequences.

At this time the position was further complicated by the demand for high-speed running on main lines that could be met only by a large scale improvement in curves and a very high standard of maintenance on the running lines. The weight of locomotives had also increased that necessitated the renewal and strengthening of over bridges, thus preventing any reduction in expenditure in that direction. This being the case track improvement was maintained throughout the worst periods of the depression and, in the years preceding the war, the amount of complete relaying of the running lines was the highest on record, achieving a total of 672 miles in 1938.

The downside of this was that the Civil Engineer's responsibility for the maintenance of stations, goods sheds, warehouses, and engine and carriage sheds were neglected as most of which were old, obsolete in design and requiring constant attention. Summing up, the general position before the outbreak of war was that the track was in a better position than ever before but structures were in general in a much less satisfactory state.

Before going further it is timely to consider how the Chief Engineer's Civil Department was organised prior to WW2, as these were the staff that formulated the wartime policy and then had to implement it. The original organisation had been in place for some twelve years before the Board Meeting, on 18th April 1935, minute 3208, decided to re-organise the department that consisted of seventeen English Districts and five in Scotland, all coming directly under the Chief

Engineer and his assistant with no Divisional Engineers. There were five supporting disciplines, New Works, Permanent Way, General Assistants, Staffing Assistants and an Architects Department each having support staff, all of which also came directly under the Chief Engineer and his Assistant. The new arrangements came into being on 1st August 1935. The Chief Engineer was W. K. Wallace .

District Engineer, Crewe, moving on to Manchester in 1921. On the 15th January 1929 he became Divisional Engineer, Derby, his salary being £2000pa. On 1st August 1935 he was appointed Assistant Engineer (Permanent Way) St. Pancras on £2500 and on 1st January 1942 Assistant Engineer Watford (HQ), on £2750, retiring on 31st October 1945. On 1st November 1945, James Briggs was appointed as his replacement, also on £2750pa, by which time the war was over.

Photo – Railway Gazette.

The wartime activity of the Civil Department was written by F. E. W. Cox

Chief Engineer William Kelly Wallace MICE was born in Ulster in 1883 and commenced his railway career on the Belfast & Northern Counties Committee in 1900 as a pupil of B. D. Wise. In 1922 he was appointed Engineer and Locomotive Superintendent of the NCC. Whilst in that position he was responsible for the new coaches for the narrow gauge boat express and also for the operation and maintenance of the NCC fleet of motor omnibuses. In 1930 he was appointed LMS Chief Stores Superintendent before being appointed LMS Chief Civil Engineer, his salary being £3250, succeeding Alexander Newlands. By 1945 his salary was £5500. Wallace was a great innovator, initiating the use of flat-bottomed rails. W. Wood (the President) held him in high esteem as he could be depended on in any circumstance. He retired in 1st September 1948 He was President of the Institution of Civil Engineers in 1955 and died in May 1969. His Assistant throughout the war was Edward Henry d'Esterre Darby who commenced his railway career on the LNWR as a pupil of the Civil Engineer. In1905 he was Resident Engineer, Garston Docks before being appointed Assistant District Engineer Walsall in 1910. In 1920 he was

Francis Edgar Wildsmith Cox, the author of the report, "History of Civil Engineer's Department during the War of 1939-1945" upon which part of this book was based. He was born at Hendon on 2nd August 1887 and entered the service of the Great Northern Railway in 1903 as a pupil of Alexander Ross, the Chief Engineer. He became Assistant to the Resident Engineer on the construction of part of the Great Northern, Piccadilly and Brompton Railway in 1905. In 1907 he entered the Engineer's Department of the LNWR at Euston. In 1915 he was Assistant to the District Engineer at Manchester and was later transferred in a similar capacity to the Crewe District. In November 1927 he was appointed Indoor Assistant to the Chief Engineer, Euston, his salary being £700pa later increased to £1000. On 1st August 1935, when the Engineer's Department was re-organised, he was appointed General Assistant to the Chief Engineer, on £1350pa increasing to £1600 by the time he retired on 31st December 1947.

Photo TNA Rail1156/21

THE PRE-WAR SITUATION ON THE LMS RAILWAY

Preparation for war began in 1937 and proceeded continuously but erratically for almost three years before war was actually declared. The tempo rose and fell depending on the fluctuation of the political international situation. In July 1938 the LMS Railway set up a Standing Committee with the objective "to establish a full measure of inter-departmental co-ordination in connection with the arrangements generally, and to provide a focal point to the Management in the regulation of work to be done and the expenditure involved". The Committee was formed to obtain decisions and not to avoid or defer them and sat at frequent intervals, sometimes daily.

The development of the aeroplane as a war weapon was the dominant factor on the maintenance of the railway as experienced in the Spanish Civil War. Bombing of the railway was expected and the main problem was to foresee the extent and effect such bombing would have in order to devise means by which railway communications and services could be afforded a measure of protection with speedy repair following damage. Would the attacks be concentrated on particular targets or dispersed over a wide area? Would they be by day or night, or both? Would traffic be disrupted over whole areas of railway or confined to individual, points? What resistance would railway-engineering structures offer to high-explosive bombs? Would the situation be affected by the use of poison gas? Clearly these were questions to which there were no answers. The only experience in this field was the experiments in high explosive blast and the experience of such bombing in Spain that would bear little resemblance to the might and strength of the German Air Force. The simple fact was that there was no real experience to fall back on and that the Civil Engineers were 'groping in the dark'

This extract, dated May 1938, was an attempt to consider the situation as to which bridges would be the target of an air attack- " It would appear that, assuming the air attack is coming from the south east, the railway routes the air attack will follow are much more likely to be the LMS than the GWR, with the possible exception of an attack in the Birmingham-Wolverhampton area assuming their objectives (apart from London) are large industrial centres such as Coventry, Sheffield, Liverpool, Manchester, Nottingham and Leeds". "Even if this was the case, the bulk of the explosives would surely be dropped as near to those centres as possible, and not just indiscriminately along the railways leading to such places. Presumably also, these large centres will be sufficiently protected to cause direct hits on bridges to be a matter of improbability rather than a certainty…. Excluding the Metropolis for the moment, it would appear that attacks directly aimed at the above industrial centres, would not follow or cross any of the main lines of the LMS south of Rugby or Kettering, and I incline to the opinion that damage south of these points, apart from the Metropolitan area, could be deemed negligible".

The difficulty in dealing with the problem can be seen with the number of assumptions in the above extract.

The provision of air raid shelters for staff was also a difficult question as should shelter be provided for all staff, or only those expected to remain in the vicinity of their work during raids? Should all areas of the country be treated on the same basis, or preference given to those areas more likely to be bombed? If shelters were provided for "essential" staff at a railway centre, how could it in practice be reserved for them? A comment in an ARP (Air Raid Precautions) stated – "At those points where we provide for the essential staff it is difficult to see how other personnel there can be prevented from endeavouring to use the shelter provided for the essential staff, which will not accommodate both parties of men".

It was decided that the railways must provide for –

1. Bombing by day and night.
2. Intensive attacks on large industrial areas, and on key positions on the railway such as junctions, traffic marshalling yards and bridges on important routes both inside and outside of industrial centres.
3. The cutting of railway communications to such an extent as to render the peacetime organisation inoperative and throw increased responsibilities on the Districts until communications were restored.
4. The possibility that large numbers of the staff would not be able to reach their work for long periods, so that essential work would have to be carried out by a limited number of "key" men for whom special shelter protective arrangements would be required.
5. The cessation of work during air raids by staff not immediately concerned with the operation of traffic.
6. The provision of adequate shelter for the staff in close proximity to their work, and of special protection for those who would be expected to continue their work during air raids.
7. An organisation to deal with the difficulties involved in carrying out repair work under conditions outlined above, complicated by the lighting restrictions and the possible use of poison gas by the enemy.

Initially only exploratory work was done by the Engineer's Department in 1937 as war seemed only a remote possibility at that time. The main concern being how to cope with air raids and the measures required to repair the consequent damage, also lighting restrictions. Selected personnel were trained in anti gas precautions but it was not until 1938 that schemes were definitely formulated for emergency organisation and the protection of staff and equipment. A sample scheme was prepared for the London District that was then circulated to all Districts dealing with air raid organisation, warning systems, lighting restrictions, protection of personnel, instructions to employees, protective clothing. de-contamination squads, rescue parties and gas detection.

The organisation provided for a Controlling Authority for the whole twenty-four hours. In normal working hours this was the District Engineer with his Chief Clerk as Deputy. Outside normal hours the authority was to be the District Engineer with a Works Sub-Inspector and a Permanent way Sub-Inspector as deputies for alternate weeks. Under the Controlling Authority, and a telephone call away were the "key" men, the Permanent Way and Works Inspectors and Foremen, whose duty was to get in touch with Gangers and charge-man over the District. Decontamination squads were formed, drawn from permanent way staff. Extra gangs, and eight squads were provided for the London District, each consisting of six men and a leader. These men were trained and equipped for gas decontamination work and were "on call". Six rescue squads of nine men each were formed from the Artisan staff with a competent charge-men and equipped to rescue staff in bombed buildings and structures.

In addition to the above it was necessary to plan for large-scale damage. From this it was realised that stocks of specialised material and equipment must be stored at convenient centres at which emergency gangs could be formed so that both materials and labour could be consigned to repair the damage. The obvious concern was the repair of permanent way and the replacement or repair of bridges. As far as permanent way was concerned it was decided that each Company should prepare a list of additional material (except ballast) and its value required to provide a reserve based on three months of its normal requirements. In addition, to cover the repair of bridges, a reserve of timber baulks (that could also be used for other purposes such as the shoring of buildings) steel joists etc. The value of the LMS reserves amounted to £119,000 made up of Permanent way £72,000, Timber £18,000 and steel joists and sundries £29,000. In addition reserves of plant such as cranes, welding and burning plant was provided. The permanent way material amounted to 22 miles of plain track, 130 sets of points, 130 sets of crossings with the required points and crossing timbers.

During 1938 ten centres were selected as focal points and the organisation of the emergency gangs determined. In each case an existing District Depot was utilised. These were:-

Cricklewood	To cover the London district and the southern part of Watford District..
Northampton	To cover the Northampton District, the northern part of Watford District and Birmingham
Nottingham	To cover the Derby South and North Districts
Crewe	To cover the Crewe District, Walsall District north of Birmingham, Stoke District, North Wales District, and a small part of the Manchester District.
Liverpool (Edge Hill)	To cover the Liverpool District, part of Blackburn District and part of the Lancaster District.
Manchester (Newton Heath)	To cover the main part of Manchester District, part of the Blackburn District, part of the Lancaster District, part of the Bradford District and the whole of the Barrow District.
Greetland (near Halifax)	To cover part of the Bradford District and the whole of the Leeds District.
Newton	To cover Glasgow District and part of the South Western District.
Carstairs	To cover the whole of the South Eastern District and part of the South Western District.
Perth	To cover the Northern and Highland Districts.

This and opposite page - *Gas exercise at Drumclog, Ayrshire, c1941. Engine No. 14330 has been deliberately derailed with the breakdown crew in the unenviable task of restoring it to the rails in full respirator gear. The fortunate ones are those detailed to watch the performance of their colleagues - the image of the crane driver probably sums it up best.*

The crane is from Motherwell of 50ton capacity and was built by Cowans-Sheldon of Carlisle in 1931 as a 36 ton crane, being strengthened in 1938. The crane was withdrawn c1987 and is owned by the Great Western Society at Didcot. Caledonian Railway Dunalastair II Locomotive 14330 was withdrawn in February 1941 but continued as a stationary boiler at Greenhill Creosote Works for nearly four years before being cut up at St. Rollox in November/December 1946. The ex Caledonian line to Drumclog was closed on 11th September 1939.

The views are from the camera of S C Townroe, a Southern man, but who had been seconded several hundred miles from his normal abode. Notice in the lower view the crane is literally dragging the casualty backwards. Mr Townroe was also fortunate in being to source film at that time, was this because it was a semi-official visit? Knowledge so gained able to be shared on the Southern.

S C Townroe / R Blencowe collection.

To give the reader an idea of the amount of planning and preparation that was made to deal with what was conceived to be the wholesale destruction of the railway, the arrangements at the Cricklewood Emergency Centre was as shown under the next heading. Needless to say the arrangements for these emergency Depots and the equipment held, were revised with experience gained, such as provision for the repair of railway over-bridges. The Board meeting held on 24th October 1940, minute 4170, approved the "establishment of special repair department recruited from all districts for restoration of railway property damaged by enemy bombing". In 1940 a pocket size pamphlet was issued in which the full emergency organisation was set out enabling those responsible to have all the required information to hand at any time by day or night. This was amplified in 1942 with a supplement based on experience gained, with both issues kept up to date as alterations took place.

The LMS Arrangements and Organisation for dealing with Air raids.

During the heavy "blitz" period in 1940/41 an organisation was set at Headquarters Watford and other key centres whereby staff would be available throughout the twenty-four hours to collect and convey immediately by telephone to those concerned all available details of railway damage arising from enemy action. Also to go out to the scene of the damage to gain an idea of what was required by way of men and materials to make the necessary repairs as soon as daylight returned. To this end, every Area Technical Assistant was equipped with a Post Office telephone, with certain Chief Officers as well as the Executive registered with the Post Office as being entitled to special priority calls. In most instances this emergency organisation was joint between the Chief Civil Engineer and the S&T Engineer with alternate turns being worked by their respective staffs. In view of the expense involved, this organisation was cancelled during the comparatively quiet periods in 1942/43 but could be reinstated at very short notice if circumstances warranted it. Prior to the outbreak of war the country was divided by the Government into air raid warning areas that were later adjusted, making some of the areas smaller in order to localise the warnings as much as possible and minimise interference to the life and work of the nation. Immediately it was determined by those responsible that an air raid warning message should be issued, an advice was transmitted giving – the nature of the message, the area or areas to which it applied and the time of its application to the Operating Department Headquarters by means of a teleprinter. The railway therefore had the information as to the air raid warnings applicable to any part of Britain within a minute or two of them becoming operative. These warnings were then plotted on a map by means flags upon which the air raid warning areas were delineated. A statement was maintained of each warning, and at the close of each 24hour period ending at 6am, a map of Britain was marked up to show the warnings during the preceding 24 hours. Any damage to LMS property was indicated thereon by means of a star. The responsibility for the assembly and distribution of particulars of air raid damage devolved upon the Operating Department. In Districts the reports converged on the District Control Offices whence they were at once disseminated to the District Officers of the Engineering Department and passed forward to Headquarters, the channels for reporting occurrences being shown.

Incidents on line, at Stations or Motive Power Depots	Incidents at Goods Terminals	Incidents in workshops and other departmental Premises
Signalmen or other local representative	Local representative	Local representative
Station Master Yard Master or Dist. Loco. Supt.	Goods Agent	Local departmental
	Dist. Goods Manager's Office	

District Control Office

Div'l Sup't of Operation	District Engineering Officers	Regional Transport Commissioner (of serious line blockages)	Regional or District Commissioner (of unexploded Bombs or Mines)

Chief Operating Manager

President	Vice Presidents	Dept'l Chiefs.	R.E.C.	Regional Commissioner (re unexploded Bombs or mines).	Head of Dep't.
			Ministry of Transport.		

Air Raid precautions in an LMS goods yard, 1 December 1939. The men with the tin hats are reported to be goods yard staff.
Hulton Getty Archive 80928357

Serious operating difficulties were created by unexploded and parachute mines falling on or close to LMS property that required movements to be stopped which led to a special examination of the subject by the Railway Companies and the Ministry of Home Security and the Ministry of War Transport. In consequence of which, the following procedure was adopted. The presence of unexploded bombs or parachute mines was immediately reported by the Station Master, Yard Master or Goods Agent, giving certain prescribed details as to position, traffic affected, etc. to the District Control Office, to the local ARP Controller, and to the Permanent-way Inspector or ganger. On receipt of the information the District Control Office advised – 1.The Regional or District Commissioner, and at the same time gave the telephone number of the appropriate District Engineer. 2. The District Engineer. 3. The Divisional Control Office.

The Divisional Control Office then gave the necessary information to the Chief Operating Manager at Watford who,

in turn, notified the Railway Executive Committee and took action with the Regional Commissioner concerned, giving him particulars of the traffic interference and placing the bombs and mines in one of the under mentioned categories for priority of removal.

A - Bombs or mines, the immediate disposal of which was regarded as essential for the war effort.
B - Bombs or mines, the disposal of which was important but less urgent.
C - Cases not necessarily calling for immediate action.
D - Bombs that could be left for an indefinite period.

The responsibility for removing the bombs rested with the Bomb Disposal Officers attached to the Regional Commissioners, whilst the responsibility for dealing with unexploded parachute bombs lay with the Admiralty who were advised through the Regional Commissioners, but in practice this led to some delay in these advices reaching the Admiralty in London, particularly from the provinces, so the custom was adopted of advising the officer responsible for this particular duty at the Admiralty direct, immediately on receipt of particulars. A secret memorandum was then issued to Supervisors giving certain specified details that, in many cases, enabled traffic to be permitted to pass bombs only, at caution, between the time the bombs were discovered and the time they could be examined by a bomb disposal Officer who could give further directions. Additional appointments were made to enable an Assistant District Controller to be on duty at night in the District Control Offices in the areas that were being attacked or were liable to attack, to deal with reports of damage as they occurred. He maintained close liaison with the offices of the Engineering Departments, which were also manned by responsible officers to receive and sift information and take preliminary action to cope with the damage. Small gangs of Engineering Department men were stationed at or near Control Offices during the night so that when preliminary reports of incidents were received, men could be sent out to ascertain the facts, in order that the relative seriousness could be determined and all possible prior arrangements made for dealing with the damage as soon as daylight arrived, as experience showed that very little actual repair work could be undertaken the same night.

As soon as the facts had been ascertained, the District Controllers consulted the District Engineering Officers who estimated the probable duration of any blockage, the District Controller then transmitted this information to the Chief Operating Manager through his Divisional Superintendent of Operation. Having decided what train services could be run, the District Controller made the necessary arrangements with the District Passenger Manager with regard to passenger train services, and the latter arranged any bus services required and took steps to advise the public by means of posters, blackboards and loud speakers. Freight services were re-arranged by the District Controller in collaboration with the Divisional Superintendent of Operation, who consulted with the Chief Operating Manager as necessary. At headquarters, members of the staff of the Chief Civil Engineer and Signal and Telegraph Engineer were on duty each night, working alongside the Chief Operating Manager's staff who collated particulars of incidents as they became available. By the morning following an attack, sufficient information was assembled at Headquarters to enable the situation to be evaluated, and conferences held between the appropriate Chief Officers with a view to determining the order of priority in which repairs should be undertaken and making arrangements for concentrations of men, materials, and equipment. The reparation of damage was naturally beyond the capacity of the existing staff in the Engineering Departments that had been depleted by calls of the services, and extra repair gangs were organised although considerable difficulty was experienced in obtaining additional staff with the required qualifications. Priority was given by the District Goods Managers to the needs of the Engineering Departments for road vehicles for the quick movement of men, tools and materials.

As referred to earlier, ten centres were selected as focal points when major damage required emergency gangs to be utilised – as an example, the arrangements at the Watford Depot are given in the next column --

Following on from the above were several pages listing emergency materials including – 2 miles of complete permanent way, 12 various switches, 13 various crossings, materials for 24 bridges of various spans, high and low trestles, materials for eight sleeper cribs for the construction of temporary bridges, tools, protective clothing that included blankets, respirators, steel helmets, oilskins and gumboots, 8 sets of BBZ wagons, locomotives to be provided by Kentish Town MPD and also cranes. Provision was also made for the availability of road vehicles. Rations were provided to last seven days for 53 men that included such things as 9ozs preserved meat per man per day that totalled 216 lbs, 60lbs bacon, 24lbs margarine, 192 1lb tins of condensed milk etc etc.

As far as staff was concerned – 52 were listed that included a chief permanent way inspector, 2 joiners, 2 bricklayers, 1 crane driver and deputy, 1 messenger (motor) and labourers and gangers.. There then followed the appointment of the "caller-out", instructions for the marking and stacking of materials and tools and the action to be taken on advice being received of a state of emergency. The arrangements required a locomotive to proceed to the Engineer's Workshops and the assembly and loading of the train. Instructions were given as to who would give the orders to proceed to the site of the emergency work, manage telephonic communication and the replenishment of emergency stocks. Nothing was left to chance and note – these arrangements also applied to nine other depots.

The Cricklewood depot was an amalgam of two Engineering Districts, Watford and London. The career details of the two named District Engineers – J. N. Peck and E. Hope as follows - Lt. Col. John Norman Peck OBE MC BA AMICE MInst T was born in Southport on 5th February 1887 and commenced on the LYR in 1909 as a pupil of D. B. Rattray. In 1924 he was appointed District Engineer, Low Moor and in 1931 Assistant Divisional, Engineer Manchester before moving to Blackburn in 1933. In 1934 he was appointed District Engineer, London on £1000pa rising to £1400 in 1945 in which year he was on the German Railways Control Commission (British Zone). He retired on 31st July 1950. E. Hope was born in 1881 and appointed District Engineer Watford on 1st March 1933 with a salary of £1000pa. In 1941, aged 60, he was given an allowance of £100 making his salary £1350pa. He was also an inventor, as the LMS granted him permission and paid the expenses to patent "an appliance for giving a visible indication to shunters of the sidings for which points are set" and also "an improved gas heater" in 1939 and 1944 respectively.

The Emergency arrangements at Cricklewood Depot. CRICKLEWOOD EMERGENCY DEPOT		
AREA TO BE SERVED	London Engineer's District – Whole of Watford Engineer's District –South of Banbury, Towcester and Roade Inclusive.	
DISTRICT	LONDON	
ENGINEER'S ADDRESSES AND TELEPHONE NUMBERS.	Mr. J.N Peck, Monksway, The Warren, Radlett, Herts Private telephone : Radlett 6108..	Office: Euston 1234, Ext. 8106.
	WATFORD	
	Mr. E. Hope, Elmdene, Kings Road, Berkhamstead, Herts. Private telephone : Berkhamstead 205.	Office telephone: Watford 2201 Ext. 12.
IMPORTANT STRUCTURES WITHIN AREA	Name	Between Stations
	Watford Viaduct	Bushey and Watford
	River Lea Bridges Nos. 32 & 33	Between Bromley and West Ham.
	Chilton Green Viaduct	Harpenden & Chiltern Green.
	LMSR (N. L. Section) Bridges 21 & 22	Burdett Road (LNER).
	Colchester line L.N.E.R. LMSR	Wanstead Park and Woodgrange Park. Harlesden & Acton Wells Junction.
	Willesden Stn. Bridges Nos. 5 & 5A Line to Broad Street also Kensington and Richmond.	At Willesden Station
	L.N.E.R. Bridges 111,Maiden Lane & Caledonian Road.112 & 113.	Maiden Lane & Caledonian Road.
IMPORTANT JUNCTIONS WITHIN AREA	Willesden	

Air Raid Shelters and Control Rooms

The protection of personnel was difficult, as to provide shelter for everyone, irrespective of circumstances, would hardly be possible. On the other hand there was no doubt that staff required to remain at their posts during air raids should be provided with good protection at the points of duty. Equally, essential control staff, motive power staff at important engine sheds, signalmen, telephone and telegraph operators received priority attention. It was vital to ensure the uninterrupted control of traffic operation during air raids and the most important centres at Crewe, Willesden, Derby and Manchester were provided with bombproof shelters to house the staff and equipment. This list was later extended to include other important control centres and when war broke out on 3rd September 1939, 21 were completed or under construction. Further centres were provided with structures that were blast and splinter proof and reasonably safe from the effects of all but a direct hit from a powerful high-explosive bomb. Signal boxes presented a problem as they could not be entirely closed and certain boxes were strengthened or rebuilt to provide walls of not less than 13½ inch thickness and signalmen were provided with a small steel shelter within the box to which he could retire when bombs were falling in the vicinity. Power and sub-stations and certain telegraph and telephone exchanges were similarly dealt with.

Motive Power and Marshalling Yard staff who remained at work were to be provided with trenches in close vicinity and where this was not practical old boiler shells were to be utilised. The problem remained for the unspecified number of staff in areas likely to be bombed, but who were not required to remain on duty. In June 1938 work was put in hand constructing an underground Control Centre adjoining the Tube Lift Shafts at Euston Station with 5 million sandbags ordered for distribution to selected centres, but only when the international crisis deepened in September 1938 was authorized work to be carried out on a large scale. The setting up of the "emergency centres" was speeded up and purchase of the agreed materials commenced. Surveys were carried out to define the positions of the trenches required in vulnerable areas and old boiler barrels positioned as and when they became available. A further crisis occurred in March 1939 that proved decisive when authority was given for protective works to be proceeded with on a large scale and treated as urgent. The trenches were manufactured at the LMS concrete works at Newton Heath, Manchester, and were reinforced concrete sections, and whilst manufacture had commenced in March 1939, it was not until August that deliveries began on a large scale, *see page 24.* Timber trenches were also constructed using second hand sleepers. The trenches were 6' 4" deep and 4' 8" wide with sleeper uprights and half-sleeper lining, a half sleeper roof was covered with earth with seats and duck boarding provided, the design of which was subsequently accepted as

A general view of Heaton Mersey Motive Power Depot taken at the end of steam. The air raid shelter can be seen on the right of the picture and is enlarged below.
Picture courtesy of the Gerald Harrop and Arthur Haynes collection

Opposite *- Figure 1. The plan and section that shows the construction of an Type "A2" Bomb Proof Control Shelter. Note Section A-A showing the overall thickness of the roof some 10 feet thick and the sand filling between the two walls.*

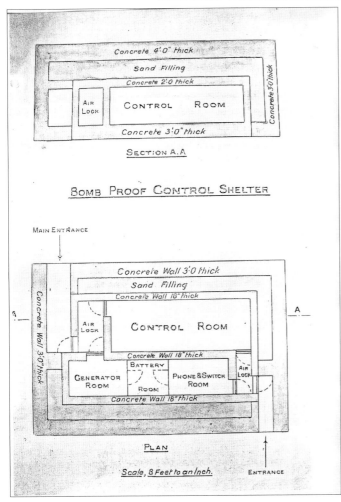

Concrete 4'0" thick
Sand Filling
Concrete 2'0 thick
AIR LOCK
CONTROL ROOM
Concrete 3'0" thick
Concrete 3'0" thick

SECTION A.A

BOMB PROOF CONTROL SHELTER

MAIN ENTRANCE

Concrete Wall 3'0 thick
Sand Filling
Concrete Wall 18" thick
AIR LOCK
CONTROL ROOM
A
Concrete Wall 3'0" thick
Concrete Wall 18" thick
GENERATOR ROOM
BATTERY ROOM
PHONE & SWITCH ROOM
AIR LOCK
Concrete Wall 18" thick

PLAN

Scale, 8 Feet to an Inch.
ENTRANCE

consideration was given to the Spanish experience and the assistance of the War Office, it was decided to make provision for the possibility of a direct hit by a 500lb high explosive bomb by constructing the shelter with two independent shells see **Figure 1**..

The outer shell was 3' 0" thick with a roof 4'0" thick and a 3' 0" thick floor designed to resist penetration by the bomb and cause it to burst. The walls were heavily reinforced to prevent the disintegration of the structure. The inner shell was separated from the outer by 3' 0" of sand filling to act as a shock absorber and had 18" thick walls designed to resist any shock waves which had succeeded in travelling through the sand filling. Three types of Control Rooms were designed, designated Types 'A1', 'A2' and 'B2'. The former were for Divisional Staff, the others for District Staff, which in certain cases also seated Engineering staff, see. **Figures 2A to 2C**.

In Manchester the structure was constructed underground, at Derby partly above and partly below ground but the majority were built entirely above ground although at Birmingham where no suitable site was available the existing accommodation was suitably strengthened to meet the criteria. A splinter-proof shelter was provided at subsidiary Control Centres that lacked the outer shell or bursting layer, but were in all other respects similar to the bomb-proof type – see **Figures 2A and 2B** overleaf. As an additional precaution both types of shelter were equipped with poison gas filtration plants.

Black-out Lighting.

In July 1937 a General Managers Committee was formed on which served representatives of the Ministry of Transport, the Home Office, Air Ministry and the Railway Companies. Their remit was to decide on the minimum amount of visible lighting required during the hours of darkness in order to maintain the efficient operation of the railway. Experimental blackouts at large towns had provided opportunities to test passenger station working and operations under different levels of illumination. Flights were made by members of the Committee to test the visibility. In June 1938 the Committee tabled their first report that recommended three main categories of external lighting as follows –

1. Fixed lighting extinguished, and hand lamps with shades to be used.

2. A low standard of illumination equivalent to about one-tenth full moonlight for passenger stations where, even during raids, it was anticipated that some lighting would be necessary to deal with crowds.

3. A higher standard of illumination equivalent to the intensity of light about 2' 0" away from a candle when label reading or other detail work was required that was to be extinguished and work stopped during raids.

satisfactory by the Home Office. With time running out there was no time for normal authorisation procedures to be made by HQ and accordingly the District Engineers were instructed to proceed with timber trenches in the specified vulnerable areas. In places where there was reasonably good shelter such as buildings with 13½inch thick walls, or where timber trenches could not be provided due to soil considerations, action was deferred until the concrete sections became available, as this was a condition of the Government grant. A problem later arose, and considerable difficulty was encountered when it was required to establish what cost all these trenches incurred. In all, over six miles of trenches had been provided at 297 places that were sufficient to accommodate some 30,000 staff. In May 1939 instructions were given to prepare schemes for providing shelters by strengthening premises to bring them within the "provisional code" of the Civil Defence Act. These were to serve as an alternative to trenches and involved partitioning off large rooms and basements and the provision of emergency entrances and exits. By the time war commenced about £30,000 had been spent on work in progress or completed. The design of the bombproof shelter for Control staff was prepared early in 1939 when information on the effect of bombs on structures was very sparse. After

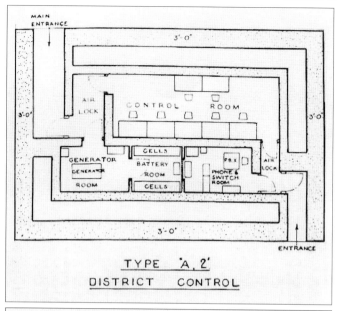

TYPE 'A. 2'
DISTRICT CONTROL

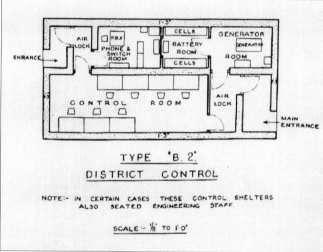

TYPE 'B. 2'
DISTRICT CONTROL

NOTE:- IN CERTAIN CASES THESE CONTROL SHELTERS
ALSO SEATED ENGINEERING STAFF.

SCALE ⅛ TO 1'0'

This column, top - Figure 2A. *Drawing showing the internal fitting out of an 'A2' type control shelter.* **Bottom** - *Figure 2B, Showing the internal seating arrangements of a Type 'B2' District Control Room where Engineering staff may also be accommodated. (Figure 2C opposite)*

All internal lighting was to be blacked out completely. Trains were to have very dim lighting, about one third moonlight, as it could not be expected that passengers would keep the blinds drawn. All engine cabs were to be hooded to minimise firebox glow. Signal boxes were a problem due to the visibility required by the signalmen for the safety of traffic and lighting therein was therefore hooded. No alterations were made to signal lights apart from colour light signals which had 2' 0" long hoods fitted and no practical way was found to prevent the flashes caused by the arcing of electric trains. With the lighting principles settled work commenced with estimates made of the amount of black out material, shades etc required that were not completed at the

time of the Munich Crisis in 1938. With war immediately possible before the materials were to hand, steps were taken to use such crude methods of dipping lamps in distemper and the removal of mantles from gas lamps leaving the flame exposed. The eventual breathing space from September 1938 was utilised to formulate a basic set of rules and codes that were circulated across the company and arrangements decentralised that enabled local initiative to make the change-over to war lighting by each department at short notice. The tremendous task in regard to the action required to every lamp on the railway was settled and the required paint, blind material smaller electric lamps, lampshades and hand lamps was issued. Lamps that were not easily accessible by a department, or those requiring special treatment were to be attended to by the District Engineer or the Outdoor Machinery Assistant. By the time war commenced on September 3rd 1939 about three quarters of the external lighting of the railway was functioning at war time intensity and the process completed by the second night, 4th September, albeit by improvised methods. In February 1945 the Ministry of Home Security agreed that half lighting be allowed in coastal zones that was previously banned. In April it was permitted to remove blackout from roofs and skylights in industrial premises but not stations and on 19th April 1945 normal lighting was resumed throughout the country except coastal areas and railways. Five days later the railways could resume normal peacetime outdoor lighting except for coastal areas that the Admiralty explained was due to submarine warfare. This obviously led to difficulties as on sections of line half a mile or more in length, that were visible from the sea coach lighting had to be screened or extinguished. Whilst discussions were taking place on that difficult problem the war ceased, and on 11th May peacetime lighting could be restored everywhere.

Building Lighting.

Lighting restrictions remained a top priority throughout the war and as stated there were three categories of restrictions on external lighting:– A - fixed lighting extinguished, B - a low standard for certain passenger stations and C - a higher standard where reading and other detail work was done, but was extinguished during raids. It was clearly a requirement to issue instructions to instigate action when an air raid was imminent that was covered by LMS Instruction ERO6643/2 dated August 1939 entitled "Form of official Air Raid messages and action to be taken in regard to extinction of lights"

With essential services such as Marshalling and Traffic Yards, Goods Sheds and Motive Power Depots coming under the latter category the effect of this instruction could have been serious if it had persisted without revision. In places such as London it would have frequently meant the stoppage of vital work throughout the night at a time of the year when the nights were at their longest. Lighting restrictions were controlled by a Committee formed of representatives of The

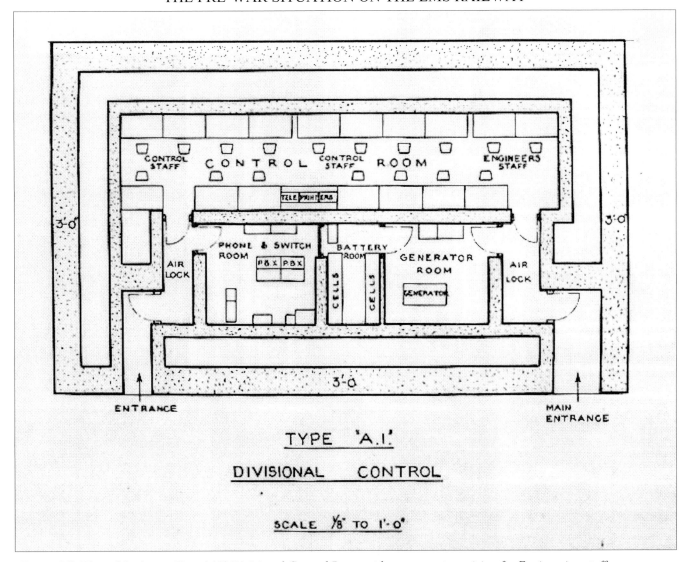

TYPE 'A.1'

DIVISIONAL CONTROL

SCALE ⅛" TO 1'-0"

Figure 2C. Plan of the larger Type 'A1' Divisional Control Room with permanent provision for Engineering staff.

Ministry of War Transport, the Ministry of Home Security, the Air Ministry and the Railway Executive Committee under whose instructions there were continuing tests and revisions. The basis of the lighting system was that it would not be visible to the pilot of an enemy aircraft at the moment the warning of approach was received with all lights extinguished. It was realised that to limit intensity only was ignoring other important factors that affect visibility such as the area of the illuminated patch, the number of lights, and the reflection factor of the ground. Tests had been arranged at Rugby in October 1940 to gain more information on these points, but were interfered with by the enemy so drastically that the tests moved to Northern Ireland that was free from raids at that time. Very useful information was gained from a series of observations made there in January and February 1941 on a wide variety of arrays of lights that simulated railway systems, eventually forming the basis of many improvements.

It was realised that the modification of the warning system was necessary if essential work was not to almost cease every time a raider or unidentified aircraft appeared that led to a "lights out" warning to take effect before the proper raid warning was given in expectation of a full raid. The result was that many men were denied the light required to perform their work, sometimes for long periods, before they needed to take shelter, and, after further tests and some pressure, the Ministry of Home Security agreed to an intermediate form of lighting between "purple" (lights out) and warning and "imminent danger". That was typical of the modifications made in the lighting arrangements as a result of experience of actual raid conditions. The openings to goods sheds were partially screened and the lighting within increased. Special lighting for close work in MPDs was installed etc. The magnitude of the work involved can be gauged from the fact that the preliminary estimate for installing war-time lighting throughout the LMS was £100,000, and by mid-summer 1943 it was just short of £300,000, around ten times the pre-

THESE **INSTRUCTIONS SUPERSEDE** THOSE ISSUED TO THE LINE DATED SEPTEMBER 28th, 1938 (E.R.O. 6643), and APRIL 28th, 1939 (E.R.O. 6643/1), WHICH MUST BE WITHDRAWN.

London Midland and Scottish Railway Company.

AIR RAID PRECAUTIONS.

INSTRUCTIONS TO ALL CONCERNED.

FORM OF OFFICIAL AIR RAID MESSAGES AND ACTION TO BE TAKEN IN REGARD TO EXTINCTION OF LIGHTS.

1. The official messages will be in the following form :—

   (i) "AIR RAID MESSAGE—YELLOW."

   Action thereon.—All precautionary measures of an unobtrusive character to be put into operation immediately.

   (ii) "AIR RAID WARNING—RED."

   Action thereon.—All lights at " exempted " premises to be extinguished or in the case of certain passenger stations to be reduced to " Fully Restricted " Standard immediately on receipt of the warning.

   As both passenger and freight trains will not cease running during air raids it is necessary, in addition to the train crews and signalmen remaining on duty, that the staff required at terminal and other points should be in attendance to deal with such trains.

   All staff not required to remain on duty to seek shelter in the places allotted to them for the purpose. Passengers, kiosk attendants, refreshment room staff, &c., to be directed to suitable shelters or given instructions as to what they should do, i.e. leave the premises and repair to public shelters nearby, &c.

   These conditions to be maintained until the Notice "Air Raid Message—Green " is received.

   (iii) "AIR RAID MESSAGE—GREEN."

   Action thereon.—The lighting conditions which prevailed previous to the receipt of the order " Air Raid Warning—Red " may be resumed.

   (iv) "AIR RAID MESSAGE—WHITE."

   Action.—Relax preparations taken upon receipt of " Air Raid Message—Yellow." In the case of a Control Office or Telephone Exchange whose duty it is to pass on to Control Circuit Points or Exchange Extensions, the codes mentioned in paragraph I must be used.

   NOTE.—The Yellow and White messages are confidential and should not be made known to the public.

FORM OF PUBLIC WARNING SIGNALS AND ACTION TO BE TAKEN IN REGARD TO EXTINCTION OF LIGHTS.

2. The public audible warning signals will take the following form :—

   (i) AIR RAID WARNING : * a fluctuating or " warbling " signal of varying pitch
   * a succession of intermittent blasts

   Action there on.—All lights at " exempted " premises must be extinguished or reduced to " Fully Restricted " Standard immediately the warning is heard. These conditions to be maintained until the signal " Raiders Passed " is heard.

   (ii) RAIDERS PASSED MESSAGE : a continuous signal at steady pitch.
   Action thereon.—The lighting conditions which prevailed before the Air Raid Warning was heard may be resumed.
   * It will be necessary to ascertain locally which signal is to be employed.

   NOTE.—When local public Air Raid Warnings are heard, these should be acted upon without waiting for the official telephone message.

EUSTON STATION,

August 22nd, 1939.   BY ORDER.

E.R.O. 6643/2.

as October 1943 pressure was still being brought to bear and further relaxations obtained. It was agreed that certain areas of the country, (roughly 50 miles from the east and south coasts and with the exception of areas of special importance), Traffic Yards and MPDs could have their lighting raised to 0.7 f.c. – an increase of 3½ times.

Train Lighting.

Train lighting was also typical of the changes in outlook as the war developed. Initially the blinds were not drawn and a dim blue light was sufficient for a passenger to see if a seat was available – but not always. The restricted lighting on trains required 150,000 light bulbs to be replaced. When the anticipated air attacks did not materialise there was a demand for better lighting to which the Ministry of Home Security reluctantly agreed with the use of shaded white reading lights, with the blinds drawn on long distance trains. When the dining cars were reintroduced, full lighting was permitted with the one problem in that any defect in the blinds meant all lights were extinguished within the compartment or coach. Suburban stock with no blinds were permitted a heavily shrouded light, barely sufficient for reading purposes. These arrangements applied during the 1940/2 air attacks, but following the relatively quiet period that followed demands were made in the press for still more light that led to several concessions being made, notably the provision of white lights in suburban stock. This resulted in three relighting programmes for rolling stock, with work being carried out by the Carriage and Wagon Departments, with the testing, submission, arguing and obtaining approval being the responsibility of the Engineer's Department. The Lighting and Heating Section of the Department was also involved with the arrangements for the supply of oil gas as an emergency measure should the normal gas supply be cut off. The oil gas was manufactured by the Railway Company and was used mainly by the dining cars. It was compressed to 150lbs per square inch and distributed through high-pressure steel piping or travelling tank wagons. When the oil gas piping was in the vicinity of a coal gas main, the two supplies were connected, but where there was no oil gas main at the supply point, a travelling tank wagon of oil gas was placed at the most convenient point. The extension of this method of supplying gas to meet wartime emergencies worked well in practice. In September 1940 the Shed lighting and certain furnaces at Camden Motive Power depot were kept going for a week; Coventry Station and Goods depot were supplied for

war rate of expenditure on lighting work. LMS Form ERO 6404 was issued for stations and depots to list their electric, gas, oil and hand lamps that required shades or restricted illumination.

The increase in the number of category C installations was also significant as before the war it was planned to have 400 but by mid-summer 1943 there were 1200. This was due to constant pressure on the Ministries concerned to convince them of the operational need for lighting and the harmlessness of increases scientifically worked out. As late

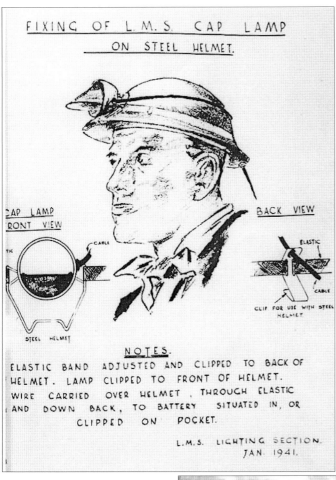

FIXING OF L.M.S. CAP LAMP ON STEEL HELMET.

CAP LAMP FRONT VIEW

BACK VIEW

CLIP FOR USE WITH STEEL HELMET

STEEL HELMET

NOTES.

ELASTIC BAND ADJUSTED AND CLIPPED TO BACK OF HELMET. LAMP CLIPPED TO FRONT OF HELMET. WIRE CARRIED OVER HELMET, THROUGH ELASTIC AND DOWN BACK, TO BATTERY SITUATED IN, OR CLIPPED ON POCKET.

L.M.S. LIGHTING SECTION. JAN. 1941.

two weeks in November 1940 and the gas supply difficulty was overcome at Sheffield and Bristol during and after the raids on these places. Drivers of electric trains were requested to 'coast' over points and crossings to avoid arcing. Steam engines required sheeting from the cab across to the tender to avoid firebox glow and likewise in sheds the glow of ashes were a problem as were braziers lit to keep water columns from freezing.

Poison Gas.

During the air raids there was always a great deal of anxiety to the effect on repair work should the enemy ever use poison gas. The problem was a national one as far as the contamination of personnel was concerned and the ARP provided machinery for dealing with railway staff in co-operation with local authorities. Decontamination squads were formed in the Districts, and some instruction given, but experience of actual conditions during the raids indicated that very serious delay would occur if liquid blister gas had to be dealt with before repair work could commence, and, if blister gas became general, the Railway Company's stock of bleach powder was insufficient to cope with large areas of contamination. It was also considered, that, in many cases, it would not be necessary to decontaminate the site before repair work commenced. Whilst the enemy did not use poison gas during the 1940/41 raids, it was deemed prudent to provide for such contingency should it be used at any time during the later stages of the war. Accordingly it was decided to carry out experiments to settle the question as to

Above - With the black out in force it was desirable to provide staff, in goods sheds for example, with a suitable lamp that was hands free. Initially the first lamp to be tried was unsatisfactory in as much as the light was thrown between the legs when bending down to pick up a package. This was overcome with a miner's type lamp that could be worn on the forehead, a cloth cap or a steel helmet. It was manufactured by Messrs Oldham's of Manchester and powered by an accumulator carried in the man's pocket as it was considered that dry batteries may come in short supply should the factory be bombed.

Right - 'Dig for Victory'. Near Harrow on 4 March 1940 an embankment is being prepared to grow crops. Hulton Getty Archive 81002536

whether repairs to permanent way could be achieved without decontamination. To this end contact was made with the Chemical Defence Research Department of the Ministry of Supply and the disused Melbourne loop in Northamptonshire was selected as the site on 20th November 1939. The Royal Engineers blew a crater in the track to represent damage by a high explosive bomb, and the whole site was then heavily contaminated with liquid blister gas A gang of permanent way and signal and telegraph men previously instructed by lecture and film, were brought on site in a special train, that included one of the ARP Instructional Units who dressed the men in their protective clothing that included secret impregnated suits. Special equipment was also carried that enabled the men to be undressed at meal times and redressed after in the same contaminated clothing. The impregnated suits were an essential part of the organisation as these protected the body against vapour, enabled lighter oilskin clothing to be worn and also did away with the necessity for the men to wash their hands on completion of the work, a matter of real difficulty in isolated areas.

The working gang was divided into halves, each working for 30 minutes and resting for 30 minutes. During the rest period the hoods and respirators were removed by special dressers, and replaced by them on the resumption of work. One of the Railway's chemists was in attendance as a Gas Safety Officer. He defined the area of liquid contamination and took readings of the vapour concentration to advise on the amount of protective clothing to be worn by the men at differing stages of the work. As an example, after the crater had been filled in, the men were allowed to continue without hoods or respirators. This experiment was completed without a single casualty and was so successful that it formed the basis of an organisation to deal with repairs to contaminated permanent way and signal and telegraph apparatus. The ten ARP Instructional Units were suitably altered with the required equipment provided. These were then stationed at convenient points to cover the whole system and a specially trained squad was attached to each unit to be available at any point where their services were required. The training of these squads was carried out at selected sites on isolated and little used lines on which the Melbourne's experiment was repeated and improved on. As a result the problem of dealing with contaminated lengths of track was brought within manageable proportions. The Melbourne branch was handed back to the LMS on 1st January 1945.

Camouflage.

The LMS architect, W. H. Hamlyn (see below) began to study this subject in 1938 at the RAF Station at Farnborough becoming the Camouflage Liaison Officer for all railways. Lists were prepared on all the railways of places on the systems that may require camouflage, collaborating with the various Companies and with the organisation which was later

An ash pit at a locomotive depot in use for LMS Home-Guard training, 11 December 1942. 'The sunken track makes an ideal trench to practice bomb throwing.' Hulton Getty Archive 3320663

to become the Directorate of Camouflage of the Ministry of Home Security. When war broke out each Company became responsible for carrying out the schemes on its system as agreed in the programme. At one time there were no less than 17 major schemes simultaneously in hand on the LMS. The work was not as straight forward as one might think as the preliminary instructions issued by the Ministry in outline, had to be developed and reproduced on models from which the contractors could work. The architects became the supervisors for the often in-experienced contractors in this class of work as they were treating many differing varieties of roof and wall surfaces not to mention complicated structures on which initiative was required in the interpretation of the camouflage scheme. The use of compressors and sprays was considerable as at Wolverton works for instance, approximately 3,250 square yards a day were completed. Another complication was that roof lights to the Company's works had been covered by bituminous hessian treatment as a safety precaution meaning that this had to be embraced in the camouflage work. In co-operation with the LMS Paint Technologist, F. Fancutt, types of paint and methods of application were developed in order to secure lasting results and it is worth mentioning that most of the original camouflage schemes in the country generally required frequent re-painting. The Stonebridge Park Power Station scheme was regarded as a model of its kind and was so satisfactory two years after its application the Ministry's representatives, on making their inspection, found repainting unnecessary.

William Henry Hamlyn was appointed Architectural Assistant in the Civil Engineer's Department in 1933 with a salary of £1100pa where he obviously made a good job on the reconstruction of the Queen's Hotel, Leeds, as Board Minute 3057 wished to give him "tangible recognition" for his work. This was likely achieved when, on the retirement of R. W. Owen, he was promoted to LMS Architect on 1st August 1935, his salary increased to £1350, that rose to £2400 in 1943 when he was sufficiently high ranked to be transferred to the Special Minute Book, a preserve of those only in the top management tier.

Miscellaneous Railway Defence Arrangements.

Minute 4100 (30/5/1940) listed the following in connection with the above, which included such things as preparing bridges for demolition, measures to prevent the use of ports, immobilisation of rolling stock and giving instructions to staff on measures to be taken. There was the formation of local defence volunteers to guard vulnerable points on the railway as part of the military defence organisation, arrangements to segregate secret documents of military importance for quick removal or destruction and the withdrawal of large-scale maps and folders likely to be of use to the enemy. Also emergency arrangements in the event of interference with telegraphic communications, e.g. despatch riders. Details of the 159 aliens employed by the

Frank Fancutt MBE, FRIC AMIChemE was born at Stantonbury, Bucks, on 23rd January 1897. In 1912 he entered the service of the LNWR and in 1916 was appointed chemist at Crewe. In 1935 he became the LMS Paint Technologist at Crewe and in 1950 the Chief Chemist on British Railways. In 1954 he was appointed Assistant Director Chemical Services BTC before becoming Assistant Director of Research in 1959 from which position he retired in 20th June 1961. In 1935 he patented, at LMS expense, a cellulose and polish reviver and a paint remover.

Photo TNA Rail 1156/26.

LMS were given to the Ministry of Transport and the appointment of railway liaison officers to link with regional transport commissioners in event of complete breakdown of communication between regions and railway HQ requiring 6 or 8 LMS officers. Other items as far as the arms drive were concerned related to making skilled railway staff available for aircraft construction (dealt with later). No annual holiday shutdown of railway workshops. Holiday trains withdrawn and the cancellation of the Whitsun holiday as elsewhere in the country. Workmen's tickets to be issued on Sundays and passenger and goods train services to meet weekend working requirements. The Army was particularly impressed with the potential value of Signalmen as lookouts for hostile troops by reason of their position in elevated signal boxes all over the country. This all the more so as they had the availability of an independent telephone system whereby reports could be quickly transmitted to Station masters and District Control Offices.

*Driver and 'van boy'. Actually a combination
of Mr and Mrs - William and May Garrard,
24 February 1941. A propaganda image of
everybody 'doing their bit'.*
Hulton Getty Archive 80843846

3

WAR IS DECLARED

NEW WORKS BY THE
CHIEF CIVIL ENGINEERS DEPARTMENT

With the preliminary tasks completed with shelters, blackout arrangements and control buildings all underway and with no initial air raids, the Civil Department was able to concentrate on other important activities, albeit made more difficult with a shortage of materials and labour.

There were a great many problems to be faced once the war commenced, such as the diversion of traffic from the east to the west coast ports and the many alterations to the flows of traffic with the new ordnance factories, Government storage facilities, new airfields and training camps etc being constructed. Such things as where would railway bottle-necks occur and what if the bridges across the Thames were demolished by the enemy bombing? The main railway companies all had their termini on either side of the Thames with few north to south bridges that would be extremely important in getting troops, munitions and supplies to (and from) the channel ports. Would the existing line capacity be overtaxed and were the exchange facilities with other railways adequate? In respect of the above, nine problems were classified and carried out, as under, by the end of 1943:-

Description of work	No. of schemes	Cost £
Additional facilities provided on the LMS system in connection with the diversion of traffic from the East to the West Coast ports.	7	27,670
Additional facilities in which the LMS was interested provided in connection with alternative routes for traffic across the Thames.	16	195,267
Railheads on the periphery of London and large provincial towns.	6	50,348
Additional running facilities and siding accommodation required for the working of war time traffic.	151	1,673,480
Additional facilities provided for particular flows of war time traffic.	4	20,890
Additional goods terminal accommodation.	13	38,072
Improved facilities at Motive Power depots and accommodation for enginemen.	9	19,450
Works carried out at railway owned docks.	5	13,017
Improved telephone facilities.	37	98,946
Total Expenditure	**248**	**2,137,140**

New munitions factories were being constructed as well as supply depots containing sidings that were generally laid by the contractor with the connections to the sidings made by the railway. In 1937 a new Royal Ordnance factory was built at Chorley in Lancashire that involved carriage sidings and loops as well as a marshalling yard and a new bridge, all carried out by the LMS costing some £225,000 with further additions as the site developed. In the same year extensive sidings were laid at Bishopton in Scotland. From 1938 the munitions industry developed rapidly, not to mention facilities for the Army, Navy and Air force, many requiring rail connections, some of the principal schemes are listed below :-

Place	Description	Date	Approx Cost £	Ministry
Swinderby, between Newark & Lincoln.	Siding accommodation for RAF Factory	1938	13,000	Air Ministry.
Tutbury, near Burton.	Siding accommodation for new Royal Ordnance Factory	1938	11,500	Air Ministry.
Sankey Junction (CLC) - *see illustration see opposite top.*	Siding accommodation for new aircraft repair depot.	1939	5,100	Air Ministry.
Heysham	Sidings in connection with fuel reserve depot.	1939	7,000	Air Ministry.
Badnall Wharf, between Stafford & Crewe.	Marshalling sidings halt etc for new ROF depot at Swinnerton,	1939	37,800	War Office
Donnington, between Stafford & Shrewsbury	Sidings and main line connections And additional opening under bridge for Royal Ordnance Factory	1939	68,000	War Office
Radway Green Near Crewe - *see illustration opposite bottom.*	Sidings 7 mainline connections, halt with passenger lines, extension of Radway Green Stn. Platforms, road bridge and footbridge for Royal Ordnance factory.	1939	14,500	War Office.
Rainford Junction, Near Liverpool	Main line connections to Royal Ordnance factory.	1939	12,700	War Office.
Capenhurst	Sidings and connections, extension of Station platforms, new footbridge and roadway for Royal Ordnance depot	1940	30,500	Office of Works
Disley (CLC). - *see illustration page 34.*	Sidings and connections and halt for Royal Ordnance factory.	1940	42,700	Ministry of Supply
Ashchurch	Siding accommodation in connection with RASC depot	1940	23,500	War Office.
Ouirinish - *see illustration page 35.*	Siding accommodation	1940	18,200	Admiralty.
Fodderty	Siding accommodation	1940	11,700	Admiralty
Bandeath	Siding accommodation	1940	13,500	Admiralty
St. Brides.	Siding accommodation	1940	10.700	Admiralty.
Connel Ferry	Siding accommodation	1940	15.700	Admiralty
Gretna	Siding accommodation	1940	32,800	Admiralty
Paisley	Siding accommodation	1941	19,000	Ministry of Supply
Cairnryan	Siding facilities for exchange traffic with military railway.	1941	16,500	War Office.
Aviemore	Siding accommodation.	1943	2,500	Ministry of Supply.

Top - *Sankey Junction (CLC, near Warrington), Siding accommodation for the Air Ministry.* British Rail

Right - *Chorley Sidings, main line connection and station for the Ministry of Supply. This site was known as Euxton Royal Ordnance Factory and had two new signal boxes, Euxton Nos. 1 & 2.*
British Rail

Bottom - *Radway Green (Between Crewe and Kidsgrove). Sidings and main line connections and Halt for the War Office.* British Rail

In addition to the above schemes requiring direct railway access to Government Works, many others both large and small were needed and authorised by the Ministry of War Transport to facilitate the additional wartime traffic. Several loops were laid in the line from Oxford to Cambridge and additional connections with the main North to South lines were made at Sandy, Bletchley, Calvert and Oxford together with a new marshalling yard at Swanbourne, near Bletchley. An additional connection was made from the Stratford-on-Avon line at Broome Junction and improved running facilities were made on the Birmingham to Gloucester line. A down loop was laid in at Sutton

Weaver on the main line to Liverpool and the connecting line between the LMS and GWR at Bordesley near Birmingham was doubled. Additional running facilities were also laid between Challoch Junction and Castle Kennedy. In addition there were many smaller schemes, but the two of major importance were the Gloucester and Cheltenham widening and the quadrupling of the main line immediately north of Carlisle.

The most important siding schemes authorised by the Ministry of War Transport are listed below:-

Place	Description	Date	Approx. Cost £
Cricklewood	Brent loaded wagon sidings. Additional siding accommodation.	1940	17,800
Crewe – Gresty	Additional siding accommodation	1940	11,500
Gloucester- Barnwood	Additional siding accommodation	1939	24,000
Northampton	Additional traffic facilities at Castle and Bridge Street Stations	1941	61,000
Coventry	Warwick Road Goods Yard. Additional, and alterations to existing siding accommodation and provision of road access.	1940	12,600
Kings Norton	Extension of and alterations to sidings and extension of bridge.	1941	19,600
Liverpool – Edge Hill and Breck Road.	Additional siding accommodation	1940	20,200
`Carlisle – Kingmoor	Additional siding accommodation	1939	15,300
Stranraer	Additional carriage siding and goods yard accommodation	1941	13,400
Kilmarnock	Additional traffic yard accommodation	1941	12,300
Law Junction	Additional traffic sidings.	1941	31,800
Elderslie	Additional marshalling siding accommodation	1942	23,000
Inverness	New marshalling yard	1943	26,200
Shieldhall	Siding facilities to serve inland sorting depot	1941	58,200
Harlescott Crossing	New marshalling yard	1941	50,000

Disley, (CLC between Warrington and Glazebrook). Sidings, main line connections and Halt for the Ministry of Supply.

British Rail

Ouirinish, (near Kyle of Lochalsh). Siding accommodation for the Admiralty.
British Rail

In order to give the reader an idea of the work involved, the following is an account of work at Northampton Marshalling Yard, the Gloucester and Cheltenham widening and the work in quadrupling the line north of Carlisle.

Northampton Castle Marshalling Yard and Additional Traffic facilities.

The scheme included the following –

1. Provision of seven new dead end sorting sidings to hold 464 wagons and a cripple siding in the Down Marshalling Yard together with the re-modelling of the connections to the existing storage sidings.
2. A new Down Goods line.
3. Extension to the Up Marshalling Sidings to provide additional accommodation for 70 wagons and a new shunting neck.
4. The extension of the existing shunting neck to form a new Up Goods Loop to hold an engine, brake and 79 wagons.
5. A double junction between the Rugby and Peterborough lines and a facing connection in the Up Rugby Line leading to the Up Peterborough line with a new signal Box (Kingsthorpe Junction).
6. Additional watering facilities.

The scheme involved 64,000 cubic yards of excavation, of which 10,000 yards was required for filling an embankment for the extended Up Sidings, shunting neck and loop. A portion of the surplus excavation was tipped on the site of an abandoned loop of the River Nene that was straightened by the River Nene Catchment Board, the railway company purchasing the land for this purpose. The remainder was tipped into a clay pit adjoining the railway and on a tipping site to the north of the Marshalling Yard. The work was carried out by the Works Section of the Department

employing direct labour and utilised a steam shovel navvy. The permanent way work was carried out by the District Engineer and programmed so that the work could be handed over to the Operating department in seven stages taking fifteen months to complete from the time of authorisation.

The Gloucester and Cheltenham Widening.

Under the terms of the 1836, 1838 and 1842 Acts, the line between Lansdown Junction and Tramway Junction was built at the equal expense and for the equal use by the Cheltenham and Great Western Union Railway and the Birmingham and Gloucester Railway Companies, the former to maintain from Lansdown Junction to the Midway Board at Churchdown, and the latter thence to Tramway Junction with Churchdown station treated as a joint station. The signalling between Cheltenham and Gloucester was provided and maintained by the GWR.

This scheme doubled the six miles of. line between Gloucester Engine Shed Junction and Lansdown Junction at Cheltenham. (**See overleaf.**) As stated half of this length was owned by the GWR with the other half by the LMS, but by arrangement between the companies the LMS undertook the work of the actual widening with the respective Companies laying their own portions of permanent way. The work involved the excavation of more that a ¼ millions cubic yards of which 140,000 was required for embankments. The transportation of the material for the embankments used side tip Yankee wagons hauled by steam locomotives, the maximum haul being two miles. The longest cutting was 1mile 48chains with another being 59chains with a maximum height of 40 feet. As the ground on which the embankments were formed was water logged a large amount of surface drainage was required before the tipping could be commenced. The longest embankment was 1mile 24chains.

Gloucester and Cheltenham Widening.
Remodelled Lansdown Junction.   *British Rail*

Construction work included the extension of seven under bridges, five new openings under existing over-bridges, the extension of ten culverts and long lengths of retaining wall, the longest being 860 feet long and varying in height from 5 feet to 25 feet above rail level. Five new signal boxes were constructed with 11½ miles of plain track and 3½ miles of points and crossings. The total cost was some £345,000. The work began on 11th September 1941 and running commenced over all four new tracks on 23rd August 1942. Note that Engine Shed Junction was renamed Barnwood Junction on 26th May 1968, and also the line reverted back to double track in 1967.

New bridge over the River Eden and the quadrupling of line between Caldew Junction and Kingmoor – Carlisle.

At this point on the main line from England to Scotland, the whole of the traffic was conveyed over two lines of rails. This scheme required a new bridge alongside the existing to carry two additional lines and the quadrupling of track from Caldew Junction to Kingmoor Yard. By this means alternative lines were available should one of the bridges be damaged by enemy action, not to mention the facilities for increased traffic on what was a vitally important route. The new viaduct consisted of seven main spans 48 feet long with two approach spans of 35 feet each. The piers were octagonal concrete piles arranged in two rows of five each that were driven through an average of 19 feet of clay, sand and gravel. Substantial concrete caps were required to carry the superstructure of pre-cast concrete beams 4' 3" deep and 2' 0" wide. The structural work included a bridge of four spans each 22' 0" long south of the river for flood openings, the construction being a continuous reinforced concrete slab 2' 6" deep with concrete retaining walls for a portion of its length. The widening of the formation required about 15,000 cubic yards of filling for the embankment, half of which was obtained from the excavation required at the south end of Kingmoor Yard. The LMS Works Section carried out the work, with the permanent way laid by the District Engineer.

The prefabricated concrete sections were manufactured by the LMS at the Newton Heath Concrete Works. The cost of the scheme was about £90,000.

The scale of the work involved can be roughly gauged by the fact that over 300 miles of track were required in these schemes that were a priority. The position had been eased by deferring new works sanctioned prior to the war or ceasing work on those that were in the early stages of construction, as labour had to be conserved. This enabled the Civil Department to concentrate on the completion of ARP measures etc without seriously affecting the day-to-day maintenance and renewal work. As previously mentioned building and structure maintenance was ignored although 343 miles of track were completely re-laid during 1940 with a further 95 miles re-sleepered with old rails put back.

Carlisle - work in progress on the new bridge over the River Eden.   *British Rail*

The total number of schemes for the provision of additional new works to facilitate the working of wartime traffic up to the end of December 1945 was 288, the total estimates for which amounted to £2,234,295.

Carlisle. The completed bridge over the River Eden.
      British Rail

4

WARTIME PREPARATIONS AND NEW WORKS BY THE SIGNAL AND TELEGRAPH ENGINEER'S DEPARTMENT

*T*he Signal and Telegraph Department's "History of the War Years" was written by A. F. Bound and covered the years 1939 up to the end of March 1944, thus the final months are not covered, but the following gives an account of most of the major problems that were dealt with.

On 27th January 1939 A. F. Bound, The Chief Signal and Telegraph Engineer wrote the following to his staff "*It behoves us all to do everything in our power to push forward our preparations with a minimum of delay. This department is very heavily involved in the various precautions which are proposed and the Government specify that in order to qualify for grant everything must be in hand by May, and whilst this may suffice as a guide to starting, I am sure you realise from the international situation it is impossible to say how soon completion may be a necessity and, therefore, I am anxious that you get this matter in the right perspective. ARP from now to completion must not be regarded as a subject outside your ordinary duties to be picked up just as opportunity offers, but it must be regarded as the live and vital issue, of primary importance in your daily work, and only when you have dealt with it as far as you can go at the time should you revert to your ordinary routine duties. I, therefore, want each of you to have this subject uppermost in your thoughts; do not let a day go by without taking stock of the situation, and resolve that every day you will do something to help forward the work of preparation, so that, if and when another crisis comes, we can say that WE ARE READY*".

Arthur Frank Bound, MIMechE., MInst T,. AMIEE, MIR SE, auhor of the Report "History of the War Years - S&T Department' .was born on 23rd. August 1878 at 10 Cambridge Street, Tunbridge Wells, the child of Frank (who was a grocer) and Jane Minter Bound He commenced work on the London Brighton and South Coast Railway in Brighton Works in 1894 as a premium apprentice under R.J. Billington. In 1898 he moved to Vickers as a Draughtsman. In 1903, he was appointed as outdoor assistant with The British Power Railway Signal Company working on the low pressure signalling schemes on the London and South Western Railway.   In November 1903 he took a post on the Great Central Railway as Assistant Signal Superintendent, and in April 1906 became the Signal Superintendent, later to become Signal Engineer, Southern Area of the London and North Eastern Railway following the 1923 amalgamations. He was appointed Signal and Telegraph Engineer of the LMS Railway on 20th. May 1929 with a salary of £2000, increased to £2500 on 1st December 1931. On 1st June 1932 the Board increased his rank to that of Chief Officer.   He was President of the Institution of Railway Signal Engineers in 1925. Bound reached the age of 65 on 23/8/1943 when he was relieved of his day to day duties in order to prepare detailed reports with regard to signalling in the post-war years, by which time his salary was £3500. He was placed on superannuation on 31st. August 1944 but retained as a consultant with a fee of £1750 p.a. W. Wood succeeded him. He died on the 5th.October 1957 at Bognor Regis aged 79.   Photo TNA Rail 1156/22

William Wood MIEE, M. inst. T was born in 1886 and began his railway career in 1904 as a Premium Apprentice under A. F. Rock on the north Staffordshire Railway. In 1911 he was appointed Assistant Telegraph Superintendent on the North British Railway becoming Telegraph Superintendent in 1912 before taking over the electric power and lighting of that Railway. In 1908, under the Territorial Army Scheme he raised and trained the North Midland Company RE with men from the Post Office and the Railway with its HQ in Birmingham where he was the Commanding Officer. In 1923 he was responsible for all electrical and telegraph within the Scottish Area of the LNER. On 1st July 1933 he was appointed Assistant to the LMS Signal and Telegraph Engineer (A. F. Bound) and when P. D. Michod retired on 30th June 1933 Wood became Principal Assistant on £1500 pa. With the eventual retirement of Bound Wood was appointed Chief S&T Engineer. on 1st August 1944 with a salary of £2500 rising to £3000 on Nationalisation He was President of the Institution of Railway Signal Engineers in 1930/1. The Railway Gazette

There could be no doubt about his concerns for the country's immediate future.

The LMS S&T Department had been re-organised with effect from 1st July 1938, retaining the four Divisional Offices but reducing the English Districts from 17 to 12, the Scottish Division having four Districts as before. When A. F. Bound retired in 1944, he was succeeded by W. Wood.

Communications.

One of the first jobs was at Euston where emergency accommodation in the underground Tube Station was equipped with a switchboard and teleprinter circuits to Crewe, Derby, Manchester and Birmingham and standby carrier systems for the Euston and Derby trunk lines. All trunk telephone circuits were connected to the emergency exchange together with tie lines to the other Companies Local Exchanges, Post Office exchange lines, and a selected number of extensions. Suitable connections had also to be made to the LMS Wartime Headquarters at "The Grove" at Watford, the Railway Clearing House and the Railway Executive Committee. Permission was sought in 1937 from the Home Defence Committee to use Wireless Telegraphy for both long and short distances, but no such facilities had been granted up to the outbreak of the war. *Circuit Construction-* New telephone circuits were provided to meet the Chief Operating Manager's requirements indicated by the fact that over 4,000 single wire miles of 200-lb copper wire (over 350 tons) were erected throughout the System, together with several miles of multi-core air spaced cables. The gangs achieved nine to ten miles of single wire per week, a very creditable performance. Transport to the work sites and the feeding of the men were major wartime problems only solved by whole-hearted co-operation of the gangs and their supervisors. Assistance was rendered by squads of Royal Engineers from Edinburgh placed at the disposal of the LMS in connection with improved telephone facilities on the Highland Line. Work commenced in August 1941 with two Officers and sixty other ranks supplementing the railway gangs with the work proceeding in the following order:-

Inverness to Wick and Thurso.
Dingwall to Kyle of Lochalsh.
Inverness to Keith – Aviemore and Perth.
Perth to Aberdeen.

The Highland scheme was completed in September 1942 when the party was split up with 20 men being transferred to the LNER with the remainder assisting railway gangs in the erection of the new Perth - Balquhidder leg of the Perth – Oban circuit. Assistance was also given by a number of men from the above squad with additional men from Edinburgh in connection with the work at Dunragit on the Dumfries – Stranraer Line.

Aerial Route – Renewals.

Continuous attention was required to pole routes and a heavy programme of deferred work built up. The problem was different from signal renewal in that a pole line being continuous it was possible to extend the life by dealing only with the weakest link concentrating on the maintenance of the most important circuits. This was not the ideal policy but the force of circumstances left no option, leaving heavy arrears to be dealt with later:-

	Authorised For 1939	Completed 1939 To 1943 inc.	Average Per annum
Poles	2,820	3,015	603
Arms	26,750	32,620	6,523
Stay wire – cwts.	2,055	2,895	579
Iron wire – cwts.	8,040	13,950	2,790
Copper wire –cwts.	1,685	3,090	618
Insulators	55,570	99,100	19,820
Insulator Bolts	69,700	112,150	22,430

From the foregoing one can readily appreciate the problems building up on the railways of Britain following cessation of hostilities by way of a tremendous backlog of maintenance. It is not surprising that the railways took several years to get back to anything approaching the pre-war standard as additional funds were not forthcoming for the backlog of work post-war.

Miscellaneous wartime communications work.

To meet flying requirements of the RAF in the vicinity of Aerodromes, there were about 200 places where the aerial route was either replaced by multi-core air spaced cable or the aerial route was rebuilt and reduced in height. Aerial routes were also diverted or cabled to clear sites for new sidings, running loops etc. About 250 signalling schemes were authorised by the Ministry of War Transport for emergency purposes that required some 3,000 single wire miles of 200lb copper wire being erected. Over 200 schemes for distribution of air raid warnings from spotters' posts involving the installation of approximately 1,500 loud sounding bells. Provision of hundreds of telephones throughout the system for ARP Controllers, Railway Transport Officers, etc and the fitment of telephone attachments to 1,000 Civilian Duty Respirators with associated alterations to telephones to provide for continuous operation under gas conditions. The provision and maintenance of about 200 radio broadcast receivers for use in special trains, Emergency Offices, Staff hostels, etc. *Public Address systems.* With a great deal of congestion at stations and to aid communications and facilitate traffic operation in marshalling yards it was necessary to make a considerable increase in the use of public address equipment, and to this effect 18 stations and 22 sidings were installed equipped with some 1,200 loud speakers.

At the beginning of 1945 there was no further need to expand telecommunications for wartime purposes as the facilities already provided were adequate. Attention was therefore given to the need to focus upon the re-organisation, consequent on the decision to establish District Operating Managers to plan for the post-war era to meet the need for the swift communication that had been established during the war, and to take into consideration developments in manufacture, design and techniques that were featured under wartime conditions in all fields of telecommunication. As a result 22 additional railway trunk telephone circuits and three telephone exchanges were authorised at an estimated cost of £93,100. When the war in Europe terminated much work was involved in the discontinuance of practices instituted for war purposes such as withdrawal of wires and apparatus provided for the Home Guard, dissemination of air raid messages etc. Where a need for ARP lines was evident for general user need, either immediate or prospective, these were retained. The wireless network licence that was eventually obtained to cover the LMS Railway for wartime purposes was cancelled by the Postmaster General, with the stations dismantled and the equipment withdrawn.

Signal Box Lighting.

It was laid down in May 1939 that signal box lighting was to be fully restricted and that no action was to be taken in regard to screening cabins beyond the provision of special lamps and lampshades. These instructions proved to be too drastic, but it should be appreciated that to reduce the peacetime lighting of some 4000 signal boxes to war time level in a few hours meant that clear instructions had to be given that could not be misinterpreted. There were three methods of illumination – electricity, gas and oil, with all signal boxes supplied with the necessary screens and lamps etc. sometime prior to the outbreak of the war. Soon after the wartime lighting was introduced, signalmen in some boxes found difficulty in carrying out their duties, when in such cases, the box was visited and adjustments made to give the maximum amount of illumination the Government restrictions allowed. The statutory Rule and Order governing lighting was not issued by the Secretary of State for Home Affairs until 1st. September 1939, but the Railway Technical Committee (formed July 1937) proposals had been circulated, and in August 1939 the MoT advised that proposed measures would be active from the outbreak of war – the Sept 1939 Order was just a rubber stamp which stated that lights essential for the internal illumination of signal boxes be exempt from the general instruction with regard to the extinguishment of lights provided they complied with the following conditions :-

1. That they were so screened that no light was thrown above the horizontal.
2. The intensity of illumination was reduced to the minimum necessary for the operation of signals.
3. That no light was thrown on any part of the window area of the box.

It was also agreed that the lights did not have to be extinguished during an air raid. There was also no need for the windows to be "blacked out" or curtained for safety reasons. These restrictions made the lighting very poor and although experiments were made up to the end of 1942, no satisfactory solution was found. However, in 1943 a system of indirect lighting proved successful whereby lamps were fitted with metal bowls directing the light into the roof of the box giving a diffused light over the whole of the interior of the box.   This enabled the signalman to see all his instruments, lever numbers, clock etc. without strain, also without any glare the view through the windows was improved.   Not all boxes were equipped with this system. It was obviously essential that signalmen should remain at their posts at all times even though a raid may be in progress. As previously stated, to provide signalmen with the best possible protection, a steel shelter was provided that was placed on the working floor of the box allowing the signalman to take cover at times when he was not concerned with traffic. To protect signalmen from flying glass, the windows were covered with a total of 112,000 sq. yds. of cellophane and 33,350 sq. yds. of hessian. Although thousands of signal box windows were shattered by bomb explosion in only one case did flying glass injure a signalman.

Signal boxes

Signal Boxes were extremely vulnerable to bomb damage and blast, especially the over-line type, the vast majority of boxes being constructed with a wood base and all had plenty of glass on the working floor level. Initially it was proposed that all boxes with 9inch brickwork should have the wall increased to a thickness of 14inches, but the idea was abandoned, not only being difficult but would take too long. The solution adopted to protect the locking as well as those sheltering in the lower portion of signal boxes was by either bricking up the lower windows or covering them with ¼ inch steel plates, both front and back. In all 12,950 boxes were plated and 950 had their windows bricked up. In addition 1,405 doorways were protected by a traverse of 14inch brickwork slightly higher than the doorway with one end being turned at right angles and bonded to the main wall. With the bottom windows permanently blacked out artificial lighting had to be provided using Tilley lamps when

Windows "blacked out" using black curtains. The windows were also covered with cellophane or hessian to avoid flying glass injuring the signalman. During the war a total of 1,890 stirrup pumps and 5,679 buckets were supplied to signal boxes to minimise the risk of serious fires due to enemy action. Between September 1939 and August 1945 102 fires in signal boxes were dealt with using the stirrup hand-pumps, and accordingly these articles were retained as standard equipment.

British Rail

The interior of Watford No.1 Signal Box on 16th October 1939 showing the indoor air raid shelter provided for the protection of signalmen as they were required to remain on duty at all times. Altogether 5,582 such shelters were provided.
British Rail

Signalman's Air Raid Shelter, Watford No.1. 16/10/1939

electricity or gas was not available. Sixteen of the most important signal boxes in the London area were converted to 14inch brickwork up to the working floor level, the remainder being dealt with by reinforced shelters in the bottom room protected by sandbag traverses inside the structure, 2' 0" from the shelter doors. This provision required a further 354 steel shelters with associated 1/4inch mild steel plating, angle brackets, bolts and 26¼ cubic feet of granite chippings per shelter. In addition there were a number of important boxes carried on girders over running lines or sidings, the girder work being supported on stanchions of cast or wrought iron, and being very susceptible to bombing. It was decided that these should be replaced, wherever possible by a ground level signal box to the ARP specification. In some of these cases the box in question took over the working of an adjacent box and in all cases a new locking frame was required. Crewe North and South signal boxes were two other very important boxes each having "Crewe" type all-electric frames that could not be readily replaced. Accordingly two ARP specification boxes were built to replace them, the North box being brought into use on 25th August and the South box on September 22nd 1940. There were other special cases such as the replacement of cast iron columns supporting the girders carrying the signal box by mild steel stanchions at Huddersfield No. 1.and Chester No. 3A. At Manchester, London Road Nos. 1 & 2 a 9inch ferro-concrete roof was constructed over the existing roof – *see illustration overleaf*. It was also proposed to do the same at Glasgow Central, but the idea was scrapped as it would have added too much weight on the Clyde Bridge resulting in a different, more complex solution being adopted. Ditton No.1 box was carried on wooden trestles at the rear that were replaced by 14inch brickwork. A reserve of S & T materials was built up to the value of £317,000, the amount agreed by the Ministry of War Transport. Eleven stores were set up covering material not of a bin and rack nature (large items such as signal posts, frames and signal boxes) and 53 Districts that

had bin and rack stores for smaller items used daily. All-wood signal boxes valued at £11,400, were constructed as spares with four allocated to each LMS Division. Their value came to the fore when Shoeburyness, Birmingham (New Street) No.5, Birkenhead Green Lane, Salford Incline, Sheffield No.1, Liverpool Exchange and Liverpool Park Lane Goods were destroyed. Locking frames of 50 levers were stored on each of the three English Divisions as well as a 150lever frame built by, and stored on the Railway Signal Company, Liverpool premises. Scotland had 2,800 existing spare levers at various depots. As far as power frames were concerned £6,000 was allocated for spares – sufficient "Crewe" type all-electric spares were available for Manchester (London Road) and Camden, Glasgow Central had been specially protected as referred to, Southport was not considered vulnerable to attack and Bolton would revert to mechanical operation if necessary, thus only leaving the Westinghouse Company type to consider. The decision was to purchase a 227 lever spare style "L" frame that would cover damage to any of the frames currently in use e.g. Manchester Victoria & Exchange and Central, Glasgow St. Enoch and Crewe North and South. The frame was stored at Meliden near Prestatyn, North Wales. A total of eleven DC transportable generating sets of 1,500 and 3,500 watts as well as eight 360 watt generators for supplying isolated colour light signals and signal box common batteries were purchased and distributed accordingly. The functioning of the bulk of S&T apparatus relied on batteries of several types, and prior to the war the LMS maintained a three months supply in stock with the annual cost amounting to £367,800. This was increased to six months for dry cells, fifteen months for wet cells and zinc batteries three years. As soon as the war commenced instructions were given that all signal box and platform name boards that were so located and of sufficient size so as to be visible from low-flying aircraft were to be obliterated or hooded. Initially it was applied to lettering over 9" high, but in June 1940 this was reduced to 4"that then made it applicable to all signal boxes

London Road No 2. Signal Box of wood construction complete with an ARP reinforced concrete 'Umbrella' to protect the box from incendiary bombs. London Road No.1 was similarly treated. The train is the 12.10 to Buxton on 9th May 1962 hauled by 42368.

B K B Green / Initial Photographics

as the standard was 6" high lettering. Only those with a non-geographical name remained. Even the removal of the name from the signal box diagram was requested by over enthusiastic Military and Police. Two years later the order was rescinded provided no letter was over 6" high and the signal box name boards were reinstated.

The ARP Type Signal Box

Reverting back to the ARP type signal boxes, the

responsibility for the design fell on the shoulders of H. E Morgan, the Divisional S&T Engineer at Crewe who set about designing a signal box to withstand, as far as possible, the effects of enemy attack. The design utilised 14" brickwork walls with a reinforced concrete floor and roof. ARP signal boxes in Scotland were similar but of different design. A total of 65 were built as listed below.

Portrays Carlisle No.12 Signal Box of ARP design. Apart from the basement windows and a steel staircase, the construction is as the drawing.
The box had a 90-lever frame.
Peter Robinson.

LIST of LMS 'ARP' TYPE SIGNAL BOXES

Location	Opened	Closed	Levers	Remarks
Acton Grange Junction.	5/5/1940	17/9/72	40 35W	Replaced an over-line box
Aintree S.S. No.1,	Plan dated 1943.	12/7/1964	55	Frame in front of box that had 5 window bays, the central 3 down to floor level to improve vision, as the box was a busy shunt frame.
Badnall Wharf	3/3/1940	8/10/1961	100	Reduced to shunt frame 8/10/1961
Bicester No.2.	9/11/1941	29/10/1973	30	
Birchills Power Sidings.	20/11/1949	4/6/1967	45	
Bordesley Junction.	6/4/1941	24/8/1969	25 22W	
Broom West.	27/9/1942	1/7/62	30 15	2 levers for double wire points
Burton Dassett	14/6/1942	4/5/1968	30	
Bushbury No.2.	1941	14/8/1965	65	
Burtonwood	?	?	?	
Camden No.1.	30/6/1940	26/9/1965	57	Replaced an over-line box
Camp Hill	23/2/1941	24/8/1969	30	
Capenhurst	15/9/1940	13/10/1968	65 56W	
Carlisle No.12	19/5/1946	3/6/1973	95 82W	
Cold Meece	3/8/1941	3/8/1959	?	
Crewe Bank (Shrewsbury)	1943	Still Open	45 37W	
Crewe Coal Yard	10/12/1939	Still Open	65	Replaced an over-line box.
Crewe North Junction	25/8/1940	19/7/85	2 x rows of 107 levers	New power signalling scheme Preserved in working order.
Crewe South Junction	29/9/1940	6/6/1985	227	New power signalling scheme
Dale Lane No.1	8/5/1940	2/9/1975	36 30W	
Dale Lane No.2	1941/2	9/9/51	15	Within MOD Sidings
Donnington No.3	20/10/1940	25/7/71	30 26W	
Dunham Hill No.1	19/7/42	2/9/1969	40	
Dunham Hill No.2	9/7/1942	25/11/1951	20 16W	
Edge Hill No.2	5/7/1947	28/8/61		
Engine Shed Junc. (Glos.).	22/2/1942	26/5/1968	105	
Etterby Junction	7/2/1943	18/2/1963	65 58W	
Fordhouses	1941	14/8/1965	75 5S	
Glazebury	15/3/1942	2/10/1965	20	
Greetland No.2	1941 date on diagram	7/2009	55	
Hope & Penyfford	2/3/1944	2/2/1970	25	
Hoscar	c.1941/2	20/8/1967	25	
Lime Street	25/1/1948	Still Open	95 89W	Power frame – still in use 2011
Millburn	?	?	?	
Mold	8/6/1944	28/2/1967	25	
Mold Junction No.4	15/12/1946	26/2/1978	55	
Mollington	6/10/1940	12/11/80	25 21W	
Northampton No.5	17/5/1942	14/2/1965	35 31W	
Polmadie Bridge	16/6/1940	25/2/1973	85	Replaced an over-line box
Portobello Junc.	?	14/8/1965	20	
Queniborough (Syston)	9/11/1941	19/12/1976	65 60W	
Rangeworthy	25/1/1942	19/10/1969	10	
Runcorn	7/1/1940	Still Open	45	Replaced an over-line box
Rockcliffe	?	18/2/1963	25	
Simonswood	1/2/1942	4/5/1965	40 35W	
Sankey Junction	21/11/1943	3/3/1969	45	
Sefton Junction	1942	13/4/1986	90	
Stevenston No.1	16/6/1947	14/9/1985	?	

Location	Opened	Closed	Levers	Remarks
Swanbourne Sidings	15/2/42	29/7/1984	30 24W	
Swynnerton Junction	5/8/1940	21/11/1965	20 13W 3S 4S	
The Oaks	15/11/1942	25/10/1966	20	
Thornhill	1943	Still open	30	Has various non-standard features.
Town Green	3/7/1949	10/2/1994	25 21W	The Last One Built
Tuffley Junction	7/12/1941	11/8/1968	50	
Wakefield West	1/9/1940	25/4/1982	95	Replaced an over-line box
Wapping Park Lane Goods	1941/2	1/11/1965	10	Built into arched cutting wall
Water Orton West Junction	18/4/1943	10/8/1969	65	Was re-named Water Orton West Junction 12/5/63.
Watery Lane (Tipton)	1942	Out of use 26/10/1969. Demolished w/c 12/12/2011	50	Frame removed, replaced by IFS Panel by 09/05
Wellingborough Junction	27/6/1943	13/11/1983	60	
Whateley Siding	24/2/1946	28/10/1962		
Whitebirk East	4/2/1943	23/9/1973	25 22W	
Wigan No.1	31/8/1941	1/10/1972	85+40 +74 switches.	New power signalling scheme
Wigan No.2	31/8/1941	1/10/1972	65 45W + 15 switches	Ditto
Wigan Wallgate	27/7/1941	Still Open	75 55W +39 switches	Lever frame & switches replaced by N/X panel 11/10/2004.
Windsor Bridge No.1	23/4/1940	29/6/69	95	Replaced an over-line box

This list of 65 boxes is from information supplied by Tony Graham, Mike Addison, Bruce Bennett, Reg. Instone, Alan Roberts, Trevor Moseley and Bryan Wilson, and was compiled on 25th January 2012. The Ministry of Transport practice of signalling inspections fell into abeyance and by the end of 1943 286 places were on the list of works awaiting inspection that applied to many of the signal boxes listed above.

Tuffley Junction 'ARP' Signal Box opened on 7th December 1941 and closed on 11th August 1968, having had a 50-lever frame, basically as on page 42.

Authors Collection

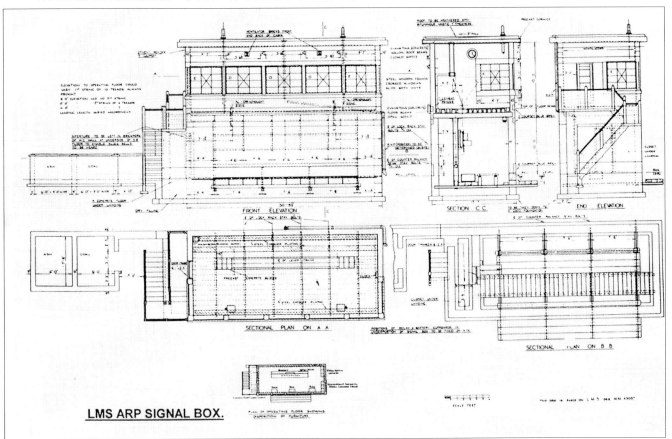

LMS ARP SIGNAL BOX.

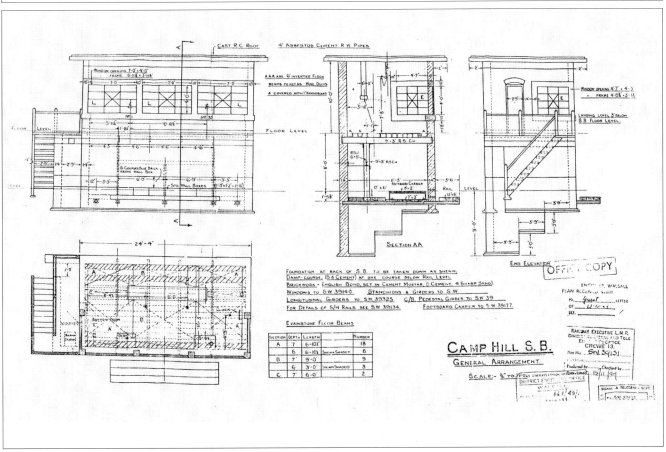

Signals

Signal Renewals. These were ongoing all the year round with the Sighting Committee continuously employed viewing all signals reported for renewal recommending any desirable alteration in the site, construction or height of the replacements. This work came under the Chief Operating Manager (COM) with all recommendations reviewed at HQ by the COM and S&T Engineer. The pre-war target for renewals was in the region of one thousand per annum. During the war only the most urgent cases could be dealt with which left a heavy programme of signal renewals awaiting the cessation of hostilities as follows :-

Year	1939	1940	1941	1942	1943	Total Deficit
Completed	864	500	494	621	892	
Outstanding Balance	136	500	506	379	106	1,629

Many signals had their life extended by heavy timber slabbing or "grandfathering" (also known as "godfathering") at the base of the post, additional guying or even heavy props produced from old telegraph poles.

Semaphore Signal Lights

Aerial observations were carried out in 1938 that established that semaphore signal lights were unlikely to give much assistance to enemy aircraft. The same could not be said for colour light signals when it was decreed that such signals should be provided with a hood 2' 0" long which were all in place prior to the war commencing. Banner signals were also hooded, dependent on type. The very few oil lit signals that were visible from the sea were also screened in various ways.

There were three types of long burning signal lamps in use, the ex Midland Railway No.10 and the LMS Adlake Nos.12 and 22 that would all burn for eight days without attention, and all used the highest quality oil known as Grade 1 Petroleum. During the war oil resources were pooled and controlled by the Petroleum Board who then introduced Pool "Signal" Oil and Pool "Burning" Oil, the former being the equivalent to the Grade 1 Petroleum. Towards the end of 1940 "Signal" oil was in short supply and tests were carried out as to the suitability of "Burning" Oil when it was agreed that it could be used should the situation worsen In January 1942 no further supplies of "Signal" oil could be imported and that mid-week inspections of the lamps may be found necessary. Early in 1943 considerable difficulty was found with the No. 22 type lamps and numerous instances occurred with them being blown out during gales. The question then arose as to whether this was due to inferior Oil or a design defect in the lamp. Exhaustive tests took place, but no final conclusion was reached at that time and the No. 22 continued to be unreliable, with no problems as far as the Nos. 10 and 12 were concerned.

Colour Light Signals

The very intense air raids in August and September 1940 caused the Government to think that, in spite of the hooding, colour light signals were aiding the Luftwaffe. Reference to the

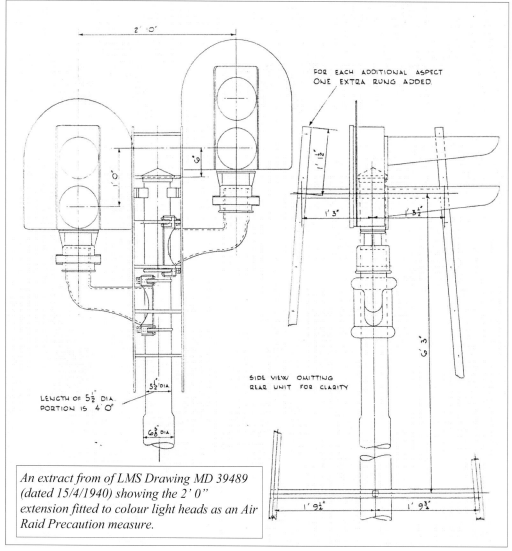

An extract from of LMS Drawing MD 39489 (dated 15/4/1940) showing the 2' 0" extension fitted to colour light heads as an Air Raid Precaution measure.

extension of the hood to two feet in length was referred to above, but this proved to be still too bright during the hours of darkness. To obviate this switches were provided enabling the signalman to reduce the intensity of the lights by approximately 60% of the voltage and the light to 6% of normal, and turned to the "dim" position at the commencement of the "blackout" period, except when fog prevailed. Under normal conditions the 12volt lamp was run on 11volts that materially increased the expected life of the lamp and still gave a beam that could be seen upwards of half a mile even in bright sunlight. Tests were made when it was found that a reduction to between 5½ and 4½ volts was equal to that given by a long burning oil lamp. Arrangements were then made for dimming the lamps during blackout hours except during fog when the voltage was maintained as during daylight. On the large colour light installations run at 110volt dc for signal lighting the voltage was reduced by half during black-out hours. An interesting situation arose at Barking on the Southend line that had been re-signalled with colour light signals. East London was the subject of heavy bombing and the locals considered that the Luftwaffe was following the colour light signals and threatened to destroy the lights if they were not switched off, this in spite of the fact that they had been dimmed. Although the staff assured them that they were no threat at the height the planes flew, a few signals were interfered with. In addition to the dimming of 1,878 colour light signals referred to above, certain other signals such as banner signals, route indicators and semaphores that were electrically intensified were similarly dealt with. To safeguard against failure of the current supply to colour light installations, a number of mobile generating sets were stabled at strategic points throughout the LMS system, so that they could be taken to any place where a failure had occurred.

Major new S&T works

At the outbreak of the war, the LMS was committed to certain new works that, for various reasons, could not be deferred indefinitely and by arrangement with the Ministry of War Transport were proceeded with providing the war effort was not hindered. These were:-

Rugby – Colour light signalling and track circuiting of the main running lines, the purpose of which was to reduce the headway through Rugby from five to three minutes. No new signal boxes.

Crewe – Colour light signalling and full track circuiting together with the provision of two signal boxes built to the Air Raid Precaution specification.

Wigan – Re-signalling with colour lights and full track circuiting when three new electro mechanical ARP type signal boxes replaced twelve mechanical boxes.

Camden to Sudbury – Colour light signalling and track circuiting of running lines to gain improved headway between these points.

Materials

As with the Civil Engineer's Department the S&T Dept had the same difficulty with the shortage of materials, particularly steel, timber and aluminium that became worse as the war progressed. It was only due to the pre-war foresight of the Signal Engineers in pressing for a 12 months' supply for emergency repairs that kept much wartime work from being seriously delayed. As far as timber was concerned, in October, 1939, a licence had to be obtained from the Ministry of Supply (Timber Control) before any item of timber could be supplied that stated – the quantity and the exact purpose for which it was required and the period during which the timber would be used. In January 1940 the situation became so serious that further restrictions were issued that stated - "consumers may only use their own stocks under licence from the Ministry of Supply". Railway Companies were exempted provided the timber was used for – the construction of any new work or equipment to the direct order of the Government or the maintenance or renewal of works or equipment necessary for the operation of essential transport services. In addition the railways were asked to conserve supplies, restrict their use, pool their resources and only draw on existing stocks for work of vital use. In June 1942 further instructions were received that any timber required for Government Contracts must be obtained specially out of the quota of the Government Department concerned. Had this instruction been acted upon literally it would have formed a most efficient brake on the progress of a number of Government Contracts on which the S&T Department was engaged. For example - in an urgent order for a new loop or fan of sidings, one of the first moves might be to construct a new pole line before removing the line of poles that occupied the site of the new work to enable the Civil engineer to make a start on the site. The obvious thing would be to use our own poles and give the earliest possible release to the Engineer but this became an illegal act and work, therefore, had to be held up in such cases pending the heavy machinery of control being set in motion and poles supplied out of the MoWT quota. There were therefore likely occasions when the zeal of the Company's Officers for the war effort might have seen the Chief Stores Superintendent prosecuted. Other items such as zinc were in exceedingly short supply that led to the Crewe galvanising plant being shut down in July 1940. A legacy of this was that the channel rodding used for points could only be protected by a coating of hard tar varnish that resulted in all channel used during the 1941/2/3 period having a much shorter life. Other steel items such as Signal wire and telegraph pole fittings were also similarly affected. As far as the re-use of materials was concerned - Board minute 4124 dated 25th July 1940 included a report by Sir Harold Hartley dealing with redundant assets and the salvaging and re-use of what in pre-war days would have been scrap. All the LMS Works were involved and photographs included of what had been achieved. The S&T Department had several examples one of which was a single post signal - *see overleaf.*

An LMS single post signal at Way and Works, Derby on 17th May 1940 utilising a 5½" diameter ex locomotive smoke tube as the main stem with a 6 ½" diameter bottom portion of new material. It is understood in the long term the post quickly deteriorated. Also in the picture are two air raid shelters under construction using pre-cast sections made at the LMS Newton Heath Concrete Works near Manchester as referred to in Chapter 2. The coaling plant is the No.1 pattern of which only a few were constructed, other sheds gaining new plant being Crewe North and Longsight.

BR DY27008

Road Transport

Prior to the war the S&T department possessed no road motor vehicles, in fact arising out of the rail and road controversy of pre-war days, it was a matter of personal pride, not to say prejudice, to make the minimum use of road services, but the war altered that viewpoint and experience gained since 1939 made road transport essential. Road transport proved to be a highly effective time and a money saver as with a restricted wartime train service, not to mention no service at all due to enemy action, the movement

of men and materials by road proved to be of paramount importance. The first vehicle was a 10 cwt. Fordson motor van delivered to the Barking Depot for use throughout that area which was somewhat remote from the rest of the system.

Following the restriction of train services, a further van was obtained for the Rugby Depot which proved to be such a valuable aid that as soon as they could be obtained, similar vans were supplied to Manchester, Sheffield, Chester, Bristol and Glasgow. Additionally, vans of 30 cwt capacity were supplied to Stoke, Warrington, Bedford and Perth. Watford Depot was of such importance to the London Area that a 3ton lorry was substituted for the 10 cwt van. Each van was fitted with tool cupboards, equipped with essential tools and a short ladder. A suitable man was trained to drive by the Road Motor Department. The vans proved to be a very great asset in moving men and materials from place to place, especially in country districts where the train service was restricted. In the case of air raid damage it was possible to commence, and at times complete, repairs long before men would have been available by train service. In connection with new works the maximum amount of time could be spent on the job without it being necessary to have regard to the timing of the last return train, the coming of darkness being the deciding factor, thereby hastening completion of the work and generally effecting a considerable saving in travelling time and/or lodging expenses. The view opposite portrays a trailer fitted out as a mobile workshop. In view of the possible necessity for transporting heavy stores and men in an emergency, arrangements were made with the Chief Operating Manager and the Chief Commercial Manager that the S&T Department had an A1 priority call on the services of a heavy motor lorry and driver at thirteen specified centres. During the heavy "blitz" on Liverpool this assistance proved invaluable both for men as well as material as in various directions transport had entirely broken down with the lorry collecting the gangs in the morning and returning them home at night. Road bolster vehicles were also similarly used for the transport of stores of unusual dimensions such as signal posts and telegraph poles. An appreciable number of supervisory staff possessed their own motor cars and when petrol restrictions came into force such cars were maintained by the Company and run on petrol drawn from the Company's supply solely for use on Departmental business. The Company provided cars for key personnel.

Rail Transport

Following the severe damage by enemy action in the early part of the war and more particularly that at Liverpool, the LMS set up a system whereby a dining and kitchen car coupled to a 3rd class sleeping coach were stabled at eight places throughout the system to accommodate and feed men hurriedly called away from their home depot in connection with repair of serious damage necessitating continuous effort during the hours of daylight. A temporary telephone was

A 10cwt Fordson van, fleet No. 175-S at Radcliffe, Manchester on 2nd.December 1940.
Nelson Twells Collection.

A trailer fitted out as a mobile workshop (No.1MWS), complete with Blacksmith's hearth, jacks, vices, portable generator, grinding wheel etc.
Nelson Twells Collection.

fitted in each of the kitchen cars to enable the number of meals required and the time of the men's arrival to be advised. A stock of non-perishable food was kept permanently in the cars for this purpose. In addition to this, four mobile canteens were provided for emergency repair gangs of the Chief Civil Engineer and the S&T Engineer dispensing hot soup and tea as well as corned beef, bread and margarine - *see next page.* These canteens were under the control of the District Civil Engineer's and located at Northampton, Walsall, Blackburn and Glasgow. They were available for despatch to any point required, either by road or rail according to the circumstances, crane power being

required at the destination to lift the canteen off the carriage truck or road motor trailer. For normal work necessitating men living away from home for an extended period, in view of the difficulty of finding lodgings under war conditions, the use of dormitory coaches was considerably extended. Prior to the war the use of such vehicles was confined to Scotland where, north of Perth, habitations are scattered. The five pre-war vehicles were extended to seven and in view of the isolated nature of the surrounding country, the men's evening amusement was catered for by the provision of dart boards, cards and games. South of the border nineteen dormitory coaches were provided by the conversion of holiday caravan

A Commer15cwt van, fleet No. 178-S, fitted out as a mobile canteen, with one allocated to each of the four Divisional Civil Engineers.
Nelson Twells Collection

coaches, each having provision for eighteen men per coach. These vehicles served a very useful purpose when so many Government works were in hand, but they had the disadvantage of requiring siding accommodation that on occasions meant a walk of several miles to and from the site of the work. Portable huts were provided on the Western Division, built in sections and secured by lynch pins enabling erection to be completed within an hour. Each hut housed eight men and contained bunks hinged from the wall and swung out of the way during daytime leaving room for a table and forms for mess purposes. These huts proved to be of great value when constructing telephone lines as they accommodated a construction gang and could be moved along as the work progressed and so provided the maximum time on the job. Difficulties continually arose in connection with rations with schemes being approved and accepted in certain areas and being turned down by Local Food Officers in other areas and it was not until September 1943 that the Ministry of Food approved a scheme that was satisfactory to both the men and the Company. In pre-war days most S&T gangs were provided with rail vans in which were stored and transported all necessary tools, ladders, ropes etc. These

vans, when placed in an adjacent siding could also be used as a workshop and as a place where meals could be taken under cover when other accommodation was not available. The stock of forty-nine vans was augmented by a further sixteen to cater for the additional gangs necessitated by war conditions.

War damage.

Restoration of the instances of major damage that were incurred at the main centres are referred to in the following chapters was typical of the widespread destruction that affected hundreds of other centres during the "blitz" period. The immense amount of restoration work involved to preserve continuity of communication services threw a terrific strain on the Department's labour and material resources, and the successful carrying out of the work was a magnificent achievement on the part of all S&T staff. Restoration work had to continue long after the actual event, as repairs, initially of a temporary nature, had to be made permanent later, and indeed had priority over everything else. Work was undertaken with the utmost expediency, often under very difficult and dangerous conditions with an "alert " still in progress, which, under "blackout" conditions, made it a matter of wonderment that at times communications were restored before the "all clear" was sounded. The provision of new, and the preservation of existing services by the S&T Engineer's staff facilitated in no small measure the task of the Operating Department. The Chief Operating Manager's successful and efficient traffic working was therefore an adequate testimony to the work performed by the S&T Department.

Military Assistance was afforded by the Royal Engineers at the time of the intensive bombing in 1940/1 in rendering appreciable help in repairing air raid damage, usually consisting of 12 men with an officer in charge. Such help was given at Willesden, Barking, Liverpool, Birmingham and Bristol. Unfortunately no real forward planning could be carried out as these squads were all liable to recall by the Military Authorities at a moments notice, which led to little reliance being placed on such assistance. Scotland was more fortunate with considerable military assistance being given to the LMS over an extended period to provide many miles of new telephone circuits. Up to the end of 1943 there were 1,768 incidents involving damage to S&T equipment of

	1939/ 1940	1941	1942	1943	Totals
Enemy Action	599	665	41	10	1,315
British Aircraft	9	15	11	25	60
Ack Ack Gunfire	23	14	2	19	58
Barrage Balloons coming Adrift, Trailing Cables	177	108	21	28	334
British Floating Mine*	-	-	-	1	1
Totals	**808**	**802**	**75**	**83**	**1,768**

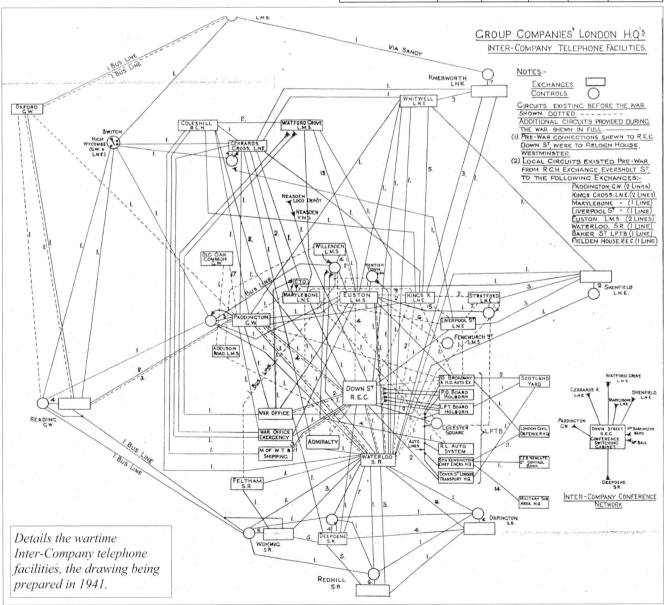

Details the wartime Inter-Company telephone facilities, the drawing being prepared in 1941.

which 1,315 were directly caused by enemy action, the remaining 453 cases were due to various causes mentioned in the summary on the previous page.

*The unusual floating mine incident was at Abergele, North Wales on 3rd. January 1943. The mine exploded off the shore when the blast caused damage to the windows and roof of an adjacent signal box. The majority of cases were of a minor nature, but there were several major incidents of enemy action such as Birmingham on 19th October 1940 and Manchester on 23rd December 1940. Up to March 1944 seven signal boxes had been completely destroyed and three were seriously damaged but repairable and one dispensed with by amalgamation.

The staff.

There is no doubt that the S&T staff responded fully to the heaviest calls made on them, particularly during the period of heavy bombing in 1940/1 when a large amount of lodging away from home was necessary, often leaving their families to face the blitz alone. Many were recognised for their efforts e.g. F. Renshaw, a Rugby Locking Fitter was awarded the BEM. In 1938 the Department employed 4,511 staff of all grades of which 89 were female. In 1943 the total had reduced to 4,273 of which 171 were female.

Bicester No.2 'ARP' Signal Box opened on 9th November 1941 and closed on 29th October 1973, having had a 30-lever frame.
Authors Collection

5

THE RAILWAY EXECUTIVE COMMITTEE AND FINANCE

THE LMS – PRELUDE TO WAR – PLANNING AND DELIVERING

Introduction

Great Britain in the 1930's was in a period of slow but steady change. The adoption of holidays-with-pay for many workers had made travel and leisure more accessible for ordinary families. Road transport grew exponentially with bus companies and road hauliers providing alternatives in public transport and the development of the private motor car had allowed many to relinquish their reliance on public transport and on the railways for leisure travel.

Against this background of limited prosperity, the prospect of another war with Germany and its allies grew year on year. Many people in Great Britain, especially those who had been through the First World War and those who were in business, war with Germany seemed inevitable; ordinary people were resigned to it, businesses felt they had to plan for it. The LMS, like other railways, saw the need to prepare for it. The railways had, on one hand, to attempt to preserve their traditional traffic and compete with road transport, whilst planning for the national emergency that would accompany a war in Europe. Set out below are accounts of the way in the

The 'Square Deal' campaign.

Men of the Moment

Sir Josiah Charles Stamp

Sir William Valentine Wood

Sir Ralph Wedgewood

Sir Cyril Hurcomb

Thomas Roydon Bart

Sir James Milne

LMS, in concert with the other railways, dealt with the situation and made itself ready for war.

LMS Commercial Position in the 1930's

The four main line railways were private companies, each with a board of directors serving the interests of shareholders. However they were not private companies like other industries as the way in which they were managed and how they discharged their business was governed by the Act of Parliament, which brought them into existence in 1923, the 1921 Railways Act. All of the railways charges and fares were fixed, subject to adjustment by the Railway Rates Tribunal, and the profit of the companies was defined by the 1921 Railways Act, which included the concept and definition of "Standard Net Revenue". The companies were not allowed to exceed "Standard Revenue" and the Act placed a duty on the Railway Rates Tribunal to adjust fares and charges to ensure the railways did achieve "Standard Revenue". The LMS, as did the other companies, suffered from poor financial results from the time of its formation. The amount of profit the companies were allowed to earn, as

"Standard Revenue", was based on the results for the pre-grouping companies in 1913; the act set this at £51.4 million for the four line companies. However none of the companies, including the LMS, individually or collectively achieved "Standard Revenue" for any year during their entire existence. In the 11 years preceding the outbreak of war, the companies were in arrears of £175 million or 3½ years of Standard Revenue; the cause of the deficit, apart from economic circumstances at the beginning of the 1930's, was the unregulated competition from road transport, not foreseen at the time of the 1921 Railways Act and the more favourable treatment given to coastal shipping. The railways had to do something about the declining situation and did so through the Railway Companies Association (RCA) and negotiation with the Government.

Railway Management and the Government

The railway companies' delegates to the RCA were directors and general managers and three figures became prominent from the companies in which all of the negotiations with the Government:-

	Standard Revenue Railways Act 1921		Actual Results		Deficit	Balance
Year	Return on Capital %	Standard revenue / £ millions	Return on Capital %	Actual Revenue / £ millions	£ million	Cumulative deficit £ millions
1923	4.70	51.4	4.40	48.1	-3.3	-3-3
1924	4.70	51.4	4.00	43.7	-7.7	-10.9
1925	4.70	51.4	3.60	39.4	-12.0	-23.0
1926	4.70	51.4	1.90	20.8	-30.6	-53.6
1927	4.70	51.4	4.00	43.7	-7.7	-61.2
1928	4.70	51.4	3.80	41.6	-9.8	-71.1
1929	4.70	51.4	4.20	45.9	-5.5	-76.6
1930	4.70	51.4	3.50	38.3	-13.1	-89.7
1931	4.70	51.4	3.20	35.0	-16.4	-106.1
1932	4.70	51.4	2.60	28.4	-23.0	-129.0
1933	4.70	51.4	2.80	30.6	-20.8	-149.8
1934	4.70	51.4	3.10	33.9	-17.5	-167.3
1935	4.70	51.4	3.10	33.9	-17.5	-184.8
1936	4.70	51.4	3.30	36.1	-15.3	-200.1
1937	4.70	51.4	3.50	38.3	-13.1	-213.3
1938	4.70	51.4	2.60	28.4	-23.0	-236.2
The cumulative deficit from 1928 to 1938 was £175 million						
Under Government Control, the results to 1942, were:					Deficit	Balance
			Return on capital %	Actual Revenue £ millions	£ million	Cumulative deficit / £ millions
1939	4.70	51.4	3.40	43.00	-8.4	-8.4
1940	4.70	51.4	3.50	43.00	-8.4	-16.8
1941	4.70	51.4	3.60	43.00	-8.4	-25.2
1942	4.70	51.4	3.60	43.00	-8.4	-33.6

From the LMS: -
Sir Josiah Stamp **(Note 1)**   President of the LMS 1926 to 1941.
Sir William V Wood **(Note 2),** President of the LMS 1941 to 1947.
From the LNER:-
Sir Ralph Wedgwood, **(Note 3)** General Manager of LNER 1923 to 1939.
From the Government, Ministry of Transport, later Ministry of War Transport.
Sir Cyril Hurcomb **(Note 4)** Secretary to the Ministry of Transport..
Sir Leonard Browett KCB; Permanent Secretary to the Board of Trade later the Ministry of Transport
These individuals feature regularly in the account of the discussions that follow. The Ministries of Transport and Shipping were merged to form the Ministry of War Transport on 9th May 1941.
Other personalities who are referred to below are:-
Lord Royden, **(Note 5)** Chairman of the LMS, 1941 to 1945
Sir James Milne, **(Note 6)** General Manager, Great Western Railway, 1929 - 1947

The "Square Deal" campaign

The companies, led by Sir Ralph Wedgwood, supported by Sir William Wood, launched their campaign for a "Square Deal" in November 1938. The campaign aimed at removing from the railways the restrictions placed on them by the 1921 Railways Act to allow them to compete on fairer terms with other forms of transport. The Government understood the financial position of the railways acknowledged in a memorandum to the Cabinet dated 21st December 1938 CP 278 [38] *"The Finances of the Railways"* which stated in paragraph 3:-

"Finances have been declining for years. This year the decline in gross receipts is £6 million and the increase in the cost of wages and materials is £4 million. It is estimated that the Net Revenue for this year is £28 million against £51.5 million under the 1921 Act. The LNER is in the worst position."

Not withstanding the memo, the campaign was unsuccessful, being abandoned on the outbreak of war in September 1939. Thus in the lead up to the Second War, the railways were very short of cash to service their capital; the effect on the LMS from the Government's failure to heed the railways' claim for equality with other forms of transport were outlined by Lord Stamp, President of the company, in a speech to the Glasgow Chamber of Commerce on 15th February 1939, when speaking of out-dated anti-monopolistic legislation (the 1921 Railways Act), he said, *"it was the clearest warning that Britain's railways would be forced into bankruptcy, if legislation was not changed".*

It was against this background that the LMS began preparations for war in October 1937.

Preparations for War – Government Control of the railways

All of the discussions held with by the railways with the company were through the RCA. Officers from the companies attended these meetings as delegates of the RCA and spoke on behalf of all railway companies. At a meeting on 14th December 1937 at the Ministry of Transport, attended by Sir William Wood and Sir Ralph Wedgwood, the railways asked the Government for its proposals for an agreement to take control of the railways in the event of a national emergency. In the First World War, the Government had taken *possession* of the railways under the 1871 Regulation of Forces Act *using a weekly (Statutory) Order,* which would be renewed until the railways were advised to the contrary. The railways, wishing to avoid a similar arrangement, understood and accepted that the Government would take *control* in a national emergency but as Sir William Wood said at the meeting, the railways needed to understand on what terms control would be exercised to enable the railways to make adequate plans. Matters such as compensation for deterioration of properties through arrears of maintenance, use of stocks and stores, interest on additional capital required, allowance for new works and special arrangements for the use of ships owned by the railways amongst others, were discussed in principle. The railway companies raised the matter of the appointment of a shadow Railway Executive Committee as the meeting to prepare for control once it was taken by the Government. Sir William Wood prepared a memorandum dated 13th December 1937 for the LMS Board. He also undertook to draft for Sir Ralph Wedgwood, a scheme covering the principles of Government control which he did. The note, as submitted to the Government through the Ministry of Transport, survives in the National Archive (RAIL 424/15). It covers the principles of use of the railway companies assets and the compensation to be paid by the Government. Sir Ralph Wedgwood and Sir William Wood continued the discussions with the Ministry of Transport for a further 20 months without conclusion; the LMS, along with the other companies found themselves in difficulty in planning for any emergency, due to the absence of any agreement. An insight into the background of these discussion and the worries of the individuals involved, may be obtained by reference to a letter written to Sir William Wood by Sir Ralph Wedgwood in September 1938; the letter discusses the matters which needed to be resolved with the Ministry of Transport; dictating his letter on Saturday 19th September 1938 three days after Neville Chamberlain's return from his meeting with Adolph Hitler in Munich, Sir Ralph says in the final paragraphs:-

"I hope you won't think me a nuisance if I send you, for your personal consideration, a fresh statement of our case, which I wrote out on Saturday morning, It is, I think, shorter and more cogent than that which I have circulated, and is influenced by the conversation I had with Browett. My only excuse for this untimely activity is that I find the

consideration of the compensation question a useful antidote to the kind of mental toothache which I suffer while contemplating Hitler's shameful bluff and Chamberlain's all to probable surrender".

On 4th October 1938, Sir Ralph Wedgwood sent the railway companies' proposals to the Ministry of Transport, which acknowledged receipt of them on 6th October 1938. Even in those dark times, there appears to have been little urgency on the part of Government and little progress was made. An internal memorandum to the Board of the LMS, dated 16th May 1939, initialled by Lord Stamp, entitled *"Emergency Arrangements – Compensation"*, noted that:- *"Sir James Milne has recently ascertained that the Ministry of Transport are not yet able to move in this matter and the position is as it was last September".* The memorandum went on to record that:-

Evacuees.

Hulton Getty Archive 3301336

"a memorandum (copy attached), setting out in detail the railway companies' case for their proposals and the considerations, which in the railway companies' view can be urged against the arguments put forward by the Ministry, was sent to Sir Leonard Browett by Sir Ralph Wedgwood on 4th October 1938.

*Sir Leonard replied that he would have the memorandum examined **without delay** and hoped to be able to fix an early date for a meeting.*

The position was reported to the Railway Companies Association on 3rd October (1938), when the General Managers were requested to continue the negotiations, it being agreed that before any scheme is accepted, the Chairmen would require to consult their respective boards"

With the international situation worsening, the General Managers of the four companies held a meeting in the LMS offices at Euston on 13th July 1939 at which they expressed their concern at the continuing difficulties in planning. Sir James Milne, General Manager of the GWR, wrote to the Ministry on 17th July 1939 asking for decisions, the Ministry acknowledged the letter on the 18th July 1939, stating that *"we are, as you know, doing our very best to get this difficult question settled and I hope to be able to let you have a decision at an early date".* However the reply was further delayed as the civil servant dealing with the matter, Sir Leonard Browett, was on holiday on 4th August 1939. War was now less than 4 weeks away! Later that month, with war inevitable, the Government took control of the railways, with no control agreement to do so in place after almost two years of discussion. However the 1921 Railways Act, with the concept of Standard Revenue, remained in force and so the railway companies were therefore bound by its provisions.

Control passed to the Government on 1st September 1939 under the Emergency Powers (Defence) Act 1939, Defence Regulation 69; this allowed the Government to retain control of the railways for a minimum of one year after the end of the War. All of the discussions between the railways and the Government had been based on the Government taking *possession* as its predecessor had done in 1914. However in the conflict, the Government took *control.* The difference between the two procedures would lead to much difficulty in resolving disputes between the parties

Pre-war preparations – Air Raid Precautions

The railway companies had asked in their earliest meetings with the Ministry of Transport, who would deal with items such as air-raid precautions and how they would be paid for? So - who did pay for these works? At the Board meeting on 23rd January 1939 (minute 3866) it was disclosed that the Minister of Transport had agreed to defray the Railway Companies up to £3,250,000 to implement schemes to ensure that the railways could continue to operate in the case of an emergency, providing the Companies would carry out at their expense such part of the work necessary for the protection of their personnel which would fall normally under the obligation to be "good employers". A condition of the offer was that the railways would be taken into the possession of the Government in the event of war. Railway Companies Association on behalf of the four main line Companies accepted the offer without prejudice to any basis that may ultimately be agreed or determined in regard to the compensation to be paid to the Railways. The LMS share of this amount was £1,359,700 to be allocated as follows:-

	£
Administrative and control centres	267,000

Signal boxes	245,000
Power station and substation	73,000
Civil Engineer – Emergency stores (3 months supply)	129,000
Signal & Telegraph Engineer (Emergency Stores 12 month's supply)	317,000
Chief Mech. Engineer – Emergency stores (Loco spare parts – 3 months supply).	140,000
Lighting restrictions	85,000
Extra protection for essential staff at certain vital yards & depots	113,000

All companies between them were to provide :-

Twelve 35-ton steam breakdown cranes	120,000
Welding and burning plant	10,000
Emergency telephone connections with the GPO circuit	25,000
Improved hydraulic power plant at Brentford Docks for wartime coal supplies	113,000

Each of these items had been foreseen by the railways and representatives of the railway companies had met the Ministry of Transport on 14th July 1937 to discuss the ARP necessary; the outcome and the remaining items were then raised by Sir William Wood and Sir Ralph Wedgwood in their discussions with the Ministry of Transport from 1937 onwards. This left the LMS railway, under it's obligation as a "good employer" to consider the following:-

1. Training of air raid precaution services.
2. Work in preparation of schemes of precautions
3. Arrangements for giving air raid warnings.
4. Provision of reasonable splinter proof shelters.
5. Provision of protective clothing.
6. Additional fire fighting appliances.
7. Lighting restrictions.

By the end of 1944 the LMS had spent £3,740,000 on ARP work (all railways total £11.5m) with an additional £2,367,00 for on-going maintenance, fire-watching etc. This may seem high, but work would have stopped without adequate staff protection and the damage bill would have been much higher had fire-watchers and other ARP staff not been on duty.

The Control Agreements – 1940 and 1941

War had been declared and the Government had control. However there was no agreement in place defining the railway companies' responsibilities and the manner in which they would be compensated (paid) for the use of their assets. On 4th October 1939, the railway companies submitted their request to the Government for Standard Revenue, as defined in the 1921 Railways Act, of £51.5 million per annum, which equated to return on capital of 4.7%; Sir Leonard Browett replied on 8th November 1939 saying the Government did not accept the proposal but wanted a partnership with the railways, under which the railways were not concerned with

revenue and would not incur risks. The Government then decided to include the LPTB in the financial arrangement, which further complicated matters, as LPTB did not exist at the time of 1921 Railways Act. Furthermore LPTB's revenue was in decline, as it had no freight handling facilities, so the burden of the decline was placed on the freight revenues from the other companies. Given the serious position in which the LNER found itself, see above, thus the burden effectively fell on the LMS. The LMS Directors discussed the Government's proposals at the board meetings on 23rd November, 15th December and 21st December 1939; at the last of these meetings, the minutes record *"that up to the present, agreement has not been reached with the Government or between the companies themselves"*. Lord Stamp outlined the form of settlement under consideration and suggested that *"there was a possibility of an inter-company arrangement which would remove the present inequalities between the LMS and LNE companies on the one side and the G W and Southern Companies on the other, at which it was hoped would not be at variance with the settlement come to the railway companies (excluding the LPTB) and the Government"*.

Notwithstanding the railway companies' objections to the inclusion of LPTB in the financial arrangements, the Government refused to exclude LPTB, so at the LMS Board Meeting on 17th January 1940, the LMS Directors agreed to accept the Governments decision.. Therefore three years after negotiations started and five months after the Government assumed control of the railways, the First Control Agreement [Cmd 6168] came into effect. Put very simply, the amount paid to the companies and the LPTB amounted to £43.5 million per annum plus a 50% share of any sum above this figure until the companies reached the Standard Revenue set down in 1921 Railways Act. Although an agreement was reached and applied, the details were never agreed owing to the need to include the decisions of the Railway Rates Tribunal (RRT) regarding the effects of increased prices of labour and materials on passenger fares and freight charges and to modify it to comply with the War Damage Compensation Scheme (PRO MT47/277). In consequence the agreement was never signed. However it became known as the "First Control Agreement" In January 1941, an internal memorandum within the Ministry of Transport, for use by the Minister, discussed the financial effects of Government control of the railways; the covering note to the memorandum, written by Sir Leonard Browett, stated:-

"I advocate maintaining the present Agreement (subject to amending for War Damage). If that is politically impossible, the only alternative is a flat guarantee and I suggest it should apply from 1st January 1941. (PRO MT47/277).

At the end of January 1941, the Treasury wrote to the Ministry of Transport to say that:-

"Railways should be told that the Agreement needs revising due to War Damage." (PRO MT47/277).

On 17th June 1941, the Railways submitted proposals for a new Control Agreement for a payment of £50 – 55 million; Three days later, Sir Cyril Hurcomb, accompanied by Sir Leonard Browett, attended a meeting with the Railway Companies Association at which Sir Leonard Browett said that *"it was agreed that the present Agreement should be terminated"*. Sir William Wood denied this and pointed out that the first 20 weeks of 1941 were a 100% improvement on 1940 and continued by adding *"that the Government proposals on maintenance were unsound if the Government was trying to subsidise users then they should pay the Pool for it"* Sir William Wood's intervention was not favourably received by the MoWT and shortly afterwards, on 11th July 1941, a White Paper WP [41] 158 entitled *"Future of Railways"* was prepared for the Cabinet; the paper discussed the need to revise the present (first) Control agreement and to limit the cost to the Exchequer of war damage to £10 million. The proposals were discussed at a meeting between the Minster of War Transport, his civil servants and the railway chairman. Lord Royden, Chairman of the LMS, pointed out on behalf of the railways that *"the Government's intentions to drop the previous agreement and to negotiate a new Agreement had no regard to the past or obligations already incurred"*. The MoWT memorandum of the meeting records that *"Sir Cyril Hurcomb told the Railway Chairmen that the Government would consider amalgamation or reorganisation after the war"*. (PRO MT47/276). This was taken by the railways as a warning to accept the revised rental agreement or face nationalisation. After a period in which meetings and discussions between the Companies and the MoWT, the Railway Companies Association wrote to the MoWT on 22nd August 1941 confirming that the Companies would accept the sum of £43 million envisaged by the revised agreement but pointed out that this sum did not adequately cover the increased costs of operation. The RCA agreed to the Government's proposal as an accommodation to meet the urgent representations of the Government at a time of national emergency (PRO RAIL 424/18 & MT47/278). On the same day, 22nd August 1941, Sir Cyril Hurcomb met Sir James Milne and told him that the Government would revert to the *political scheme* if its latest offer was rejected. The political scheme was not defined but presumably it referred to nationalisation. The LMS Board after the reading of a memorandum regarding this agreement approved it at its meeting on 28th August 1941 (Minute 4342). In addition to the rental payment and the term of the agreement, it was to last for one year after the cessation of hostilities, it provided for time for the railways charges to be adjusted in line with the requirements of the 1921 Railways Act. Thus the "Second Control Agreement" [CmD 6314] came into force, providing the controlled undertakings with a fixed rental of £43 millions of which the LMS share was £14,749,698 per annum.

The LMS Board minutes refer to acceptance of the rental payment under the first and second control agreements, what is not mentioned is the charges the railways had to make by law. Between 1937 and 1946, there were only two increases in charges both of which were subject to public enquiries. The situation was also acknowledged by the Minister of War Transport who told Parliament that but for the restrictive effects of the First Control Agreement; the railways would have earned the Standard Revenue defined in the 1921 Railways Act. The effect on the LMS was to reduce its earnings from £19.13 million under the Act to £14.75 million as included in the Second Control Agreement. The condition in which the Government would hand back the assets to the railways remained in contention right up to the time of nationalisation.

Equitable agreement?

In March 1944, the Parliamentary Secretary to Minister of War Transport, Mr Philip Noel-Baker, when asked to back his claim that the Railway Control Agreement was fair to stockholders, by publishing correspondence and records of meetings, refused. His reason was that they were confidential and it would be contrary to public interest; he declined to do so in wartime or even after the war *"even if both parties agreed"* (Hansard, vol 374, col 847) The financial agreement with the Government under the second control agreement, provided for all net revenue due to the four mainline railways and the London Transport to accrue to the Government. The net revenues according to "British Railways in Peace and War" published in 1944 by the companies and London Transport, was in 1941, £65.1 million and in 1942, £89.1 million; the balances accruing to the Government after payments in each year of £500,000 to minor railways, were 21.6 million and £43.6 million respectively.

The Railway Executive Committee (REC).

As with the First World War, the Government exercised its control through the Railway Executive Committee, originally formed in 1912; the principle function of the REC was to act as adviser to, and the agent of, the Ministry of War Transport, so as to issue instructions covering the movement of men and war materials, and the distribution of essential supplies, being so planned that they could be executed by each of the railway companies through their existing organisations, with officers remaining responsible to their own managements and boards as in peacetime. The LMS found itself trying to reconcile two obligations; to carry out economically and efficiently the instruction received from the REC covering Government needs and policy and to maintain the integrity and smooth working of the company, discharging its own innumerable day-to-day functions in which the Government had no real or direct interest. This was not an easy task given that the LMS remained a private company bound by the provision of the 1921 Railways Act. Board Minute 3993 on 29th September 1939 recorded that the Company had received a letter from the Ministry of

Transport on 1st September that enclosed a copy of the order taking control of the Railways from that date. The companies involved were subsequently referred to as "controlled undertakings" in accordance with the pre-war discussions over such definitions. The Companies involved were:-

SR, GWR, LMS, LNER, LPTB, All Joint Committees of these companies i.e. S&DJR, M&GN etc, the East Kent Light Railway, the Kent and East Sussex Light Railway, the Kings Lynn Docks and Light Railway, the Mersey Railway Company, Shropshire Railways and the Shropshire and Montgomery Light Railway.

It was reported at the Board meeting on 30th May 1940 that the Railway Air Services together with their relative staff had been also taken over by the Government. Some LMS shipping, various hotels, ambulance trains, the School of Transport at Derby and the Chellaston Branch line were all requisitioned by the Government requiring payments to be negotiated and paid. Of the equipment requested prior to the War by the Government, by 30th May 1940 the LMS had already supplied 14 diesel shunting engines to the War Office with a further 22 wanted between July 1940 and October 1941.

The Minister appointed the following as the Railway Executive Committee:- Sir Ralph Lewis Wedgwood CB CMG, Chairman, Sir James Milne KCVO, CSI, Mr C. H. Newton, Mr Frank Pick, Mr Gilbert Savil Szlumper CBE, Sir William Valentine Wood. Mr G. Cole Deacon was appointed Secretary to be the Ministers agent "for the purposes of giving directions under the order and any directions in writing signed by any two members of the REC or by any member and the Secretary of the Committee shall be a valid exercise of the authority hereby given to the Committee".

The LMS Chairman (Lord Stamp) then drew attention to a sentence in the covering letter that said – "You will carry on as usual subject to the directions of the REC".
Many members of LMS staff were seconded to assist REC; the salaries and wages of all of the railway staff, whether members of the REC or clerical staff, seconded to the REC were paid for by the companies, the LMS was no exception; the Government made no additional payment so the hard bargain driven by the Government in respect of the first and second control agreements (and the annual payments) was made even harder.

War damage

The liability for meeting the cost of war damage delayed the completion of the First Control Agreement and it was not agreed at the time of the Second Control Agreement. Liability for the cost of war damage and the moneys to pay for it were not agreed until 1949. Compensation for war damage, generally, was first considered in 1939, [Cmd 6136] when the Government *undertook to pay the highest compensation possible at the end of the War"*. The basis of reinstatement will as between as willing buyer and a willing seller. In 1940 a further paper [Cmd 6197] was issued for agriculture and, finally, in 1941 a third paper [Cmd 6403] was issued for public utilities (including railways), which were excluded from the provisions of the first two papers, as *"they are not appropriate"*. In the third paper the Government reduced its liability from 100% to 50% of the cost and told the railways that they had to pay their share from the rental payment and not from working costs. On 15th January 1943, an internal MoWT paper on Post-war railways said that the amount of war damage to the end of 1942 was £19 million and was estimated to reach £25 million by the end of war; how that could be calculated in 1942 when the war had not turned in the Allies favour is difficult to understand. The LMS proportion of the damage sustained to the end of 1942 was £4,660,000 on the companies own lines and on its share of joint lines. It was stated on 29th January 1943 that the government Bill dealing with war damage had still to be submitted to Parliament. By Treasury Order in 1949, the Government paid £24.8 million as its share of the railways claim for compensation or 72.1% of the claims made by the railways; the monies were paid to the BTC in 1949.

So much for the legal and financial discussions, what was the practical effect on the LMS and its employees?

Note 1.

Sir Josiah Charles Stamp GBE,, DSc,(Lond), FCIS, President and Chairman of the LMS 1927 to 1941.
He was born in June 1880 and educated at London University taking the degree of BSc with First Class Honours in 1911. He entered the Civil Service in 1896 in the Inland Revenue Department. In 1898 he was appointed to the Marine Department of the Board of Trade. In 1900 he went to the Taxes Department of the Inland Revenue Department, being transferred in 1914 to the Secretariat and becoming Assistant Secretary to the Board in 1916. In 1918 he received the CBE becoming KBE in 1920. Following WW1 Earl Lloyd George described Lord Stamp as the greatest living economist. In 1919 he resigned from the Civil Service to become Secretary to Nobel Industries, Ltd. On 1st. January 1926 he was appointed President of the Executive of the LMS Railway and on 1st November 1927 became Chairman of the Company on the retirement of Sir Guy Granet, remaining President of the Executive Committee. His salary was £20,000pa. Stamp had the ability to translate into everyday terms the most abstruse and technical subjects, of which there was no shortage on the LMS Railway. In 1938 he was raised to the peerage as Baron Stamp of Shortlands in the Birthday Honours list In the early months of the war he travelled to distant parts of the railway listening to any problems the staff may have had and helping them to overcome them. He died as Josiah Charles Stamp, First Baron of Shortlands in a London air raid on 16th April 1941 together with his wife Olive Jessie and his eldest son The Hon Wilfred Carlyle Stamp. On 31st November 1941 the Board subscribed £1000 to a memorial.

Josiah Stamp was a very highly respected and well-known economist who had sat on several UK national organisations and government and international committees between the Wars. As Sir Josiah Stamp, he was:-

A Governor of the Bank of England
Member of the Economic Advisory Council

Advisor on Economic Co-ordination to Ministerial Committee 1939 to 1941.

President Abbey Road Permanent Building Society and Member of the Committee on Taxation and National Debt, 1924.

British representative on the Reparation Commission's (Dawes) Committee on German Currency and Finance, 1924 and (Young) Experts Committee, 1929.

Lord Stamp's advice and assistance was requested by the Government before the outbreak of the war when it became obvious in 1939 that all hope of averting war was rapidly vanishing. In March 1939, Sir John Anderson (afterwards Lord Waverley), the Lord Privy Seal, wrote to Lord Stamp, on behalf of the Prime Minister, Neville Chamberlain, enquiring if he (Stamp) would be prepared to be nominated for the appointment, in the event of emergency, as Regional Commissioner for the North West. Lord Stamp, after consultation with some of the directors of the LMS declined the invitation, on the basis that his duties at such a critical time lay in London. Sir John Anderson

LMS Home Guard using rail wagon for cover.   *Hulton Getty Archive 80185649*

was undaunted, feeling that in discharging his duty as Minister of Civil Defence, he should press Stamp to accept the appointment on a temporary basis until 1st November 1939, when another well-known public servant had agreed to take his place.

Lord Stamp, once more, declined the invitation, stating *"in all its bearings with my directors (of the LMS sic), I have never reached a responsible decision with more certainty as to its correctness. But with more regret in having to convey it, in the knowledge that it may well be misunderstand. My Directors are in full accord with it."*

On the outbreak of War, when the Government took control of the railways, Stamp was immediately invited by the Government to become an advisor on economic co-ordination. Lord Stamp wrote a personal note, which exists in his private papers, clarifying the situation but also to remove the apparent inconsistency in having refused to become Regional Commissioner earlier in the year. The note runs to eight paragraphs, which are reproduced in full below:-

*The Railways are now under Government control. Lord Stamp is under whole time contract with the LMS and although Lord Stamp theoretically is able to give up the Directorship, he is not free to **resign** from the Presidency of the Executive. In view of the changes for the time being in the onus of daily management, the LMS Board agree to **second** him for the proposed Government duties, on the clear understanding that he continues as Chairman, and is allowed to give enough time as President to maintain his hold on matters of major LMS policy. The Minister of Transport has acquiesced.*

The Government duties are unpaid.

*At the present time the "Compensation" question between the Government and the Railways is unsettled. It is a matter in which there is strong feeling on the part of the shareholders and their Boards. Lord Stamp feels that he is in a position of trusteeship on the conduct of the discussions and is honour bound to see them through as an **independent** representative.*

He considers he ought not to relinquish his duties for three reasons –
The trusteeship referred to:

*The best national service he can render is to continue to handle those major issues (in a sphere which is **also** national defence) in which he now has a great experience that cannot be immediately made good by any other person. (The consideration is reinforced by the fact that the Vice-President, Mr. Lemon, has been seconded to the Air Ministry as Director of Production for the duration of the War, and Sir Harold Hartley is also giving much time to Government service*
The contacts which the railway and Bank of England give Lord Stamp continuously first hand with industry and finance all over the country, and through which he is accustomed to keeping himself informed to make economic judgements, are in his view directly related to his competence as an advisor. To be cut off from them and to be forced to improvise or rely on new ones, he regards as likely to reduce his efficiency.

*The actual time given to these Government duties in September **(1939)** amounted to 35 hours per week and 29 of his railway and bank activities. Any other private interests are entirely in suspense.*

*Lord Stamp has been Chairman of the Government's Economic Information Committee (under the Economic Advisory Council) since he was appointed by Mr. **(Ramsey)** MacDonald some eight years ago **(in 1931)** and in that capacity has sent many confidential reports to respective Prime Ministers.*

*He has expressed his personal willingness, within the limits indicated, to give his service in what ever form may be deemed best, and is of course in no way responsible for the **particular form** which the whole question of economic control has now taken. But he made it a condition that he should have the full assistance of the two well-known economists, Mr. Clay and Mr. Henderson, seconded from their public positions.*

At the same time he and his Directors, with a more exact knowledge of the railway situation than outsiders can have, will always feel it their duty to express their opinions about the relative national values of proposals for time and energy of this kind. It was for this reason they repeatedly declined, earlier in the year, Ministerial requests for Lord Stamp's whole time services in another capacity which they judged to be on balance a less effective use of his experience.

With this request declined and concluded, Lord Stamp should have been able to continue his duties with the LMS and his pursuit of an equitable agreement on the "compensation" issue for the use by the Government of the railways. However this was not so, as early as 9th October 1939 the problem of economic planning in wartime was raised in the House of Commons, with pressure placed on the Government to appoint a Minister of Economics. Lord Stamp wrote a private document on the subject for the Government pointing out that such an appointment would lead to much confusion. In the debate that followed, the Prime Minister, Neville Chamberlain, indicated his intention and referred to the appointment of Lord Stamp as advisor on co-ordination, which gives a strong indication of the faith the Prime Minister had in Lord Stamp as an economic expert.

This faith lead in turn to the final effort by the Government to obtain Lord Stamp's services; the doubts harboured by the Prime Minister about the adequacy of the Chancellor of the Exchequer, Sir John Simon, came to a head at the end of 1939 leading to what Lord Stamp refers to in his private papers as "*The Chancellor Episode*"

On Tuesday 2nd January 1940, the Prime Minister requested Stamp to meet him the same evening. What followed was probably the most important event in Stamp's public life. The request received by Lord Stamp at the Grove, Watford *(LMS Wartime headquarters)* asking him to meet the Prime Minister at 6.30 p.m. Stamp promptly cancelled his evening engagement for dinner at Mill House (*part of the estate at the Grove, which was used to provide overnight accommodation for Directors or Vice-Presidents of the LMS)* and left for London at about 6.00 p.m.

At the meeting the Prime Minister came quickly to the point, saying he had the feeling that "*all was not well at the Treasury*" and having looked round all of his colleagues in Cabinet and in the House of Commons, said "*that his choice (as Chancellor of the Exchequer) fell on me (Stamp)*". Stamp discussed the request with the Prime Minister pointing out the difficulties, beyond those referred to earlier, in accepting the post as he had no political experience, he was a peer and therefore barred from sitting in the House of Commons and that he was in the forefront of the struggle with the Chancellor of the Exchequer to agree adequate compensation terms for the railways for their use by the Government.

The Prime Minster pressed Stamp for an answer, to which Stamp asked to be given time to consider, he was given until Thursday 4th January 1940. On Wednesday 3rd January 1940, Lord Stamp met the Governor of the Bank of England, Sir Montagu Norman, to discuss the approach. The Governor confirmed that he had been to see the Prime Minister about the need for change at the Treasury but was totally unaware of the PM's approach to Lord Stamp.

On Thursday 4th January 1940, Lord Stamp replied to the Prime Minster in a private letter setting out the issues surrounding an appointment and there the matter rested. The feeling within the country was growing that the Prime Minister and his Government were unequal to the task that lay ahead of them, which materialized with the appointment of Winston Churchill on 10th May 1940. Churchill subsequently invited Stamp to be become chairman of an important Government Council, details of which were never published, and which went with Stamp to his grave in 1941.

What is very clear is the esteem in which Lord Stamp was held by all politicians, the business community and bankers alike. One can only conjecture what influence he would have had on the negotiation and agreement of the compensation terms for the railways; the Second Control Agreement was approved by Parliament in August 1941, five months after his death, and what position he would have held in the British Transport Commission in 1948, had he lived we will never know.

Note 2.

"JOSIAH STAMP – PUBLIC SERVANT – THE LIFE OF THE FIRST BARON STAMP OF SHORTLANDS – J Harry Jones MA LLD – Sir Isaac Pitman & Sons, London 1964..

Note 3.

William Valentine Wood KBE, Vice President and later President of the LMS, 1930 to 1947, was born in 1884 and joined the staff of the Belfast and Northern Counties Railway in 1896 in the "Accountants Office". In 1917 the Government took over the Irish Railways when he was appointed Secretary, and later a member of the Railway Accountants Committee set up by the Irish Railway Executive Committee. When the Ministry of Transport was formed Wood came to London as the Ministry's director of transport accounting, being appointed as Accountant to the Committee in 1921. On 1st December 1924 he joined the LMS as Assistant to the Accountant General with a salary of £1850 pa. On 1st January 1927 he was appointed Controller of Costs and Statistics, his salary rising to £2200. On 1st January 1930 he was appointed as Vice President for Finance and Services on £4500. He received his Knighthood in 1937. In 1940 his specialist responsibilities to the Railway Executive Committee saw his salary increase to £8000 and to £10,000 in June 1941. On the death of Lord Stamp he became President until Nationalization on 1st January 1948. He had also served as Chairman of the Railway Clearing House. He retired on 1st September 1953 and died on 25th August 1959.

Note 4.

Sir Ralph Wedgwood, 1st Baronet CB, CMG, was born on 2nd March 1874 and was educated at Clifton College and Trinity College, Cambridge. He became Chief General Manager of the LNER on 1st January 1923 until his retirement in July 1939 and Chairman Railway Executive Committee September 1939 to August 1941. He died on 5th September 1956.

Note 5.

Sir Cyril Hurcomb. (raised to the peerage as Baron Hurcomb of Campden Hill in the Royal Borough of Kensington in 1950); died 7th August 1975.

Note 6.

Thomas Royden Bart., Chairman of the LMS 1941 to 1946., was born in May 1871 at Holmfield House, Mossley Hill, Liverpool and was educated at Winchester College and Magdelen College, Oxford. He then went in to the shipbuilding and ship owning firm of Thomas Royden and Sons of which his father was senior partner. He moved to railways on election to the L&Y Railway Board, LNWR Board and LMS Board in turn. He was Conservative MP for Bootle from 1918 to 1922 when pressure of business forced him to retire. On 15th March 1940 he was elected Deputy Chairman of the LMS Railway and on the death of Lord Stamp in 1941 became Chairman on £5000 pa. In 1923 the total remuneration for all Directors was not to exceed £35,000 and it was regretted that the Board could not pay him £10,000 pa as this would exceed the limit that still stood, however the limit was later amended and on 25th March 1943 he did receive his £10,000 fee. He retired in 1946 and was succeeded by Sir Robert Burrows.

Note 7.

Sir James Milne KCVO, CSI General Manager GWR, was educated at Campbell College, Belfast and Victoria University, Manchester. He joined the GWR in 1904 in the CME's Department at Swindon as a pupil under G. J. Churchward. He transferred to the Traffic Department and then the General Manager's Office in 1908 and was appointed Head of the Passenger Train Running Department in 1912. In 1916 he was Chief Clerk to the Divisional Superintendent at Pontypool Road and Assistant Divisional Superintendent Swansea in 1916. In 1916 he was appointed Assistant Divisional Superintendent, Plymouth and Director of Statistics at the Ministry of Transport in 1919. He was Assistant to the General Manager in 1922. In 1923 he was the Principal Assistant to the General Manager and in 1924 Assistant General Manager and finally General Manager in 1929 from which position he retired on 31st December 1947.

6

WAR IS DECLARED

LMS Staff, 1939/40/41 and the Dunkirk Evacuations.

The First Four Days.

On reading the foregoing, the reader might think the Civil Department was solely occupied with the inevitable approach of the war, which would be quite false. The fact is that all this work was on top of the Department's day-to-day responsibilities until the last few months, when they assumed major importance and overshadowed all the normal activities. For instance - track relaying in the first eight months of 1939 amounted to 474 miles that was more than anything achieved during the years 1923 to 1927. By the end of August 1939 all glass roofs at stations and similar structures were painted or had the glass removed and the indoor lighting restrictions brought into use. All District offices were manned day and night, as required by the ARP scheme, as aerial bombardment was considered likely even before war was declared. However, protection for personnel and equipment was still a problem that was not so easily solved. (The ARP budget worked out at £3 per member of staff) The timber trenches for the somewhat unhappily described as "non-essential" staff in vulnerable areas had been completed but due to the concrete units only just becoming available the "essential" staff at Motive Power Depots, Traffic yards etc had still to be catered for. The over -ground blast-proof shelters were in various stages of construction of which only three of the 42 had been completed. As a temporary measure some structures were strengthened and other improvised methods made, such as

the use of engine pits. (As an aside – does any reader know if any of these blast-proof buildings still exist?). Over 5million sandbags were filled and utilised using local initiative, and it could be justifiably claimed that the Company had done everything possible and there were few staff that did not have reasonably good protection and equipment. So, after all that urgent effort, not a single bomb fell on LMS property during the first nine months of the war which allowed all the protective measures to be completed enabling the Civil Engineer's to turn their attention to other aspects of the "War Effort".

One of the main concerns was for the Headquarters Staff and one of the earliest schemes to be authorised was the provision of a shelter under St. Pancras Chambers to accommodate some 22 skeleton staff consisting of the Chief Engineer, his principle assistants and other key staff. A self contained set of offices complete with telephone equipment and a poison gas filtration unit was installed. The need was to maintain continuous contact with the Districts and other Departments. In addition portions of the building were strengthened and adapted so that the whole staff could be protected from blast effects with tests carried out to show that all staff could reach the shelter in a few minutes following an alarm. Initially it was understood that Head Office would remain at St. Pancras Chambers with staff such as Accountants and Solicitors evacuated elsewhere as the

What were these children thinking? Where are we going? When will I see mum and dad again? Likewise the parents must have had similar thoughts!!!

British Rail

The Grove, Watford was owned by the LMS Property Company, Lineside Estates Ltd and was the LMS War-time Headquarters. It was originally the seat of the Earls of Clarendon and the fifth in line of the second creation Edward Hyde Villiers and his second wife are buried in the grounds. Lord Stamp and the Vice-Presidents, together with their staff, utilised the ground and first floor rooms. The top floor, (ex servants bedrooms) were used by the Chief Officers. At the time this picture was taken The Grove was occupied by the British Transport Commission as the Work Study Training Centre.

Authors collection.

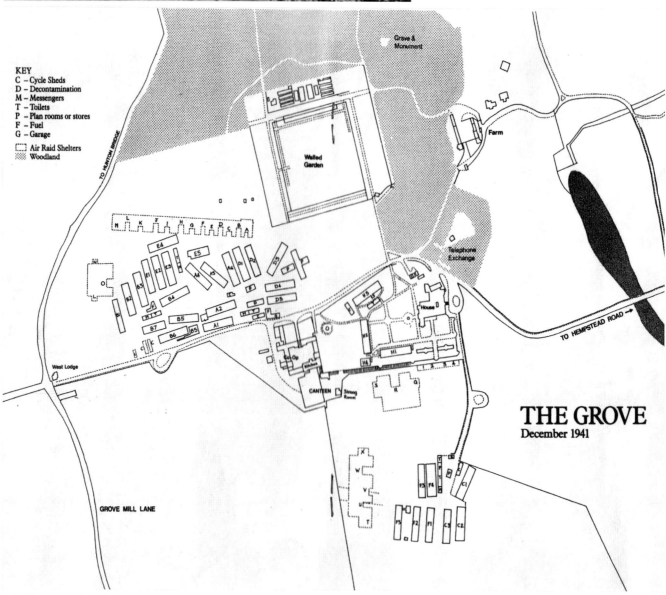

A 1941 site plan showing "The Grove" and the wartime huts and air raid shelters erected by the LMS to accommodate the Management Staff from Euston and St. Pancras.

executive and administrative staff would remain in the London Offices. As it happens St. Pancras was hit several times as described in chapters 7 and 8.

The LMS evacuation of LMS HQ staff to "The Grove" at Watford, Willow Grange and Thornton Hall, Glasgow.

The acquisition of "The Grove" by the LMS Railway was approved by the LMS Board at their meeting on 27th April 1939 (minute 3926) and consisted of sixty rooms and stood in an estate of about 300 acres, owned at that time by The Equity and Law Life Assurance Company. The sale went through on the 15th May 1939 at a cost of £89,538 and was purchased by the LMS Property Company Lineside Estates. The Board had approved expenditure of £100,000 as part of the £150,000 authorised by an earlier minute, 3866. Immediately following the purchase, £70,000 (part of the £150,000) was allocated to prepare the property for occupation by LMS staff. This included the provision of 39 huts, see figure 8, some of which were approved by Works Committee 4923 (26/5/1939) and 5008 (29/9/1939. The provision of these huts was clearly secret as their erection was referred to as Scheme "X" in the minutes. Works

Committee Minute 4923 called for Holliday & Greenway Ltd to supply 16 huts at a cost of £5,616 and to erect them for a further £11,881/2/8d also a lavatory block for £1,017/17/10d. Works Committee Minute 5008 approved the expenditure of £12,053/2/8d for the same Company to erect 16 further huts at £753/6/5d each. Air raid shelters and a movement building where staff organised wartime rail traffic were also built, the eventual total cost of which was £160,121. The overall cost of the purchase of "The Grove", huts for staff (that included drains, water, sewage disposal, roads and paths) and furniture was £270,826. The whole of this work was supervised by the LMS Civil Engineer's Department and paid for by Lineside Estates from whom the LMS rented the property. Quite clearly most staff knew nothing about "The Grove", that is until the morning of Saturday September 2nd 1939, when the Headquarters staff of the LMS Railway Company received instructions to transfer to "The Grove" at Watford. The staff was assembled and orders given, that was followed by the packing-up and despatching of correspondence, plans, personal belongings etc. to what, for most staff, was an unknown destination. So, on Monday 4th September, thousands of LMS staff made their way by many routes to the estate to squeeze themselves into their allotted hut,

Thornton Hall, Glasgow – bought by the LMS in 1941 for possible use by its Glasgow Staff that never materialised, to eventually be sold to the East Kilbride Development Corporation.   *Authors Collection*

65

although things were not helped as not all the huts were finished and some letters were dictated and typed outside in the autumn sunshine. Whilst telephone connections had been made internally and externally to the LMS system it in no way equalled the facilities that existed at Euston and a difficult period was experienced until the situation was remedied. Initially there was no catering facility, the nearest pub was a mile away and even the buses provided by the Company could not, for some time, enter the estate due to the weak bridge over the Grand Union Canal. Private offices were banned from within the huts that soon gave way as staff improvised and surrounded themselves with filing cabinets and allied furniture to secrete themselves away. The mild autumn of 1939 soon gave way to an exceptionally hard winter that led to much staff discomfort. By March 1940 a large canteen had opened and the private road remade allowing access for buses and grievances were gradually forgotten. "The Grove" remained British Rail property (and many BR staff will have attended a course there) until 31st March 1995, when it was sold for £2.5m for conversion to a hotel of the same name that opened in August 2003. Despite a return to old offices, the code name 'Grove' was used for many years after the war in connection with special trains including Royal Train workings.

Willow Grange at Watford was also approved for purchase by the Board on 24th July 1941 and bought for £10,606 to accommodate the LMS Hotel Department staff, with a further £8,894 for alterations. Willow Grange later became the headquarters of The British Waterways Board before being sold to Barratt Homes for £12.3m in 2007 to convert the office building into apartments and build new dwellings to provide 174 new homes on the 4.87 acre site.

The LMS also purchased Thorntonhall Estate at East Kilbride near Glasgow to accommodate a number of LMS Glasgow staff in the event of their offices being damaged by enemy action, as mass bombing of the Clydeside shipyards was anticipated. Purchase was approved at the LMS Board meeting on 26th July 1941, the price being £15,125. A further £50,192 was spent on huts etc and £4,925 on furniture. As far as can be ascertained no LMS Staff were evacuated there, the property eventually being sold to East Kilbride Development Corporation, the valuation being £20,000.

The total amount spent on the huts etc on the above three properties was charged to the Government "ARP" account, whilst the £26,092 spent on furniture was charged to the LMS Capital Account.

1939/40/41 Evacuations.

During the first four days of the war a massive exodus of children and other priority classes was made from many of the large cities in Great Britain. Arguably it was probably the greatest controlled mass movement of people the world had ever seen. Many meetings took place and plans had been drawn up in the autumn 1938 and considered again in July 1939. The decision was made on August 31st taking only one day to set in motion. And so, on September 1st 1939 tens of thousands of children were shepherded from school assembly points to mainline and suburban railway stations. A total of 1,735 trains were planned of which 1,372 actually ran. The number of evacuees scheduled was 1,095,718 but of this number only 43% or 471,678 actually travelled over four days from fifteen stations. The figures do not include the large number of empty stock trains. In addition to the London area, the LMS received 73 trains from junctions on the LNER evacuating children from the Newcastle-on-Tyne area. Many of the children were accompanied by their mothers, and everyone carried a gas mask, food, a change of clothing and each wore three labels. Boarding schools left the south of England for Scotland. and the Lake District. Many folk arrived from the continent to seek sanctuary in this country and Americans went to Eire en route home. On 2nd June 1940, 48,000 schoolchildren were evacuated from Kentish and East Coast towns that involved the working of 70 special trains, 12 of which originated on the LMS. All were received by either the GWR or LMS. When the bombing commenced on the provincial cities further evacuations took place from Coventry, Birmingham Liverpool and Manchester etc. In April 1941 27 special trains left Glasgow for the evacuation of registered schoolchildren. At Liverpool, in May 1941, the LMS ran entire households out of the city in controlled trains that ran every evening from 19.30 at 15minute intervals, and the next morning returned the working members to their employment. Many other evacuations were planned and carried out involving such places as Ipswich, Colchester, and the Glasgow area, too many to deal with here. During the colder months, the London County Council with the Authority of the Ministry of Health sought to provide hot meals to evacuees travelling long distances, but this was dependent on obtaining competent kitchen staff. In the event it was agreed that the helpers escorting the evacuees would assist in the serving of the meals and the subsequent clearance of tables and the washing of the dishes. The meal served consisted of soup, meat-pie or Irish stew, milk pudding, tea or milk, for which a charge of one shilling was made or 5p in today's money. On 1st September 1939 it was decided to evacuate a certain portion of the patients in London and Manchester Hospitals. To this end the LMS provided four improvised hospital trains, consisting of corridor brake-vans with a corridor third at each end for the conveyance of stretcher cases. Plans were also drawn up to evacuate hospitals in a 20mile zone along the East and South Coasts should an invasion take place. The Bank of England staff together with office records were moved by two special trains at the end of August 1939 from Broad Street to Headquarters at Trentham Park, near Stoke.

Another form of evacuation was the removal of art treasures, specimens from the National Gallery, the British Museum, the Tate Gallery and Westminster Abbey, many of which required very careful handling and specialist packing. Food was also 'evacuated' between August 31st and September 4th – 32 special trains were run by the LMS to convey meat and butter away from the London Docks. A few days later a further seven specials conveyed 1,600 tons of tea to the north.

Moving on to 1944/5, the London and the South East was still subject to evacuation as the threat of flying bombs and rockets with their limited range was still real as related in Chapter 9..

The Dunkirk Evacuation.

Virtually every south east coast port was utilised during what was a remarkable transport feat in the evacuation of the Allied armies from Northern France into waiting trains that were sent to intermediate destinations where military officers and railway officials decided the destination of the train. The number of troops requiring conveyance was an unknown factor and named "Operation Dynamo" with the whole operation undertaken at extremely short notice. All trains were controlled by telephone, as there was no possibility of

time tabling the trains. The LMS provided 44 trains out of the 186 required for the purpose.

From the 30th May to the 4th June 1940 all public passenger services on the Southern Railway between Reading, Guildford and Redhill were suspended to give free passage to the enormous traffic generated by the evacuation of the British Expeditionary Force from Dunkirk. Initially 620 trains conveyed the 319,116 troops to reception points and a further 200 trains were required from 6th June, (of which the LMS worked 123, that included three specials for French munitions workers), to return troops to Depots, many in the north, for re-equipping. As an example, the LMS was required, at short notice, to provide 23 trains to Stranraer between June 16th and 19th to transfer troops from southern depots to Northern Ireland. All this took place over a period of 16 days, with many staff often working for periods of 18 hours. Having got the forces to more permanent areas and re-equipped it was then necessary to provide further trains for the leave that followed. The Secretary of State for War published a statement in the Press recording his appreciation of the work done by the railways. Following a short lull of 12 days there were more emergencies as Allied personnel from the more westerly and south westerly coasts of France arrived at ports in the south and west of England. See also Chapter 11 with regard to shipping.

St Pancras 16 October 1940.

Liverpool – Alexandra Dock destroyed by enemy action on 21ˢᵗ September 1940.

British Rail

7

THE BOMBS BEGIN TO FALL - 1940

With all preparations in place, shelters and bunkers built and camouflage completed, the London staff re-located and with pre-conceived notions built up with little or no data as to what will really happen, it was a question of wait and see. Note that the 24hour clock system is used throughout.

Summary

Incidents caused by air activity were so numerous that it would require a separate volume of some magnitude to record them all, and it is only practicable to basically review them and their effect. Ironically the first bomb to fall on a British railway was dropped by an RAF plane on 20th May 1940 being on Mells station in Suffolk. The first incident on the LMS Railway due to enemy air action occurred on the Thames Haven branch at 05.00 on 19th June 1940, when a bomb fell 70' 0" from the railway fencing damaging the banking and block telegraph wires. Shortly after midnight at 00.51 on 24/25th of June 1940 the first bomb dropped on LMS property, being Bristol engine shed that damaged the permanent way and the roof of the shed. One running line was blocked but restored within 10 hours. At the same time incendiary bombs fell on the Goods Shed roof at Bristol St. Phillips burning a hole in the roof, but damage was restricted due to the efforts of the staff. A further incendiary hit a footbridge at Ketton on the Manton and Peterborough line, burning a hole in the timber floor. On that same morning at 03.15, a high explosive bomb landed on the permanent way at Ullesthorpe on the Leicester - Rugby line that made an 8' 0" diameter crater 10' 0" deep causing settlement to both tracks. The first unexploded bombs also fell on or alongside the permanent way at the same place causing the up line to be blocked until 18.15 that day and the down line until 19.00 the following day before the bombs were removed by the military. Serious difficulties and delays occurred with unexploded bombs due to the lack of co-ordination between the Civil and Military Authorities. The arrangements between the railways and the Ministry of Home Security for dealing with unexploded bombs were then reviewed in the light of experience and placed on a much better footing, but further experience led to more improvements in October 1940. There were seven incidents in that last week of June 1940, the most serious was the damage caused to the canal dock wall and shed at Etruria (Stoke-on-Trent) on the Trent and Mersey Canal. Bombing was intermittent during July with ten "incidents" in England and Scotland but only one being serious. Raids were spasmodic until 24th August 1940, after which they rapidly increased in both frequency and weight, becoming intensive during September. In August 1940, 85 places were bombed, 8 of which were in the London area. The first bomb in the Home Counties area fell at 18.50 on the 18th August on Shoeburyness Station, causing damage to the Signal Box, permanent way and footbridge. Traffic was blocked for six hours whilst the track was repaired and temporary signalling installed. The first real attack commenced on 7th September when the target was East London with 183 incidents during that month. The most destructive was at Poplar 'A' Warehouse and Shed on the 7th with extensive damage to Haydon Square Warehouse on the 9th. Away from London, the Liverpool District was the worst hit with 62 incidents that included the gutting of Alexandra Dock Warehouse on the 21st September and Brunswick Goods Shed on the 26th September. Railway attacks intensified reaching their maximum during October and still further in November with the London area still the main target although Birmingham and Liverpool also had severe attacks that included the highly concentrated bombing of Coventry on the night of November 14th/15th. In December the main targets were the Liverpool, Manchester and Birmingham areas followed by two months in which damage was relatively light with the Swansea and Holyhead areas heading the list of incidents. The damage that affected the running lines most seriously, and proved to be the most difficult to repair, was that caused by high explosive bombs to arches and retaining walls. Unexploded bombs and parachute mines also caused serious blockages due to the danger of them exploding from vibrations if movements were made in the vicinity, not to mention the grave risk to those personnel involved in removing them. This led to an instruction from the Government in October 1940, that such bombs were not to be interfered with until 96 hours after they had fallen, unless they were causing very serious interference with important traffic, and no reasonable alternative was available. The delays caused by unexploded bombs and mines can be gauged from the fact that during November 1940, there were 30 cases of unexploded bombs and 10 of unexploded parachute mines falling on or close to LMS property and lines interfering with traffic movements. Seven of the bombs and two of the mines caused serious obstruction and were placed in Category "A", i.e., to be removed urgently with delays to the railway reduced as a result of the better contact with those responsible, coupled with the skill and resource displayed by the Bomb Disposal Squads and Admiralty personnel.

Fires due to incendiary and high explosive bombs were very numerous but, generally speaking, were attacked with considerable success by the staff, occasionally aided by the

*Damage to Plaistow
Station on
7th September 1940.
British Rail*

local authorities. There were however, several cases where buildings such as warehouses and stations sustained heavy damage by fire owing to water mains being damaged during a raid causing a failure of the water supply. There were a few instances, during the very heavy raids, when the local fire-fighting services were overwhelmed. At the outbreak of the war the LMS had three fully equipped fire trains with motor pumps and tanks stationed at Derby, Crewe and Horwich. In July 1940 orders were placed for 83 Ransomes and Rapiers 1½" self priming water pumps that could be stored at selected locomotive sheds throughout the system, ready for immediate despatch by light engine with trained staff to attack fires, water being used from the tank or tender of the locomotive if necessary. Unfortunately, considerable delay took place in obtaining these pumps and the required accessories owing to the contractor's premises sustaining serious damage during the heavy raids. With deliveries only commencing in May 1941 and completed in August, meant, that by the time the pumps were ready for use in May 1941, the heavy air raids were almost over. In spite of this they did prove useful in later smaller air raids, sufficient to state that, had they been available when expected, the damage by fire would have been considerably reduced.

At the Board meeting on 26th September 1940 it was reported that since the enemy commenced large scale bombing and damage, the Company's precautionary measures had proved effective. The provision of shelter accommodation was being extended, and all signal boxes were being provided with shelters as quickly as steel supplies allowed. Arrangements were in hand for the distribution of 65,000 additional steel helmets and 50,000 civilian duty respirators.

It was also pleasing that the instructions developed by the LMS for trains and vehicles contaminated by liquid blister gas had been adopted for general use by the REC.

From August 24th to November 1940 inclusive the LMS Railway was affected by air raids on 95 of the 99 days, the raids being heavy on 53 of those days. A brief review follows of the incidents that occurred in the above four areas during the 99 days. Only the more serious instances are listed, but here again a division will be made and only the major features will be mentioned in the text.

The strain on the staff and organisation of certain of the Engineering Districts was intense but there were relatively few occasions when the enemy succeeded in closing a line for more than a few days and very few in which limited operation was not resumed within a few hours. Even when unexploded bombs or extensive damage occurred to delay the restoration of traffic, there were usually alternative arrangements that solved the problem, as the incidents detailed below will show.

Thames Estuary, (East of Bromley).

There were eight heavy daylight raids on this area on 26th and 31st August and 7th and 15th September, and night raids on 15th and 27th September and 14th and 15th October. The worst was on the evening of Saturday 7th September when a tremendous attack was made on the Thames Estuary and East London, including the London Docks. In several places the main lines were heavily damaged by direct hits, whilst at West Ham an empty electric train was hit and the platforms and lines were so heavily damaged that the station was

Bow Junction following a raid on 14th September 1940.

British Rail

closed until 11th August 1941, (11 months later) when it was opened for electric services only. Very serious interruptions to traffic working on the LT&S Section ensued, but a steam service was maintained east of Barking with occasional interruptions by unexploded bombs, whilst a shuttle service of electric trains was generally run between Upminster and Barking or East Ham. The services were gradually reinstated west of Barking during the following week as repair work was completed, but damage on the LNE line at Stepney and Fenchurch Street held up services to and from Fenchurch Street until 17th September. In the interim the steam and electric services available west of Barking were used to the best advantage, and where neither service could be run, bus services were introduced, thus giving an emergency service throughout, whilst full use was made of the line between Barking and St. Pancras to give an alternative service. Freight trains were badly affected. Subsequently the Tilbury and Southend services were frequently interrupted at various places, and on several occasions Fenchurch Street Station was isolated owing to damage on the LNER Company's lines.

Shoeburyness - 18th August.. Two high explosive (HE) bombs dropped, one close to the station signal box and the other on the nearby permanent way. The box was practically demolished and all communications completely severed. The signalman was killed, this being the first war fatality on the LMS.

Tilbury Section - 7th/ 8th September. The air raid commenced at 17.00 on the evening of the 7th, when extensive damage was caused by high explosive and incendiary bombs. Signalling suffered considerable damage

at several places throughout the Tilbury Section, generally to signal box structures, electrical signalling equipment, power cables and overhead lines of communication, much of which was completely destroyed. The Skinner Street linemen's Depot was burnt out.

Appreciation

The Board meeting on 26th September 1940 requested the Chairman Lord Stamp to convey to Mr Wallace (Chief Civil Engineer) and Mr Bound (Signal and Telegraph Engineer) together with their staff, the Board's appreciation of their fine work in repairing air raid damage and keeping lines open for traffic.

London Area Passenger Stations.

Finchley Road Station – 2nd October. A much longer time was required to restore traffic following a high explosive bomb that landed behind the retaining wall at the Finchley Road end of Hampstead Heath tunnel. A length of 30 yards of the wall was destroyed with three of the girders spanning the line displaced. Rebuilding the wall was essential and it was not until the 17th October that one of the two lines could be used for single line working. Normal use of both lines was not possible until early in January 1941. Clearly this stretch of the old North London Railway was not as important as the previous example and required a bus service between Finchley Road and Hampstead Heath Stations for passengers who could not use alternative routes.

St. Quintin's Park - 2nd October.. Station premises extensively damaged.

Kilburn – 8th October.. At 20.30 a large calibre high

Royal Scot No. 6122 "Royal Ulster Rifleman" seen here after running into the debris caused by a bomb at Queen's Park, London. The train was the 19.30 express from Euston to Inverness.
British Rail

explosive bomb fell on the main line at Kilburn, forming a crater 12' 0" deep and 60' 0" in diameter across all four lines. The Up fast line was lifted bodily and deposited on top of the Down fast line, the whole being covered with clay from the crater and brickwork from the foundations of an old wall. The Down Slow line was lifted several inches and the Up Slow badly distorted. A further complication was that the line became flooded from a broken sewer in Kilburn High Street. This was a serious breach of a very important line, but the Down Slows were re-opened for traffic at 12.10 the following day and the Fast Lines by 17.50.

Hampstead Heath – 10th October.. Station buildings destroyed.

Kensal Green, London – 12th October.. In this incident a bomb fell on the Up Electrified line tunnel at Kensal Green between Euston and Watford, destroying a part of the segmented cast iron lining and letting in debris from above. The line was blocked until 27th October. On the 7th November the adjacent Up and Down Slow line tunnels for

steam traction were penetrated by a high explosive bomb and about 30' 0" of the brick lining was brought down with the resultant debris. The slow lines were blocked until 21st November.

North London Line. – 13th October. The North London line between Haggerston and the Broad Street Terminus was the subject of the most serious and protracted interference with traffic. A high Explosive bomb badly damaged Union Street Bridge north of Shoreditch blocking all four lines on a length of line that is elevated above the surrounding property and is carried over several streets. By the following afternoon one line opened for traffic but that same night a further bomb fell on Primrose Street Bridge, between Shoreditch and Broad Street blocking all lines again. This rendered serious damage as the abutments were badly affected, and, whilst work was in hand, yet another bomb fell on Laburnam Street Bridge between Haggerston and Shoreditch on 25th October, again blocking all four lines. Through Traffic between Haggerston and Broad Street was not resumed until 11th November when two lines were re-opened with the other two finally brought

St Pancras
16 October 1940.
British Rail

into use on 14th February 1942.

Whilst the LMS received its share of the bombing on London, there was not always a direct relationship between the incidents on the railway and the severity of the attack on the town. During the concentrated bombing on London on the night of 29th December 1940, when so much damage was done, there were only three incidents on the LMS showing how the great size of London was responsible for such disparities. On the other hand Coventry provided the best example of a concentrated attack on a limited target. Not only was Coventry served exclusively by the LMS, the greater part of the town lay within a triangle of lines one of which was the main line from London to Birmingham and the Black Country.

Highbury 14th – October.. Station premises gutted.

LMS Director **William Lionel Hichens** was killed on this night at Church House, Westminster, (see Chapter 18).

Queen's Park – 15th October. At 19.45 a bomb fell on the line in front of the 19.30.express from London to Inverness, hauled by Royal Scot 6122 "Royal Ulster Rifleman" that ran into the debris. The engine and several coaches overturned and the driver and firemen were injured but survived. About 40 minutes later a second bomb exploded a short way ahead blasting the retaining wall onto the electrified tracks towards Kensall Green Station. More bombs fell at 02.00 damaging Queen's Park No. 2 Box, blocking the line with more debris. One LPTB staff was injured at Queen's Park Station. The lines were re-opened in stages between 22.50 on 16th October and 09.30 on 26th October.

St. Pancras Station – 15th October. At 19.28 the sirens sounded for what was the heaviest raid of that month in which 400 bombers took part and 430 people were killed. The attack went on until 05.10 in the morning. At 03.25 a signalman on duty outside St. Pancras Station observed a landmine attached to a parachute suspended in the signal bracket over Nos.1 and 2 platforms, whereupon he urgently called the station staff who in turn notified the Civil Defence Authorities At 03.50 the mine was pronounced live and the station evacuated, that is apart from a gang of men who had unofficially taken refuge in the basement at the terminal end of St. Pancras Station. One can only imagine their awakening when the landmine was exploded at 05.15. There were no casualties but the station was very badly damaged. A large crater was formed at the north end of Nos.1 and 2 platforms badly damaging the permanent way. Most of the glass and slates in the high arched roof were brought down, with most of the rooms and offices in the station suffering damage. Sixty coaches and two wagons were damaged and the station lighting put out of action, as were all the telephones. With no telephones, the District Engineer's control clerk, who was on duty at St. Pancras Chambers, on his own initiative sent a runner to the Engineering Department in Kentish Town with instructions that all artisans booking on duty at 07.40 were to proceed immediately to St. Pancras Station. The permanent way Sub-Inspector, who was also on night duty at St. Pancras, also went to Kentish Town to assemble as many permanent way staff as possible. Altogether 233 men commenced work that morning in the clearing of the debris, all of whom had experience of the nightly raids for more than a month, and came from their shelters, or from civil defence duties, to help

Top left - London, Queen's Park Station showing the retaining wall damaged on 6th November. 1940.

British Rail

Top right - London, Queen's Park Station showing the retaining wall having been reconstructed.

British Rail

Centre and bottom - Damage done at Kilburn and Brondisbury on the night of 16th September 1940 and the temporary repairs to shore up the viaduct to get trains running again.

British Rail

Opposite - The damage done on 2nd October to the Stonebridge Park car sheds that served the Euston-Watford electric service. (See also two further views on page 76).

British Rail

re-open St. Pancras Station. Initially it was thought the huge roof could be unsafe as the base of one of the cast iron support columns was fractured, but two scaffolders from the District Engineering staff volunteered to make a preliminary inspection of the steelwork. Following their favourable report two steeplejacks were engaged to remove broken glass, ironwork and glazing bars. The first objective was to clear an accumulation of parcels by concentrating on the re-opening platforms 1 and 2 that was achieved, with the lines restored by 17.00 in the afternoon. The roof being devoid of any covering it was impossible to blackout the station, with work only proceeding in daylight hours. With the exception of the parcels traffic the station was closed for five days, mainly due to the need to remove all the loose glass from the overall roof. In this period 100 wagons of debris were dispatched. During the stoppage, trains were dealt with at Kentish Town, but a limited service into St. Pancras was restored on 21st October, extended on 23rd, with a full service resumed on the 16th November 1940. Of interest was, that free cups of tea were provided for the workers, but when traffic was partially restored almost everyone on the station, including troops and passengers also lined up hoping for the best. The St. Pancras Junction and Station boxes were damaged, the relay apparatus and battery huts, with all their contents such as rectifiers and transformers were destroyed. The Lineman's Depot with almost all contents was also destroyed, as well as a bracket signal. *7th November* – three high explosive bombs fell on the station, one on No.1 platform damaging the roof and the booking office, and one on the main road in front of the station. Nos. 1,2 and 3 platforms were out of use until 11th October.

Gospel Oak – 16th October. Station buildings extensively damaged.

Euston – 19th October. Incendiary bombs set fire to the roof of the Great Hall and high explosive bombs made a crater in the roadway between Nos.2 and 3 platforms, damaging the station roof and offices in Drummond Street, and the west wing of the Euston Hotel. Platforms 1 to 6 were blocked, No 6 being opened on 21st, Nos.4 and 5 on 24th, with the remaining platforms in the evening of the 27th.

Kensington (Addison Road) – 20th October.. Station building extensively damaged.

Queen's Park Station – 5th November. The retaining wall and station was damaged.

West End Lane – 16th November. Station buildings and platforms badly damaged.

London – 29th December. – The heavy raid on this date was later described as the "London Fire Blitz" as most of the LMS damage was due to fire, with the line blocked at one point only. Fires were started in several buildings, but prompt and efficient action by staff prevented all except one causing extensive damage at Whitecross Street Goods Depot, where a stable with 99 stalls was almost completely burnt out. The staff evacuated the horses safely.

Goods Stations etc.

Poplar "A" – 7th September High explosive bombs destroyed old and new warehouse and a considerable number of wagons, whilst the east quay 30 ton crane and two coal tippers were heavily damaged, six other cranes being less severely damaged.

Canning Town- 7th September. Shed demolished and office badly damaged.

The upper picture shows the damage inflicted on Stonebridge Park car sheds on 2nd October with the lower picture taken following the removal of the debris.
British Rail

Haydon Square – 10th September. Heavily damaged by high explosive and incendiary bombs. Grain warehouse and dry bond gutted, banks and shed on High Level and small warehouse destroyed. Horse cartage vehicles and equipment badly damaged

Poplar "B" – 17th September. Warehouse destroyed and other buildings heavily damaged.

Somers Town – 18th September. High explosive bomb fell in Euston road, knocking down the front wall and causing damage to shed roof and offices.

Camden – 22nd September. Princes Road stables badly damaged and damage to new warehouse and on *26th September*, four large craters caused in yard, clerks' canteen demolished and electric cables damaged.

Kilburn and Brondisbury – 16th September. Extensive damage to the viaduct

St. Pancras – 24th September. Damaged by high explosive and incendiary bombs including damage to hydraulic workshops, water main, glass roofs and ambulance room.

Stonebridge Park Car Sheds – 2nd October. Extensively damaged.

Commercial Road – 1st November. Buildings and offices considerably damaged.

Appendix 'A' details the lines blocked and the duration for the months September to November 1940 in the London area..

Birmingham, Coventry and Wolverhampton Areas.

The first raids in this area were on two consecutive nights of 25th and 26th August 1940, and were fairly heavy. The area was then free from raids until the night of 12th October, followed by further heavy raids on the nights between 11th and 31st October and on 14th, 19th and 22nd November. The concentrated raid on Coventry on 14th November led to coining of the word "Coventrated" in connection with air raids. As the particulars in **Appendix 'B'** show, the line blockages caused were numerous, and important sections of the main lines and stations, including New Street, Birmingham, and Coventry, were isolated on several occasions, whilst extensive damage was done to buildings, warehouses and stations, and to the District Control Offices at New Street. Signal boxes and signalling equipment with cable routes and overhead telegraph wires received considerable damage causing signalling operations and telegraphic and telephonic communications to be put out of use.

Special mention is made of the following raids that had a serious effect on traffic movements.

16th October 1940. Birmingham (New Street).

New Street No.5 signal box was practically destroyed by a direct hit by an HE bomb about 8pm that blocked the up and down Wolverhampton and up and down Gloucester lines for 36 hours each. The signal box was 76'3" long by 12'0" wide by 8'0" elevation, with a cellar 7'3" below rail level to accommodate the locking. It was fitted with a 153 lever Webb tumbler frame, the cellar and lower storey constructed of brickwork with a wooden superstructure from the working floor level. Virtually the whole of the brickwork of the lower storey was demolished, the blast destroying about forty levers, instrument shelf, block instruments, telephones, batteries, relays etc, and damaging the wood portion beyond repair. The following morning arrangements were made for complete possession of the running lines and debris amounting to forty wagon loads were cleared away, coincident with this an adjacent signal linesman's room was fitted up as a temporary block post by the provision of the required block instruments and field telephones. It was decided to demolish the remaining portion of the brick lower storey and to use two of the ARP 43' 3" emergency signal boxes, one being obtained from St. Helens and the other from Stafford Stores. On 17th these were loaded up and arrived, one on the same day and the other by special train early next morning. The variation in the overall length necessitated altering the corner and intermediate posts to suit, also the flooring to suit the Webb frame to which forty new levers were added, the whole frame being re-locked. The Crewe construction gang commenced on the rebuilding of the cellar portion of the old box to form the foundation for the new all timber structure and the general work of construction continued from daylight to dark each day. On the 20th a start was made on erecting the first half of the wood superstructure which had meanwhile been altered in height and also made suitable to join up with the second half. The first half, including the floor, was finished and the roof sheeted over as a temporary measure on the 22nd. The remaining half was erected in 10' 0" sections each day, commencing the next morning, to suit the progress with the brickwork of the cellar. The final stage was erected on 26th, the floor completed and the roof sheeted over the following day, when all the window sashes were fixed and gas lighting installed. The points were then coupled up to the levers which remained without interlocking, the block instruments and telephones installed, and the signalman returned to the box at 6pm on the 27th, eleven days after the mishap. Complete restoration of all interlocking was effected at 1pm on November 7th, but the roof was not finished and slated until the 19th November. During the period of disconnection, traffic operations were carried on by ground staff who operated the points and flagged trains under the instructions of the signalman in the temporary block post. Communications suffered severely, the District Control Office and Telegraph Office being completely destroyed, necessitating operating from the Shelter Control Office. Ultimately, as previously stated, new offices were provided. At Birmingham Lawley Street, prompt action by the S&T Engineer's staff enabled the automatic switchboard and associated equipment to be protected from extensive damage by fire and water, and the apparatus was ultimately overhauled and reinstated. All line cables leading into New Street Station and Lawley Street were also destroyed, involving extensive renewals. The up

Above - New Street No.5 Signal Box following re-construction in November 1940. Vic. Phillips

Below - Birmingham, New Street Station following attack on 28th October 1940. British Rail

and down Wolverhampton and up and down Gloucester lines were blocked for 36 hours each. On *24th October* the station was completely closed for 5 hours and 20 minutes following serious damage by high explosive bombs. On *28th October* – Serious damage by bombs, particularly the District Control Office, the District Passenger Manager's Office, and the Parcels Office. On *19th November* there was further serious damage to the station, whilst line blockages at the station and the adjoining areas completely isolated the station for 18½ hours, until 16.00 the following day. On *22nd November* further slight damage was caused to the station, but line blockage in the adjoining areas completely isolated the station until 12.15 on the 23rd (14½ hours), when the lines were available for Western Division trains only. The Midland Division trains could not use the station until 17.00 (10 hours).

Saltley – 17th October. The Mill Road bridge carrying four lines of railway over the roadway was badly damaged by a high explosive bomb, and only the down line to Camp Hill was safe for traffic. Single line working was put into operation over this line until the up main line was available at 17.00, 4 days and 17½ hours later, on the 22nd. The down line was not opened until the following day, and the up Camp Hill line until the 27th October.

Vauxhall and Duddeston – 1st November. Station Damaged.

Spon Lane – 14th November.

The raids on Birmingham were not sustained for so long as in London, nor so concentrated as in Liverpool but damage in and around Birmingham was heavy.

Top - Vauxhall and Duddeston Station following an attack on Birmingham on 1st November 1940.

Centre - Birmingham Central Goods Warehouse gutted by enemy action 26th October 1940.

Bottom - Birmingham Central Goods Station was hit on 26th October 1940.
All British Rail

Coventry Station – 15th November 1940. The picture is taken from the south end of the up platform, looking towards Birmingham, the branch from Leamington comes in on the left of the picture

British Rail

There was though, an ideal example of a single bomb dropped in the right place. At Spon Lane, between Birmingham and Wolverhampton, the railway consisted of two tracks supported by a retaining wall 27' 0" high adjoining the Birmingham Canal. On the night of 14th November 1940 a high explosive bomb fell on the edge of the towpath and seemingly lifted the wall and dropped it again. For 150 feet of its length it was bulged about 6inches and badly cracked, and the movement of the wall caused subsidence to the rail track. A trench was sunk at the back of the wall in order to ascertain its condition, when it was found necessary to strengthen it and carry the rails on girders to transmit the weight of the trains directly on to the foundations. The repair work was carried out under very difficult conditions, and it was not until 14th January that the Down Line was re-opened for single line traffic with the Up Line being out of use for ordinary traffic until 29th July 1941, eight months after the raid.

Perry Barr. - 11th December,

A land mine was dropped on the embankment about 30 yards from the North Junction signal box destroying the lower brickwork and badly damaging the upper wood structure. Considerable damage was done to the lever frame and apparatus, also the block instruments and telephones. The work of erecting a temporary block post was immediately taken in hand and brought into use on the afternoon of the 12th December.

In addition to damage to other passenger stations, the large goods stations and offices in Birmingham suffered heavily in these raids – the principal ones being :-

Birmingham, Curzon Street – 15th October. Destruction of the warehouse in the Top Yard detrimentally affected cartage working by blocking an extensive dray parking area.

Birmingham, Lawley Street – The destruction of, or serious damage to several sheds, and total destruction of the general offices.

Birmingham Central - 26th October – The Working Shed with warehouse above was completely destroyed and it was not until 21st September 1942 that it was possible to restore goods shed facilities of a temporary character at this place.

Coventry 14th/15th November. . This area was very severely attacked, and by 23.00 the station had been seriously damaged and was isolated by several line blockages at the station and in the adjoining areas. Perishable traffic commenced to work into the goods yard from the south end only during the morning of 16th November and freight trains commenced to pass through the station during the evening of that day, but the passenger station was not opened and the lines used for passenger trains until the morning of 17th, i.e., 2½ days after the raid.

This was the first raid of its kind during the war, when, within hours, 122 incidents occurred on the railway that was nearly twice the number on any other LMS town on any night.

The railway lines through Coventry are:-

The main line from Rugby to Birmingham passing through Coventry Station.

The connecting line from Coventry to Nuneaton that

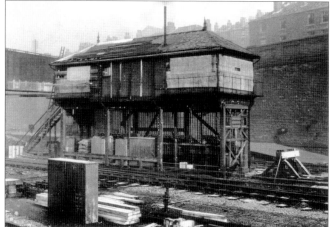

Top left - Sheffield South No.1 Signal Box that was completely destroyed on 12th December 1940 in the process of being rebuilt.
Roy Anderson Collection.

Top right - The replacement 68 lever frame being erected on Platform 5 on 12th December 1940 for Sheffield South No.1 Signal Box.
Roy Anderson Collection.

Bottom left - Sheffield South No.2 Signal Box on 12th December 1940 following an enemy air raid with the box having suffered severe bomb damage with all the wood panels blown out together with windows and roof tiles.
Roy Anderson Collection

Bottom right - Sheffield South No.2 as rebuilt taken in 1963 with Sheffield South No.1 in the background that was completely destroyed in the same raid.
Mike King.

branched off from the Rugby and Birmingham line on the Birmingham side of Coventry Station.

The "Avoiding" line, branching off from the Rugby and Birmingham line south of the station and connecting with the Coventry- Nuneaton Line near Foleshill.

The branch line to Kenilworth and Leamington, connecting up with the Rugby to Birmingham line south of Coventry Station.

Bombs were dropped on all these lines, the most intensive being on the "Avoiding" line, about 3½ miles in length. An estimated 40 high explosive bombs fell on this line, which included one delayed action bomb. Craters up to 60' 0" in diameter were created with the track damaged in many

places, though not seriously. A small calibre bomb fell on to a reinforced concrete bridge, damaging the arch and parapets. Special gangs of men were dispatched from Rugby and Nuneaton and the line was re-opened for traffic a week later on 21st November.

On the main line, several bombs fell on the station and the Rugby side thereof. The roof covering the station was damaged on both sides of the line with most glass broken. The junction with the Leamington line was seriously damaged together with a mail train standing on the branch. A further high explosive bomb landed on a freight train about two miles from the station, derailing wagons and blocking the line, traffic being diverted via Leamington. A land mine fell on the goods yard near the station and there were two unexploded bombs in the cart-ways. The down platform opened two days later with up and down trains using that platform, with normal working on the main line resuming on the 19th, just four days following the raid.

It was estimated that fifteen high explosive bombs fell on the Coventry and Nuneaton line in the vicinity of Coventry causing craters in the track and damage to the permanent way. One bomb fell on a viaduct carrying the line, partially destroying two arches, putting both lines out of action. The up line was restored on the 28th and the down line on the 30th. The story could have been different had there been a vulnerable and important railway structure within the area, but the fact was, that in the most concentrated attack experienced by the LMS, the main line was back in traffic within four days and on all lines within two weeks. The S&T equipment suffered badly. A large number of signal boxes were structurally damaged together with the signalling connections and apparatus but fortunately in no case was there a "knock-out" of a signal Box as an operating unit. Considerable lengths of overhead pole routes were brought down and cable work destroyed causing serious interference with communications.

Appendix 'B' details the lines blocked, and the duration, for the months August to November 1940 in the Birmingham area.

Sheffield - 12th and 15th December 1940 - Sheffield had its first heavy raids and on the evening of the 12th the station was hit by several high explosive bombs and buildings, platforms and roofs were badly damaged. Lines were blocked and damage was caused to passenger and goods stations. South No.1 Signal box was demolished by blast and subsequent fire along with the interlocking frame of 68 levers, and apparatus, comprising the whole of the block instruments, repeaters, indicators and telephones. South No.2 box had all windows and the roof and timber sheeting blown out, and the whole of the switchboard cabling to the two position manual switchboard at Sheffield Station Telegraph Office had to be renewed on site, service being maintained whilst the wiring was dealt with. An unexploded parachute mine also landed on the passenger station, causing the services to be suspended for passenger trains for 40 hours.

Liverpool and Birkenhead Areas.

There were seven fairly heavy raids in this area during September, viz., on the 4th, 6th, 18th, 26th and 29th, and one on 11th October and another on 28th November. The damage and line blockages were severe and the reaction on traffic operations considerable. These featured outstanding damage and destruction by bombs and fire to goods sheds and warehouses in the dock area. There was also serious damage to railway communications, particularly at Exchange Station.

Top left - Liverpool - Canada Dock Goods Warehouse destroyed by enemy action on 20th/21st December 1940.

Top right - Liverpool – Canada dock Goods Warehouse with the temporary shed erected on the same site.

Bottom right - Liverpool – Canada Dock goods yard – 24th December 1940.

All British Rail

The LMS suffered extensive damage during the three consecutive night raids from 20th to 22nd December when much damage was done to signalling. A number of signal boxes were damaged, two beyond repair, along with the apparatus and connections therein. Signals, outside connections, overhead wires and cables were all affected. The Signal Stores at Bank Hall received damage to the roof and the telephone exchange and telephones in the Canada Dock Warehouse, which burnt out, were completely destroyed.

13th October 1940, Birkenhead, Green Lane Junction. Four bombs were dropped (one delayed action) around the junction box that was wrecked. All block telegraph and telephone communications were severed and there was extensive damage to the permanent way blocking all running lines. By 16.30 the up fast line was re-opened for single line working and during the day communications were temporarily restored.

Liverpool - 20th December. A very heavy raid on Liverpool

Above - Liverpool – Viaduct between Exchange Station and Sandhills damaged by enemy action 20th December 1940.

British Rail

Top left - Manchester Exchange Station damaged by enemy action 21st December 1940.

Top right - Manchester Exchange Station having been made safe and debris removed.

Bottom left - Manchester Exchange Station, No.1 Platform, concourse and roof damaged by enemy action, 22nd December 1940.

Bottom right - The same scene with the debris removed.

All British Rail

Left - *Manchester Victoria – 24th December 1940.*

Right - *Manchester, Oldham Road Goods Station – Lees Street Warehouse and Provision Shed destroyed by enemy action on 22nd December 1940.*
British Rail

caused damage to Lime Street and Exchange Stations, and at Canada Dock Goods Station. The latter was flooded to a considerable depth owing to the bursting of the banks of the Leeds and Liverpool canal. The most serious result of this raid was the damage to three 30foot arch spans and two pier walls of the Sandhills viaduct, about a mile from Exchange station, with the result that all lines were blocked between Sandhills and Exchange Station as well as into Great Howard Street Goods Station. Temporary bridges were erected and traffic over the slow lines was resumed into Great Howard Street Goods Yard on 3rd March 1941 and into Exchange Station on 23rd March, the fast lines remaining blocked. Electric services were resumed at Exchange Station on 24th March, when the up and down slow lines were opened, but the fast lines remained blocked until 22nd March 1942. These blockages also isolated Great Howard Street Goods Station. Further damage was sustained to the arches on 3rd May1941.

Liverpool and Birkenhead 21st December. – There was a further heavy raid on Liverpool and on this night Birkenhead also suffered. Lines were blocked at 14 points and damage occurred at 17 places, including signal boxes at Wallasey, Waterloo Dock, Wapping Ford and Liverpool Exchange where Exchange Junction Box was destroyed and "B" Box damaged. In some instances the damage was serious, notably at Canada Dock where the warehouse and goods offices were gutted and records destroyed, whilst damage was caused to cranes, wagons and yard equipment. At Park Lane Goods Station the station entrance and stock warehouse were heavily damaged and the hydraulic plant put out of action.

Liverpool – 22nd December. – For the third successive night, a heavy raid affected the LMS badly. The only running lines affected were the up and down goods lines at Kirkby that were blocked for 14 hours, but much damage was caused at goods stations. At North Mersey the warehouse and other buildings were destroyed and the roofs of the loading quays and 130 wagons damaged (80 of them severely), whilst at

Great Howard Street, high explosive bombs caused damage to the boundary wall and to the permanent way and 80 wagons.

Manchester Area - Christmas Week 1940.

The city had its first raid on 22nd December, and the damage and line blockage was considerable. Manchester did not suffer from too many raids, but the two main attacks were extremely severe. In two nights of Christmas week there were 89 incidents on the railway, 69 of which were on the night of 22nd/23rd December 1940 when Victoria and Exchange Stations suffered severe damage the most serious being to Manchester Exchange Passenger Station, which was extensively damaged by fire and all lines through the station were blocked. The buildings and offices, including those of the District Engineer, were burned out and a portion of the main roof collapsed. The debris from Exchange Station was cleared, with the dangerous structural damage made safe for through traffic by 1st January 1941 with one Up and one Down platform through the station available. All platforms re-opened for limited use by the 8th January with full use of all platforms on 12th February but traffic did not get back to normal until 19th May 1941.

At Victoria the blocked lines were cleared for traffic at intervals until 20th January except for platforms 16 and 17 that were retained for Engineer's use in connection with the ongoing repair work. Serious damage was caused at Ancoats Goods Station to the main goods shed and warehouse, the latter being totally destroyed and falling on the working shed accommodation beneath. At Mayfield, the passenger station was considerably damaged by incendiary and high explosive bombs and was closed until 3rd January, when a limited service of trains commenced, but normal working was not resumed until 9th January 1941.

At Manchester, London Road Goods Station, the stables

Top left - *Bridges No.14 and 19, between Manchester Exchange and Ordsall Lane damaged by enemy action on 22nd December 1940.*

Top right - *The same bridges following re-construction.*

Bottom left - *The Manchester South Junction and Altrincham Railway, Castlefield Viaduct arches destroyed on 23rd December 1940.*

Bottom right - *The Castlefield Viaduct re-constructed.*

All British Rail

were damaged and two horses killed, and Ordsall Lane No. 4 signal box was destroyed by fire and some damage was caused by fire to the roof of Hunt's Bank Offices. The majority of the telephone circuits at the Divisional Control Office at Victoria Station were out of use. At Oldham Road Goods Station the provision shed and warehouse were destroyed and the sundries shed damaged. At Salford Goods Station the New Bailey Street Goods Shed with warehouse above was destroyed by fire, 40 wagons were badly damaged and a considerable amount of cartage equipment was destroyed. The 23rd December saw the second heavy raid when damage occurred at 16 places, with line blockages at seven, the most serious being in the vicinity of Victoria Passenger Station. At 23.45 there was a violent explosion, apparently from a number of high explosive bombs in the vicinity of the Square alongside No.16 platform, and all the buildings on Nos. 14, 15, 16 and 17 platforms were either destroyed or extensively damaged, whilst considerable

difficulty was experienced in attacking fires owing to the mains water supply failing. The damage included the total destruction of the Divisional Control Centre and many of the Divisional Superintendent's Offices whilst the Emergency Control Office, which had been provided for such happenings, was flooded and the control telephone communications put out of action necessitating a hurriedly improvised control office being provided in the cellars under Hunt's Bank Offices. Nos. 12 and 13 platforms and some buildings on them were also damaged at the west end, and most of the windows in the Hunt's Bank Offices were broken by the blast. Some damage was also caused to locomotives, coaching stock and station equipment. The Parcels Office, which was the Central Parcels Depot for the city was one of the buildings very seriously damaged and the parcels and associated traffic was disorganised in consequence. The main lines through the station were closed until 11.00 the following day, when two were available for a limited service of freight trains. Passenger trains could not arrive from the west, but a few were able to leave from No.11 platform that was the only one of the six main line platforms that could be used. On 30th December Nos. 12 and 13 platforms were opened, the latter for 100yds of its length only, and a limited service of passenger trains to and from the west was commenced and improved on 18th January 1941 when No.14 platform was opened, followed by a further improvement on 27th January, when No.11 platform was opened. Up to this time there had also been many restrictions on the main line services to and from the east. On April 12th 1941 the last of the main line platforms (No.16) was opened, but as two of the platforms were not available for their full length, restrictions were placed on the length and loading of passenger trains and the conveyance of parcels traffic until 19th May. Damage was also caused to the buildings, cranes, etc. in Heaton Norris Goods yard, whilst the District Control Office at that place sustained damage and had to be vacated for a time. The extensive damage to the passenger and goods stations and the line blockages in this densely populated industrial and commercial area played havoc with the extremely heavy passenger traffic (the following day being Christmas Eve), and the freight and coal traffic. The necessity for handling the passenger traffic and much of the freight traffic at outlying stations two to four miles away, the blocking back of large portion of the freight traffic and practically the whole of the coal traffic, coupled with the diversions of heavy through traffic (east and west, and north and south) normally passing over these main lines, reacted very seriously over an area of 30 miles radius in Lancashire, Yorkshire and Derbyshire. Exchange Passenger Station and five of the six main line platforms at Victoria were out of use. All the four main lines serving Exchange Station on the west side, the four main lines serving Victoria Station on the west side, and the four main lines serving the main line platforms at Victoria Station and also Exchange Station on the east side, were blocked. Although the bay platforms at Victoria Station were not damaged, they could not be used to any extent for the main line trains serving Victoria and Exchange Stations on the east side as they were used daily for 365 trains serving the branch lines east of Victoria. A bomb also penetrated the superstructure of Greengate Street Bridge at the Salford end of the station that exploded and killed several people who were sheltering beneath. At Victoria the roofs over platforms 12 to 17 were destroyed and the underground control shelter on platform 17 was hit and damaged with several offices gutted. The permanent way within the station was distorted with water tanks and mains fractured. The viaduct between Exchange and Ordsall Lane was also badly damaged. The slow lines were re-opened for traffic on the 27th December but the fast lines did not re-open until 22nd March 1942. It can be seen that the most serious difficulties in traffic working were overcome within a month of the raids.

The signal and telegraph equipment received considerable damage. A number of signal boxes were damaged chiefly through broken windows. In two cases only was damage severe, the Salford Incline Box being completely demolished and Ordsall Lane No.4 having the upper portion destroyed by fire. Damage was done to signalling plant, but it was more serious to S&T equipment in connection with communications apparatus and wires. At Manchester Exchange Station serious effect upon all communications was caused by the destruction of the whole of the cables and wires attached to the wall of the station buildings that were completely burnt out. On the 23rd December Victoria Station received the brunt of the attack and buildings, including the Divisional Control Office, were destroyed, the whole of the telephonic and telegraphic apparatus, including loud-speaker equipment, being destroyed. This was a major disaster and although the personnel were safe in the shelter, the structure was shaken and serious flooding resulted. All line cables and terminations were destroyed by fire, but skeleton contact with outside Control Offices was quickly given, and all Control circuits were restored using temporary cables within a few days. Improvisation of the temporary Control Office, restoration of equipment and cables to enable the shelter to be re-occupied and finally provision of a new Control Office with the Shelter as standby, involved a large amount of work at a critical period. Destruction of Manchester Exchange Station and the heavy damage in the area resulted in the destruction of many miles of multi-core cable and open line wire, and the restoration work was made more difficult by the simultaneous destruction of all the Emergency cable Stocks in the Manchester Area.

Signal Boxes destroyed by enemy action in 1940.

Shoeburyness – 18/8/1940; Green Lane Junction – 13/10/1940; New Street No.5 - 16/10/1940; Salford Incline and Ordsall Lane No.4 – both 22/3rd/12/1940; Perry Barr North Junction – 11/12/1940; Liverpool Exchange Junction and Park lane (Goods) – 21/12/1940..

Table 1 overleaf covers the period of heavy air raids from 24th August 1940 until December 31st 1940 and shows the number of days in each month that the LMS Railway was affected by raids, and the number of days when the air raids were heavy. Note that when an air raid occurred at night on say the 1st/2nd October, the particulars below count as having occurred on the 1st October only, in other words a raid commencing on an evening and not finishing until the morning of the following day counts as one day..

During the period from August to November 1940 there were 914 cases of damage of which 612 occurred in four areas as shown over the page in Table 2.
As shown in Table 2, 612 or 67% of the total number of 914 instances of damage on the LMS Railway due to enemy action in the four months under review concerned the four areas just reviewed. The remaining 302 or 33% were confined almost entirely to England and Wales with only ten

Table 1

Month 1940	Number of days in month	Number of days LMS affected	Number of days when raids were heavy.
August (from. 24th)	8	8	5
September	30	30	16
October	31	31	24
November	30	26	8
December	31	15	11
Totals	**130**	**110**	**64**

in Scotland and none were serious. The remaining incidents in England and Wales were widespread and the trunk lines were frequently, and sometimes seriously affected. The only serious instances of damage to buildings during this period occurred at Salford Goods Station on 3rd October, when the Stone Jug Warehouse was gutted, and at Bristol where St. Phillips Passenger and Goods Stations were damaged by fire, including the destruction of the goods shed and three of the goods offices on 14th November, whilst on the same day the District Goods and Passenger Manager's Offices were also destroyed.

These are the bare facts as far as the main line blockages and damage to buildings at passenger and goods stations are concerned, but there were other occurrences that re-acted severely on traffic workings. It will be appreciated the locomotive sheds, marshalling yards and carriage sidings were often provided on the outskirts of all important centres, and whilst locomotive sheds fortunately escaped serious injury, there were numerous instances where sidings, which offered larger targets than the main lines, sustained heavy damage.

Table 2.

Area	Number of instances of damage	Percentage to line total
London	328	36
Thames Estuary	54	6
Birmingham and Coventry	157	17
Liverpool	73	8
Total for four areas	**612**	**67**

8

THE BOMBS KEEP FALLING - 1941

Summary

In March and April 1941 London was again the target with severe raids also experienced in the Glasgow and Birmingham areas. The final effort was in May 1941 when sixteen out of the twenty-two Engineering Districts received bombs, with Liverpool, Birkenhead and Barrow and Glasgow being the worst hit. Liverpool and Birkenhead were attacked on seven consecutive nights from 1st to 7th May 1941 that was followed by a heavy raid on London on the night of Saturday 10th May. There were a few lighter raids later, including one on the Nuneaton area on the night of 16th May, and in the Manchester area on 1st June, with this being the last raid of anything like a heavy character affecting the LMS railway. The campaign closed, for all practical purposes with an attack on Manchester on the night of June 1st 1941 which may well be due to the German invasion of the USSR that took place later in that month on June 22nd.

Unexploded Bombs

One of the difficulties experienced during the heavy raids in 1940 and 1941 was the inability to obtain an early inspection of unexploded bombs and expert advice on relaxing standard restrictions. This was usually due to Bomb Reconnaissance Officers being stationed at central points, some distance from the site of the bomb, and to the fact that the number of Officers was inadequate to deal with these incidents promptly. During the lull in enemy activity, the Authorities increased the number of Bomb Reconnaissance Officers by training local wardens, police and railway staff in such duties, and by the end of 1943 the LMS had 108 members of the Chief Civil Engineer's staff, stationed at appropriate centres throughout the system, competent to perform the necessary inspections and give advice.

Comment.

The extent to which the Luftwaffe deliberately set out to damage defined railway targets is a subject of speculation. It might be that in some cases they saw a definite target and bombed it, but if the height at which they were flying, the strength of the defence, or the weather conditions rendered accurate bombing impossible, then they would drop their bombs as best they could in an area known to have vulnerable targets. Certain places were bombed more than once – Queen's Park between Euston and Willesden seemed to possess some attraction, but many important targets escaped totally and it could be considered that many targets were simply hit by chance. Had the enemy wished to destroy Goods Sheds and Warehouses then they did achieve considerable success in Liverpool. Manchester and

Birmingham. However if the aim was to paralyse the British railway system, then, as stated earlier, it was a failure, as even the massive damage to Exchange Station, Liverpool and the adjoining viaduct, and to Manchester Victoria and Exchange Stations were nowhere near operating disasters. Having said that credit must go to the ready response of railway officials and staff who rose to the challenge, and in particular to the Engineering, S&T and Operating Departments who co-operated fully in the task of maintaining and restoring communications. The wholesale dislocation on which the pre-war preparations were based never materialised and therefore improvisation and ingenuity was required. Certain key places such as important junctions and bridges were not often bombed and generally speaking

Derby Station was damaged on15th January 1941.

Derby Station, with the debris removes and a temporary footbridge in place.

Month 1941	Number of days in month	Number of days LMS affected	Number of days when Raids were heavy.
January	31	12	5
February	28	10	3
March	31	15	7
April	30	13	10
May (to 10th)	10	10	8
Total	**260**	**170**	**97**

damage to them was unexpectedly easy to deal with. Railway communications were not cut to the extent so as to render the peacetime organisation inoperative. Most damage was, in the main, dealt with by the extension and adaptation of normal peacetime procedures, with no particular case being considered as typical but the table bottom left following will serve as an illustration.

Derby - 15th January 1941 High explosive bombs were dropped on Derby Station killing four passengers and two staff and injuring three passengers and five staff. The roof over Nos. 4 and 5 platforms was demolished for about 100 yards and damage caused to No. 6 platform, the station footbridge and to roofs and windows of several offices and buildings in the vicinity. Damage was caused to the windows of the Station "A" and Engine Sidings No.2 signal boxes. Nos. 4 and 6 platform colour light signals were destroyed and damage was caused to crossover points between Nos. 3 and 4 platforms. Cables from the station to the Locomotive Works were damaged by blast and wiring circuits to the colour light signals referred to were destroyed. Damage was also sustained to the loud speakers and some open wires were brought down.
Avonmouth - 16th January 1941. Three boxes were more or less seriously damaged - Dock Junction, Sidings and Dock station boxes. A gantry signal was destroyed, also signal connections and a bracket signal damaged.

Liverpool and Birkenhead – 1940/1

Liverpool and Birkenhead sustained bombing that was both prolonged and concentrated, particularly in December 1940 and March and May 1941. Bombing on 12th to 14th March caused damage at 51 places including 15 instances of line blockage. All the main, branch and dock lines sustained heavy damage, some on several occasions, and important docks, passenger and goods stations, and

Right - A further view of the damage caused at Derby Station on 15th January 1941.

Bottom - The Liverpool Exchange viaduct was once again the recipient of enemy attention on 3rd May 1941.
                        All British Rail

freight marshalling depots were isolated for long periods, whilst destruction of buildings at passenger and goods stations and the docks was very extensive.

Liverpool – 3rd/4th May. The centres for the new arches on the Sandhills viaduct and the temporary bridges were again destroyed and the slow lines blocked again, with Exchange Station badly damaged. Part of the western wall of the station was blown inwards on to the platforms, causing the collapse of four bays of the main roof on to an electric train and severely damaging two additional bays. The blast damaged all the offices on the west side of the station, most of the roof glazing, and the District Goods Manager's offices were also demolished. The buildings on the eastern side of the station were gutted by incendiary bombs, and a fire in the basement caused the carriageway to collapse. It was not until July 6th that the slow lines from the station and over the viaduct were reopened for electric trains, with a modified steam service following a month later. The fast lines were eventually re-opened on12th April 1942. This was the worst dislocation to an important traffic centre during the whole of the raids, but diversion of traffic to other stations and routes

within the vicinity eased the operating difficulties. Had these alternative facilities not been available there is no doubt the repair work could have been speeded up by concentrating on the restoration of lines into Exchange Station, but this would have been at the expense of other important railway facilities in the Liverpool area. Huskisson Goods shed was destroyed. There were about ten cases where tunnels were damaged being a rare occurrence, but there were two in Liverpool. **Spellow Tunnel - 14th March**. was hit by two high explosive bombs, and whilst the damaged portion was being repaired it was hit again on 7th May in the great raids in the first week in

This page:, top - Liverpool, Huskisson Dock targeted on 3ʳᵈ May, 1941.

Middle - *Liverpool, Bootle Branch, Spellow Tunnel Damaged on 14ᵗʰ March 1941.*

Bottom - *Liverpool, Spellow Tunnel hit for a second time on 7ᵗʰ May 1941.*

Opposite top - *Marsh Lane Station on the Liverpool – Southport electrified line damaged by enemy action 4ᵗʰ – 8ᵗʰ May 1941.*

Opposite bottom - *Marsh Lane Station with the platform reconstructed.*

All British Rail

May. Although single line working was soon possible after each incident it was not until the end of November 1941 that both lines were re-opened. In the latter raid Crown Street Tunnel collapsed as a result of a direct hit. From the S&T viewpoint on 26ᵗʰ April *and* 8ᵗʰ May, 1941 a total of some eighty locations (offices, signal boxes etc.) were damaged, main multi-core cables and all open wires being down in numerous sections. Twenty signal boxes received damage, with that to Bootle Station and Dale Lane No.2 being considerable. Liverpool Exchange "B" box and gantry were badly damaged by fire. The control Office at Aintree, Telegraph Office at Liverpool Exchange Station and the Telephone Exchange at Canada Dock were demolished, a temporary board installed at Canada Dock again being destroyed in the later raid. Difficulties at the docks were accentuated by prolonged interruption of hydraulic and electric power affecting cranes, capstans etc., and the severance of connections between LMS lines and the Mersey Docks and Harbour Board Estate. The various Goods Offices and Station Telephone Exchanges were interconnected by about fifty Post Office maintained tie lines, and, owing to the extensive damage suffered by the Post Office, chaotic conditions prevailed initially. It was only due to the provision of temporary tie lines by the S&T Engineer's Department over devious railway routes that skeleton inter-communication was afforded within a week or so.

Marsh Lane Station – 4th/8th May was also damaged in these raids.

Scotland – March and May 1941.

As far as Scotland was concerned, the worst raids affected Glasgow as might be expected. Many bombs fell on the Forth and Clyde Canal during the first raid without causing too much damage. Although there were a great many incidents in the raids, there were not many cases of serious damage, if the standard of the attacks on Liverpool and Manchester was the yardstick.

5th May. The goods sheds at Greenock were the worst affected. Damage was caused to nine signal boxes, those at Greenock Central and Gourock No.1 of a serious nature. Aerial wires were brought down in many places, telephone communication and block working between Langbank and Port Glasgow and between Wemyss Bay Junction and Greenock were made inoperative necessitating all trains being run on a time interval. Study of the table on page 99 shows that the combination of attacks on Liverpool and Glasgow in the first week of May 1941 accounted for the highest number of incidents on the LMS for any week, this being the final fling by the enemy on the West Coast ports.

Birmingham Area.

Coventry 8th/10th April. The telephone exchange was completely destroyed and Nos. 2, 3 and 4 signal boxes and connections damaged together with pole routes.

Birmingham 8th/10th April. The windows of eight signal boxes were damaged. One signal gantry was demolished and two other signals blown down. At New Street all communications were cut. Main line blockages were numerous and very serious, and damage considerable. Blockages occurred on the main trunk lines of the Western Division between Stafford and Rugby, and the Midland Division between Derby and Bristol, and the reaction on traffic workings, both passenger and freight was extremely heavy and considerable diversions for important through services were made. In addition the following goods depots were isolated - Lawley Street until the afternoon of 12th April, Curzon Street until mid-day on 11th April with full access not available until 16th. and Central Goods until 13th April.

London Area.

Highbury - 19th March. The Liverpool Road over-bridge and retaining wall damaged.

London 16th April 1941 – *Sir Josiah Stamp was killed, aged 60, together with his wife Olive Jessie and his son Wilfred Carlyle Stamp.*

London, Haggerston 17th April. The signal box at Haggerston was seriously damaged, also four others to a lesser extent. A signal gantry at Haggerston was demolished. Aerial wires were brought down at several places. At River Rom a District train (empty) received a direct hit and rested on the cables, which fortunately did not affect their working.

Above - *London, Highbury Liverpool Road Bridge and retaining wall damaged by enemy action 19th/20th March 1941 and after reconstruction.*

Centre - *Bow Works was severely damaged on the North London Section on 19th April 1941.*

Bottom - *Barrow Station was attacked on 5th May seen here following tidying up.*

Opposite page *- The last heavy raid on London on 11th May saw much damage to St. Pancras Station as shown.*

All British Rail

Bow works- 19ᵗʰ April. Was hit on 19ᵗʰ April 1941.

London Area - 19ᵗʰ/20ᵗʰ, April. Nine signal boxes received structural damage and broken windows. Aerial wires were brought down and cables damaged at many places. At Broad Street New Inn Yard signal box, all block and other instruments were put out of order. Plaistow traction sub-station was damaged, putting out of use the signalling equipment.

Barrow-in-Furness – 4ᵗʰ May. There were direct hits on Barrow Central and carriage sidings. The carriage and wagon offices and warehouses were demolished and some forty coaches were damaged. Main lines were blocked and all communications were down. The station lines were cleared in 29 hours.

London Area - 10ᵗʰ and 11ᵗʰ May. Seven signal boxes were damaged, that at Poplar seriously so. Signals and signal and point connections were damaged, aerial wires brought down and cables destroyed with damage at several other places.

St. Pancras – 10ᵗʰ May. This was the last heavy raid on London with St. Pancras Station again a heavy sufferer, being closed until 19ᵗʰ May.

Blackpool Central – 27ᵗʰ August. Blackpool Central was targeted on 27ᵗʰ August 1941.

Signal Boxes destroyed / seriously damaged by enemy action during 1941:

Avonmouth Dock Junction – 16/17ᵗʰ/1/1941; Haggeston – 17/4/1941; Bootle, Dale Lane No.2 and Liverpool Exchange No.2, all between 26ᵗʰ April and 8ᵗʰ May 1941; Poplar Central 10/11ᵗʰ May/1941.

At the Board meeting held on 29ᵗʰ May 1941, (Minute 4289,) The Chairman, Sir Ernest Lemon, gave details of the damage done at Liverpool, Birmingham and elsewhere and "explained the difficulty experienced in carrying out essential repairs owing to the Government's dilatory system of priorities and licences

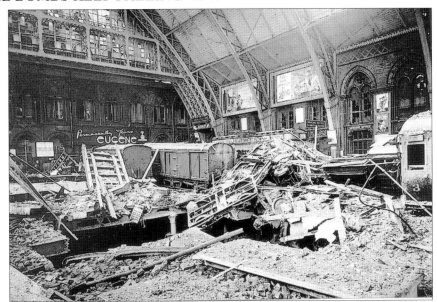

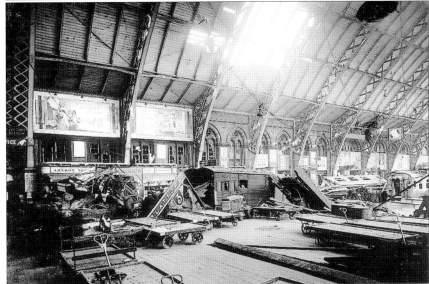

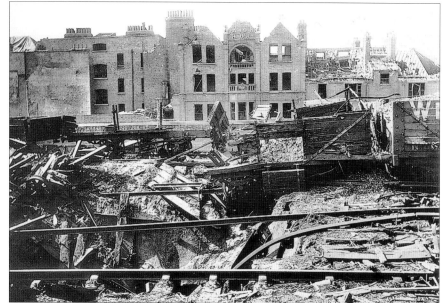

Top - St Pancras, Somers Town Goods , 11ᵗʰ May 1941.

Bottom, left and right - Blackpool Central received a visit from the enemy on 27ᵗʰ August 1941..

All British Rail

having regard to the vital nature of railway traffic in the country's war effort". The Board authorised the Chairman to approach the Government with the object of overcoming avoidable delays. (See Chapter 12 dealing with materials etc.).

Thereafter the raids tapered off and in the seven months June to December 1941 inclusive, there were only 52 occasions on which damage was done to LMS property.

The following tables are included in respect of the period 19ᵗʰ June 1940 to 31ˢᵗ December 1941.

Table 1 opposite lists passenger and goods stations that were severely damaged.

Table 2 (page 96) shows the dates on which severe air raids occurred on the 10 areas served by the LMS Railway that were principally attacked.

It will be seen that in total, from June 1940 to November 1941, inclusive damage was caused on 1,716 occasions and running lines were obstructed for total of 136,132 hours, with 67 persons killed and 462 injured. An analysis of the 1,716 incidents reveals that 1057 or 62% occurred in the Southern portion of England and Wales (south of a line drawn through Ambergate, Norton Bridge and Shrewsbury) 591 or 34% in the Northern portion and 68 or 4% in Scotland.

Classification of the heavy raids (opposite bottom) shows the following;-

Table 1 - List of passenger and goods stations severely damaged – 19th June 1940 to 31st December 1941.

Passenger Stations

London Area	Birmingham Area	Manchester Area	Other Stations
St Pancras	New Street	Exchange	Bristol St Phillips
Euston	Coventry	Victoria	Sheffield
Hampstead Heath	Vauxhall	Mayfield	Attercliffe Road
Highbury	Coleshill	Pendleton (Old)	Derby
St Quntin Park	Moseley		Swansea Victoria
Kensington (Addison Raod)	**Liverpool Area**		Holbeck
West Ham	Exchange		Renfrew Wharf
Gospel Oak	Marsh lane		Grays
Caledonian Road and	Canada Dock		Nottingham
Barnsbury	Breck Road		Barrow Central
Poplar	Kirkdale		
Bow			
Whitecross Street (Parcels)			
West End Lane			

Total 37

Goods Stations

London Area	Liverpool Area	Birmingham Area	Other Stations
St Pancras	Alexandra Road	Curzon Street	Barrow
Somers Town	Brunswick Dock	Lawley street	Bristol St Phillips
Haydon Square	Sandon Dock	Central	Avonside
Poplar 'A'	Canada Dock	Spon Lane	Heaton Norris
Poplar 'B'	South Dock	Cioventry	Leeds Wellington Street
Broad Street	Waterloo Dock		Leicester
Canning Town	Garston Dock		Nottingham Manvers Street
Commercial Road	Edge Hill		Sheffield (Queens Road)
Birkenhead	Park Lane	**Manchester Area**	Sheffield (Wicker)
Egerton Dock	Bankfield	Salford) Stone Jug & New	Sheffield Nunnery
Cathcart Street	North Mersey	Bailey sSreet)	Stoke Works
			Broadheath

Total 40

Area	Number of incidents in heavy raids	Percentage to line total.
London	425	25
Thames Estuary (east of Bromley).	96	6
Birmingham and Coventry	240	14
Liverpool and Birkenhead	269	16
Manchester	74	4
Clydeside.	50	3
Totals	**1163**	**66**

Year	London Area	Thames Estuary	Birmingham and Coventry	Manchester	Liverpool and Birkenhead	Leeds	Sheffield	Swansea	Bristol	Clydeside
1940 June									24/25	
July										
August		18th 26th 31st	25/26 26/27					17/18	13/14	13/14
Sept.	7th, 7/8, 8/9, 9/10 10/11, 15/16 17/18, 21/22 25/26, 27/28 28/29, 29/30 31st. Oct.	7th, 15th, 15/16 27/28			4/5 18/19 21/22 26/27 29/30			1/2		
Oct.	1/2, 2/3 4/5, 5/6 8/9, 9/10 10/11, 13/14 14/15, 15/16 16/17, 19/20 21/22, 23/24	14/15 15/16	12/13, 16/17 17/18, 18/19 21/22, 14/15 25/26, 26/27 28/29, 31/1 Nov.	2/3 7/8	11/12					
Nov.	7/8, 15/16 16/17		14/15, 19/20 22/23		28/29				24/25	
Dec.	¾, 8/9 29/30		3/4, 11/12	22/23 23/24	20/21, 21/22 22/23		12/13 15/16		6/7	
1941 Jan.	5/6 11/12	12/13			9/10				26/17	
Feb.								19/20 20/21 21/22		
March	8/9, 19/20	8/9 19/20		11/12	12/13, 13/14 14/15	14/15			16/17	13/14
April	16/17, 17/18 19/20	1 6 / 1 7 , 19/20	8/9, 9/10 10/11		15/16, 26/27				11/12	7/8
May	10/11		16/17	7/8	7 cons. nights 1/2 to 7/8 inc. 31/1 June					5/6, 6/7
June					1/2					

Table 2

Above - St. Pancras - repairs at an advanced stage.

Right - Not so at Nottingham. Damage to carriage sidings and stock, 9th May 1941.

Both British Rail

Following the Battle of Britain, the enemy concentrated on night bombing and the relative scarcity of raids affecting the railway in normal working hours, rendered it unnecessary to apply other sections of ARP measures designed before the war. As a result of the greater part of the staff being away from railway premises during night raids, the rescue squads were not called upon, neither had the trenches and shelters been occupied to anything like that anticipated

The table below shows the number of incidents in each Civil Engineering District – June 1940 to May 1941

Of note was the fact that, although an "Emergency Depot" (as detailed in chapter 1) was often only a few miles away, it was not necessary to call on that emergency organisation. The usefulness of such depots lay in the availability of special stocks of bridge materials, permanent way etc. In general it was crater filling that was usually the major job, whilst damage to bridges and viaducts were not numerous. There were about thirty cases of damage to viaducts, bridges and station roofs where material from the Emergency depots was required. One such case was the repair of Bridge 36 at Bulkington, between Rugby and Nuneaton on the main line to the north. This was a girder bridge carrying three tracks and damaged by a direct hit that smashed one of the main girders and threw two others into the canal. The use of emergency beams enabled both lines to be re-opened within four days, single line working having been instituted within 24 hours of the damage being caused. Emergency material was also used on the wrecked bridges on the North London line, the Sandhills viaduct and several other places.

District	Permanent way	Bridges and Retaining walls	Buildings	Total
Watford	196	52	283	511
London	173	64	196	433
Liverpool	218	63	106	387
Walsall	158	46	129	333
Manchester	159	30	108	297
Bangor	116	11	89	216
Glasgow	46	10	97	153
Crewe	34	5	41	60
Derby North	34	11	28	73
Derby South	34	4	34	73
Abergavenny	21	1	21	43
Northampton	15	4	22	41
Barrow	19	-	20	39
Leeds	10	5	14	29
Bradford	14	4	4	22
Stoke	10	-	9	19
Blackburn	11	2	5	18
Perth	7	1	6	14
Edinburgh	3	-	4	7
Irvine	-	-	5	5
Lancaster	2	-	2	4
Inverness	-	-	1	1
Total	**1,280**	**313**	**1,204**	**2,797**

Rolling Stock.

Whilst the damage to stations, permanent way and buildings

etc. has been considered, it is appropriate to enumerate the principal items of movable plant that was destroyed or damaged up to end December 1941.

Category	Destroyed	Damaged
Locomotives	1	40 Heavily damaged
Steam, electric & other coaching vehicles	151	2473
Wagons – railway owned	1038	5271
Goods motors	24	104
Parcels motors	2	34
Mechanical-horse tractors	8	105
Mechanical horse trailers	43	73
Drays	637	367
Horses	21	32 Injured.

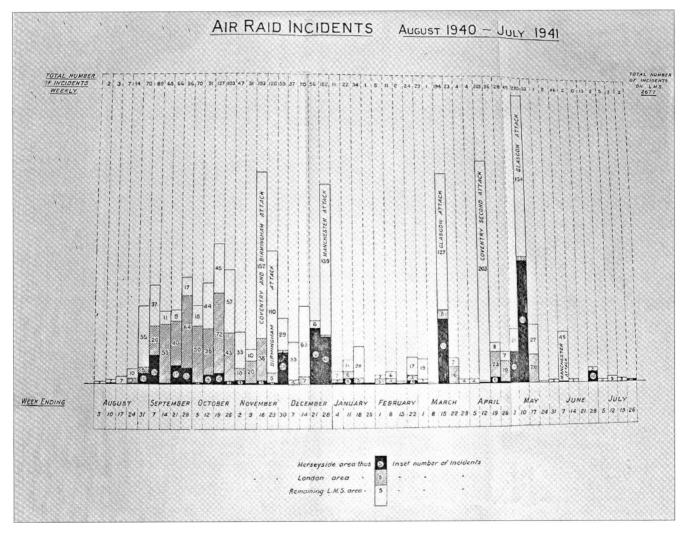

Table showing the Air raid Incidents - August 1940 to July 1941.

British Rail

Derby, 1941.

9
1942 to 1945:
BOMBS, FLYING BOMBS and ROCKETS

Bomb Damage - 1942

The technique of air attack on Great Britain changed during the latter part of 1942 from spasmodic bombing at lengthy intervals and isolated daylight raids by single enemy aircraft to sneak raid attacks, mainly on coastal areas, by fast fighter bombers coming in at zero height to elude the defences. The London area and the Thames Estuary also experienced small scale attacks in the latter part of 1943, which failed to have any appreciable effect on the normal operation of the railway. In 1942, 70 incidents affected the LMS. 46 or 66% occurring during six fairly heavy raids, the areas affected being Bath on two occasions, Birmingham also twice, Nuneaton and Wolverhampton. Phosphorous bombs were dropped at the latter place on 30th/31st July, the first such experience of this type on LMS property.

Luton – 5th September 1942. This was the most serious of the daylight raids by single aircraft when a high explosive bomb fell in the public highway to the Goods Yard, causing extensive damage to the warehouse, offices, etc. Six staff were injured. Other cases of serious damage to property occurred during 1942 as follows:-

Bath – 25th April 1942. Grain shed destroyed by fire. Goods Offices demolished and extensive damage to roofs of the Locomotive Shed and Offices. The Passenger Station buildings were also damaged.
Stockingford – 25th June 1942. Roof of warehouse extensively damaged.
Vauxhall, Birmingham 30th- July 1942. Passenger Station and Booking Office seriously damaged by fire.
Lawley Street, Birmingham - 30 July 1942. Offices and buildings extensively damaged by a high explosive bomb.
Templecombe Upper (S&D Joint) - 5th September 1942. The Southern Railway Company's portion of the Joint Station was extensively damaged by a high explosive bomb.

In none of these cases were lines blocked or the permanent way damaged and during 1942 no member of the staff was killed on LMS Property but 13 were injured.

Up to December 1942 bomb damage to all the Railway Companies was estimated to be £19,250,000, the LMS amount, including Joint Lines being £4,660,000. At this time the Government Bill dealing with damage to Public Utility Undertaking had still to be submitted to Parliament. The LMS was therefore using its own cash resources totalling £2,149,337 up to the end of 1942, mainly on repair work.

In 1943 the number of incidents affecting the LMS further declined to 24, mainly in the London area and the Thames Estuary, damage was generally light and there were no casualties. The only instance of serious damage took place at Swansea, St. Thomas, when high explosive bombs damaged the roof of the station and the old Midland warehouse at the Eastern Depot.

Moving on to 1944, with the invasion of France imminent, the Government anticipated heavy air attacks, and to ensure that essential rail and road traffic was not delayed during the crucial period of military operations, decided that some risk would need to be taken with respect to unexploded bombs. In May 1944 special instructions were issued to the District Controllers and District Engineers setting out certain modifications to the standard regulations applicable to the working of trains past unexploded bombs. These relaxations were based on the knowledge gained of the fuses used by the enemy. The new instructions were to be regarded as most secret in case the enemy obtained a copy and thus revised their tactics. In the event no such heavy bombing took place and neither did the gassing of the invasion ports or the feeder lines of communication as was anticipated. Following a lapse of two months the Government decided that there was no further justification for the continuance of these special instructions that were cancelled on and from 30th August 1944.

Comment in the Operating Managers Report for the period to 1943

"This chapter cannot be closed without paying tribute to those of all grades of the Operating Department. Railwaymen of the operating grades were more in the firing line than in any other industry, as the traffic continued to run after danger was imminent, whilst gun-fire was intensive and bombs were falling. No one, other than the men them-selves, can fully appreciate what it meant to be a Driver or Fireman of a train approaching London or any provincial city at night, with the sky full of bursting shells or be a Driver, Fireman or Guard of a train brought to a stand at a signal box with bombs of all kinds dropping in the immediate vicinity. Again, how many people would, during a raid, have cared to take the place of a signalman in an elevated box, or to be a shunter in the open without any overhead protection? But it is almost invidious to mention particular grades, because in all branches – on the passenger stations, in the traffic yards, at the locomotive depots, in the goods sheds, and elsewhere – work went on. One could not but feel a thrill of pride when, during the nightly din of bursting bombs and gunfire, with the glare of fires telling their woeful tale of

destruction, there constantly emerged the sounds of running trains and shunting movements of "the service that never sleeps". But the price of this devotion to duty had to be paid, and whilst any loss of life was deeply regretted, it will probably be a matter of surprise, having regard to the large numbers employed, that only 48 railwaymen were killed on duty, perhaps it was a case of "fortune favours the brave". By carrying on with their jobs, railwaymen performed acts of bravery every day, but they also distinguished themselves by the precision with which they tackled fire-bombs and by the more specific feats which could be singled out for official recognition. Railway men also played their part in the performance of acts of bravery as members of the Civil Defence Services as civilians, for which awards were granted".

Bomb Damage - 1944

Enemy air activity increased using piloted aircraft during the first three months of the year mainly in the London area, the heaviest attacks being on 19th and 20th February. On 19th main lines were blocked at ten places and extensive damage was done by high explosive bombs to station buildings at Canonbury and West Hampstead. During the period from 1st January to 14th June there were 83 incidents causing damage, including 32 occasions on which running lines were obstructed.

Canonbury and West Hampstead Passenger Stations - 19th February 1944. Extensive damage caused by high explosive bombs.

St. Pancras –15th March 1944. Canley Street Stables heavily damaged with two horses killed.

Flying Bombs - 1944

On 13th June the Germans introduced the use of 'flying bombs' that were a mid-wing pilot-less jet propelled monoplane, the jet propulsion unit being mounted above the rear portion of the fuselage. The overall length was 25' 4 1/2" with the wingspan varying from 16' to 17' 6", the warhead containing approximately 1,700 lbs of high explosive. These projectiles were used daily against Southern England, including the Greater London area until 31st August with the sole exception of 26th August. Altogether there were 128 flying bomb incidents on the LMS, During the peak period from the middle of June until the end of August, the missiles were sent over at short intervals by day and night especially during poor visibility, and on the 24th August there were no less than 13 'Imminent' Danger warnings between 17.50 and 21.15, the peak period for the forwarding of traffic at the main London Goods Depots. In the twelve-week period from weekended 18th June ending on 3rd September "Red" warnings operated in the Central London area for 645¼ hours or 32% of the time. The first flying bomb that caused damage to LMS property burst at Poplar on the 16th June 1944. In order to combat the flying bomb it was decided to utilise 3.7" heavy anti-aircraft guns, and to this effect 76 were moved in five special trains

from Scotland, Newcastle, Leeds and Sheffield to the South Coast within a period of ten days. In all 155 flying bombs damaged LMS property, of which 133 were in the London area. When war broke out the Nation's householders were given the option of receiving one of two types of air raid shelters. One was the 'Anderson' shelter of galvanised corrugated iron construction for partially burying in the garden and covered over with earth. The second was the 'Morrison' type for use indoors that one slept under. With the range of flying bombs limited to the London area an appeal was made for those resident in the north to dismantle their indoor type for dispatch to London to meet the emergency. The total brought to London by the LMS was 37,868.

None of the cases caused damage comparable to the worst incidents from the earlier mixture of high explosive and incendiary bombs.

The worst cases are listed below:-

Poplar – 16th June 1944. Station buildings, platforms, staff rooms, two signal boxes, retaining walls and sidings damaged.

Fenchurch Street – 18th June 1944. Control Office windows, doors, ceilings etc damaged by blast.

Wembley – 3rd July 1944. Flying bomb dropped in 6ft. way between up and down electric lines, causing damage to Sudbury Junction signal box and serious damage to the permanent way. The down line was blocked from 19.07 until 15.08 on the 4th and the up line until 18.15 on that date.

Somers Town Goods and St. Pancras Passenger Stations – 5th July 1944 - A flying bomb fell on Ricketts' Wharf, causing damage to crane, coal shutes, shed, the permanent way of four sidings, and to 67 wagons. Windows of the goods and passenger station buildings were broken. Thirteen passengers and eighteen members of the staff sustained minor injuries or shock.

Kilburn – 24th July 1944. A flying bomb dropped in Cambridge Road at the time the 10.00 express train from Blackpool to Euston was approaching. Thirteen coaches had windows and fittings badly damaged, whist 56 passengers were injured.

Purfleet – 24th July 1944. A flying bomb fell in the 6' 0" way as a military freight train was leaving the sidings. Forty five wagons sustained damage.

Commercial Road Goods – 1st August 1944. General Delivery Office and 20-ton wagon hoist demolished and thirty wagons smashed. Fourteen staff and nineteen USA personnel were injured or sustained shock.

On 24th December 1944 the enemy made his first attack with flying bombs on Northern England ie that part of the country north of a line from the Wash to the Severn Estuary. Slight damage was caused to the Company's property at Stockport (Davenport Junction), Radcliffe Bridge, and Killamarsh. On the morning of 29th December air raid alerts were also sounded in the Liverpool, Manchester, Crewe, Wigan,

Damage at Somers Town Goods on 5th July 1944.

British Rail

Macclesfield and Sheffield areas. The severity of the flying bomb attacks can be gauged by the time warnings operated in the Central London area. From the beginning of the attacks until 3rd September (12 weeks), warnings were in operation for 646 hours, or 32% of the total hours for this period, the worst week being that ending on 9th July when alerts were in operation for 98 of the 168 hours, or 58.3%. In all 116 members of the staff sustained injury or shock during the course of their duties, but no fatalities occurred. The staff most at risk were the cartage staff, who were bound to be out on the streets without shelter, and in many cases in charge of horse vehicles. The fears were not unfounded as 24 van men, carters, etc including six females, were injured whilst on duty. During certain periods of those attacks it was necessary to restrict the forwarding of certain traffic to the London Goods Depots.

The 1944 Voluntary Evacuations from Flying Bombs and Rockets

With the advent of flying bombs and rockets in 1944 a limited amount of voluntary evacuations took place of school children and some mothers to the Midlands and the North. This became apparent when, on 24th June 1944 both the 12.00 train from St. Pancras to Bradford and the 14.40 from Euston to Liverpool were seriously overcrowded with passengers standing and each leaving 100 passengers behind. The following day was much worse, as following the departure of the 10.00 train from St. Pancras there were still 700 passengers awaiting the midday service. At Euston the situation was no different with the platforms packed throughout the morning and afternoon. There was at this time restrictions on the running of additional passenger trains but the Ministry of War Transport gave permission to run relief trains for bona fide evacuees and three trains ran on Saturday 1st July being the 09.45 St. Pancras to Leeds, 09.50 Euston to Manchester and 12.05 Euston to Manchester. However it became evident that further trains were required and authority was obtained for seven further trains on 1st July that ran from Euston or St. Pancras to Manchester, Liverpool, Leeds, Derby and Leicester with an approximate total of 5,950 passengers. Interestingly permission was given to run what would have been empty stock trains back to London as Up main line relief trains, provided discretion was used.

Rockets 1944/5, the Final Attacks and Hostilities in Europe Cease

In the early part of September 1944 the enemy supplemented the flying bomb with long-range rockets. These missiles were projected by rocket propulsion into the stratosphere to fall like a shell at a very much higher speed and at an angle of about 60 degrees to the horizontal. They measured some 45' 10" long by 5' 6" wide (11'9" including the fins) and contained a warhead similar to that of the flying bomb in that it weighed about 2000lbs. The rockets were sent over at varying times during the 24 hours of the day, and, as no air raid warning was given, they were not detected by any existing device. No defence measures could therefore be brought into operation with trains running at normal speeds and the working of stations and goods depots continued. For a long time the Government did not admit their existence, that was, until the German wireless made a definite statement that they were being used and had fallen in England, following which an official announcement was made. Interestingly, in November 1944, the Germans announced that Euston Station had been demolished by one of their rockets, which, like many others, was untrue thus leaving the LMS to design a new Euston Station without the assistance of the enemy. Altogether there were 128 flying bomb and 13 rocket incidents on the LMS with fifteen flying bombs and thirteen rockets being direct hits. Damage was caused by 51 such rockets, all in the London area. The first case being on 11th October 1944, at Bow Works

Bow Works – 13th October 1944. The wagon shop at Bow Works was virtually demolished, with the roofs of most of the other buildings blown off by the explosion.

Tilbury Riverside – 14th December 1944. Rocket projectiles fell in East Sidings causing considerable damage to the passenger station, sidings, refreshment rooms, goods shed and offices. In addition 142 coaches and 13 freight wagons were damaged. Of the 142 coaching vehicles affected, 26 formed part of two ambulance trains stabled in the sidings. Four staff members and seven War Department personnel attached to the ambulance train were injured.

West End Lane - 8th January 1945. A rocket fell on the permanent way cutting the up and down lines. Shuttle electric services were instituted between Broad Street and Hampstead Heath and Brondesbury and Richmond. Windows were broken in two coaches of the 10.08 express from Bradford to St. Pancras that was in the vicinity on the Midland Division line at the time. Lines were blocked for 24 hours.

Bow - 13th January 1945. A rocket demolished the Wagon Works and damaged the Locomotive Works. The lines between Poplar and Bow and the entrance to Devon's Road Motive Power Depot were blocked by debris. Blast damaged an LPTB electric train at Bromley (LTS Section), injuring 30 passengers, one of whom died the following day.

Dagenham Dock – 7th February 1945. A rocket fell in Ripple Lane Down Sidings making the largest LMS crater being 40 feet deep and 120 feet in diameter. The up and down lines were obstructed by debris and the permanent way in the down line was damaged. Twenty-two wagons were damaged.

West Ham and Plaistow – 28th February 1945. A rocket fell in the down sidings. The down local line and three sidings sustained damage together with 29 wagons and 5 brake vans. The roof was blown off the Booking Hall at West Ham and the other station buildings suffered damage.

East Horndon - 8th March 1945. A rocket fell in Laindon Cutting damaging the down line. The up and down lines were closed to traffic from 20.20 to 03.00 the following day.

Dagenham Dock – 17th March 1945. A rocket fell in Ripple Lane Down Sidings causing a 50 feet diameter crater with 3 brake vans and 21 wagons damaged.

Hornchurch - 26th March 1945. This was the final recorded rocket recorded to fall on LMS property.

The last major attack on Britain was made on the nights of 3/4th and 4/5th of March 1945 when around 70 planes flew to convey and launch V1 missiles   In total 170 V1 Flying bombs and V2 rockets fell on the LMS as listed below.

Analysis of Damage Caused by Flying Bombs and Rockets 1944 /45

Area	Flying Bombs	Rockets	Total
London	32 (6)	23 (6)	55
Thames estuary	86 (9)	17 (2)	103
Elsewhere	11	1	12
Total	129	41	170

The figures in brackets indicate the direct hits on the railway.

The General Air Raid Warning System and the Industrial Alarm warning arrangements were cancelled on the 2nd May 1945. The last "alerts" given in the country were at Aberdeen and Forfar on the afternoon of Monday 30th April. The total number of "Red" warnings issued in the Central London Area throughout the war was 1,227 and the longest period of consecutive days on which warnings were given in the same zone was from 23rd August 1940 to 1st December 1940, a total of 101. The largest number of "Red" warnings in one day was 23 on 3rd August 1944. Folkestone has the overall warning record with 2,643 warnings. On 2nd May 1945 instructions were issued for the return of all ARP equipment to the General Stores Department, when later, arrangements were made for the staff to purchase certain of this equipment such as gum boots, oilskin coats, beds etc.

The final table of bombing incidents to LMS property, including flying bombs and rockets was as shown opposite top.

To sum up – from all the foregoing much of the preparation made to combat air raids was never tested, the trenches were rarely used and neither was poison gas and even the emergency depots were hardly ever called upon to any where near the extent envisaged.

Notwithstanding – if these thorough preparations had not been made, just consider the public outcry and the consequences, had the air attacks been as expected. All three Departments, Civil, Operating and S & T all did a first class job in keeping traffic moving and stations open.

On the lighter side – for many years the LMS was the custodian of a faked showpiece, alleged to be the fossilised remains of Ossian, one of the legendry giants who built the Giants Causeway in Northern Ireland. He was eight feet tall and weighed almost three tons. In 1876 he became a ward in

The final table showing damage to the LMS railway, by bombs, flying bombs and rockets.				
Civil Engr's District	Permanent way	Bridges and Retaining walls	Buildings	Total
Watford	242	83	400	725
London	205	53	280	538
Liverpool	218	63	106	387
Walsall	159	46	130	335
Manchester	159	30	110	299
Bangor	116	11	89	216
Glasgow	48	10	100	158
Crewe	34	5	41	80
Derby North	34	4	35	73
Derby South	34	11	28	73
Abergavenny	21	1	22	44
Northampton	16	4	23	43
Barrow	19	-	20	39
Leeds	10	5	14	29
Bradford	14	4	4	22
Stoke	10	-	9	19
Blackburn	11	2	8	21
Perth	7	1	8	16
Edinburgh	3	-	4	7
Irvine	-	-	5	5
Lancaster	2	-	2	4
Inverness	-	-	1	1
Total	1,362	333	1,439	3,134

Analysis of the Number of Incidents 1939 to 1945

Area	Number of Incidents	Percentage of Total
London	593	28.7
Thames Estuary (East of Bromley).	188	9.1
Coventry, Birmingham, Wolverhampton.	277	13.4
Manchester	74	3.6
Liverpool and Merseyside	269	13.1
Clydeside.	60	2.9
Rest of England and Wales.	592	28.7
Rest of Scotland.	10	0.5
Total	2063	100.0

Damages and Blockages by Enemy Action 1939 to 1945

	1939	1940	1941	1942	1943	1944	1945	Total
No. of occasions damage was caused	Nil	1,140	576	70	24	224	29	2,063
No. of occasions running lines were obstructed	Nil	447	204	26	5	35	8	725
No. of hours lines were blocked	Nil	43,999	92,133	6,497	99	638	98	143,464

Chancery of the old LNWR, following an ownership dispute between Showmen partners. An appeal to the Courts by the Company, to secure disposal against storage charges was dismissed and Ossian enjoyed a tranquil existence for the next 64 years, firstly at Broad Street and later Worship Street Station in London. At £11 5s a year, storage charges reached over £700 until the night of 14th October when Ossian was blitzed and could not be put back together, finally filling a crater made by a bomb – and there were no mourners.

The Evacuees Return

In April 1945 there were 500,000 evacuees in safer areas of the country and plans were formulated to return these in 610 special trains of which 200 were on the LMS. In the event it was found that most of the evacuees made their own way home and the special arrangements were scrapped, and when the LMS ran 35 long distance trains for the purpose, the number who travelled did not reach expectations. In all the LMS ran 2,036 special evacuee trains during the war conveying 840,512 evacuees. Hospital patients had all returned towards the end of 1944 and from July 9th to 16th October 13 loaded journeys were made, the furthest being from Brechin. In 1945 evacuees drifted back from America and the Colonies, generally to the Mersey, and a total of nine specials were provided for this purpose. Staffs of certain Government Departments returned to London from their evacuated headquarters, one case being the Ministry of Food from Colwyn Bay that required two special trains for the 1000 members of staff and families. Seven special trains were required between July and October 1945 for about 5,000 persons to return Channel Islanders to Southampton and reserved accommodation was provided on ordinary trains for smaller parties.

Air Raid Casualties

The idea of the Germans to defeat Britain by the use of air raids in 1940/1 was a complete failure and the V1 flying bomb and V2 rockets came too late to make a meaningful difference. Statistically the Luftwaffe dropped some 64,393 tonnes of high explosive bombs from aircraft, 5,823 tonnes as Flying Bombs and 1,054 as Rockets with 3,500 shells fired across the channel onto the Dover area. The final estimation of the number of people killed or seriously injured was 116,293 of which 80,397 were in London and 35,896 in the provinces, with the total number killed being 60,595 with damage caused to over 1 million homes.

The First World War – 1914-1918

By comparison as far as the 1914/18 war was concerned, there were 108 air raids on Great Britain, of which 29 were on Kent or at least got no further than Kent. This left 79 raids that could have affected other railways. Of the 79 raids, 49 were by Zeppelin and 30 by aeroplanes, and due to their limited range were of short duration. On the LNWR, Euston was damaged five times, mainly broken glass and damaged slates. Only some 12 incidents were reported, the worst being at Wednesbury on 31st January 1916 when the permanent way, a retaining wall, a platelayers hut, a goods shed, a weighing machine and signals were all more or less damaged. The Midland Railway records stated - "Sleeper slightly split". In the case of an air raid on 10th May 1915, it stated an incendiary bomb fell on the line between Leigh and Southend when "two sleepers scorched". In all there were 19 instances mostly concerning broken telegraph and telephone wires or panes of glass.

10

OTHER ENEMY ATTACKS AND MISCELLANEOUS WAR DAMAGE

Isolated attacks by the Luftwaffe at low level on the LMS Railway.

Such attacks were usually made using machine guns or cannon fire and in general were ineffective. The LMS was the least affected by such occurrences, the east coast lines and the GWR and Southern being targeted more often.

On 23rd August 1940 at 11.55 on the WCML Banbury Lane–Gayton Boxes near Blisworth, platelayers were machine-gunned and the telegraph wires cut, but there were no casualties.

On 3rd October 1940 the second part of the 13.10 Euston – Blackpool express was bombed and machine gunned at Stoke Hammond box, south of Bletchley. Two passengers and two staff were injured with minor damage being done to the train that was held at Rugby for two hours.

On 25th October 1940 at 17.20 the Edinburgh to Aberdeen XP was machine-gunned at Montrose with windows broken but no casualties.

On 6th November 1940, at 12.25, the station roof at Trent was reported as damaged by bullets from an overhead air battle.

On 13th March 1941 the 20.48 ordinary passenger train from Chester to Denbigh was machine gunned at Caerwys but no damage was done.

On 27th April 1941 freight engine, J37 9479, was shot up and moderately damaged between Easthaven and Elliot Junction on the Dundee & Arbroath Joint line.

On 9th May 1941 at 00.30 a Carnforth to Plumpton freight train was attacked and bombed, with minimal damage, between Arnside and Silverdale.

On 27th June 1941 at 17.45 the 16.20 freight from Dundee to Arbroath was machine gunned Elliot Junction – Easthaven (LMS/LNE Joint). The driver was injured but able to continue.

On 2nd October 1941 the 20.00 freight train from Bletchley to Cambridge was machine-gunned at Gamlingay at 01.10, but only the engine and two wagons were slightly damaged, with the line blocked for 2½ hours.

On 3rd July 1942, at 20.15, at Kirby-in –Ashfield, the engine and tender of 3F 3249 was damaged by machine-gun fire with the fireman injured.

On 3rd July 1943 the stations at New Mills and Shirebrook were gunned and a fireman was injured, but no damage to the locomotive was reported.

Attacks by Allied Aircraft on the LMS – Deliberate and Accidental.

It was the practice of the Allied Air Forces to use old locomotives on isolated or disused track for target practice. LMS HR 4-4-0 14391 "Loch Shin" that was withdrawn in July 1941 was adapted at Bow Works and used as a target at Shoeburyness in 1941/2. LMS (LYR) 0-6-0T engine 11553 was also purchased by the Government for such purposes but never used. Train busting attacks were greatly favoured by US fighter pilots as the 0.5inch guns on their aircraft were very effective should the boilers be hit. During the later stages of the war about 30 locomotives per day were being immobilised in Germany, estimated at a total of 15,000 destroyed or severely damaged. By contrast only eight had been damaged beyond repair in the UK and 484 damaged, mostly only slightly. In 1943 areas of the UK were earmarked for low flying exercises that were not appreciated by railwaymen. As an example, though not on the LMS was as follows -

On 4th January 1945 at Haughley, on the LNER, one of three low-flying USAAF Mustangs attempted a trail shoot up of the locomotive (D15, 4-4-0 7764) on the 10.35 ordinary passenger train from Ipswich to Cambridge and accidently struck the locomotive and knocked off the top of the cab and cladding and then fatally crashing. The driver and fireman were not seriously injured and no passengers were hurt, with the train being worked forward by a freight engine. It appears that there were no such occurrences on the LMS. The following is a quotation from this incident. – *"On 4th January 1945, 2nd Lieut. Sands was in a flight of 479 Fighter Group USAAF Mustangs which flew from Wattisham on a navigation exercise involving low level flying. Prior to take-off, pilots were warned to keep widely spaced, look well ahead and keep 50 feet higher than their leader. For the first hour all went well. At 11.15 the Mustangs dropped from 2,500 feet to a low level run towards the coast. Two minutes after descending, the leader of the flight flashed low over Haughley Station, Suffolk. The 10.25 from Ipswich to Bury St. Edmunds had just pulled out, trundling slowly along the tracks. Lou Massari, an NCO with the 385th Bomber Group, was a passenger on the train and saw the first Mustang streak overhead then swing up in a right turn after simulating an attack on the Locomotive. A second Mustang roared over, climbing out in the same manner. Lou heard another coming in and pressed his face to the window looking for it. Beyond the station there was a hillock. To Lou, the Mustang simply failed to pull up and hit the hillock in a disintegrating fireball. Lou was completely unaware that the Mustang had also hit the engine of the train. Driver George Baker had drawn slowly away from Haughley, and he and his fireman Cyril Broad were startled when a plane tore low overhead followed swiftly by another. The third aircraft was even lower, and Thurmann Sands' flying career ended in a terrible mis-judgement His P-51 came under the telegraph wires, ripped through a fence bordering the permanent way and clipped the locomotive. The boiler cladding and steel sheets between the chimney and cab were pulled open as the force of the impact slammed the Mustang to the ground. Sands' mutilated body was found near the end of a fire-scar across three fields. The driver had head wounds and the fireman was struck by flying glass, but their injuries were not serious. None of the passengers were hurt but their train was delayed for an hour while USAAF personnel from Great Ashfield removed the body of Lieut. Sands. Coincidentally, a B-17 from Great Ashfield was flying over Haughley, going in to land, when the crash occurred. As the Flying Fortress descended, its crew saw Mustangs buzzing the train and radioed base to report that one of the P-51s went too low and shredded itself to pieces beyond the railway line. Calling for an ambulance the B-17 pilot, Frank Wallis, photographed the trail of burning wreckage.*

Aircraft Crashes on the LMS Railway.

During the war period, the number of aircraft flying over the UK was immense, either training or on operations. The number of military airfields totalled 792 by the end of the war including landing grounds and seaplane bases. No less that 572 were located near an operational railway, with 130 being right beside the railway. It appears that some 10,000 aircraft are estimated to have crashed on land or on the shores of the UK between 1939 and 1945. Bomber Command lost 1,380 within the UK whilst outward or inward bound planes on operations and their Operational Training and Heavy Conversion units suffered a further 3,986 accidents. The UK based US Eighth Air Force alone had 1,084 planes destroyed through non-operational causes, with hundreds crashing while operational. The Luftwaffe lost about 1,500 planes in and around the UK. It therefore comes as no surprise that the number of aircraft crashes between 1939 and 1945 on or beside a railway, and reported as incidents to the Railway Executive Committee, amounted to over 200.

As far as airfields were concerned it was decided that where an aerodrome was adjacent to the railway with runways terminating within 200 yards of the running lines, in order to avoid collision with aircraft that may overshoot when landing, two types of safety signalling schemes were devised. One was to provide telephone communication together with an alarm bell circuit from the Control Tower to the nearest signal box and secondly, to provide in addition to the above, emergency colour light stop signals on either side of the aerodrome runways in cases where the existing signals were not suitably placed to give the required protection. Later, a third method required trip wires to be run along the side of the railway on posts about 10'00" above ground, that when severed, caused a bell to ring in the signal box that alerted the

signalman, and at the same time placed the signals at danger. Should the line be electrified power would also be cut-off. There were about 40 such airfields adjacent to the Railways. The first such installation on the LMS was at Hixon, and by the end of 1944 the following installations adjacent to the LMS were in place as follows;-

Dalcross (now Inverness Airport), on the Inverness to Elgin line.

Defford, Purton Siding Box, Defford - Wadborough on Birmingham to Bristol main line.

Elmdon (now Birmingham Airport) Marston Green, Rugby – Birmingham line.

Hawarden, Mold Junction Box, Chester – Holyhead main line.

Broughton & Bretton, Chester-Mold-Denbigh line.

Hendon, Silkstream Junction and Mill Hill Station Boxes, St. Pancras-Sheffield main line.

Hixon, Hixon (Colwich) WCML Rugby-Stafford.

Kimbolton, Kettering- Huntingdon line.

Longmans, Inverness.

Montrose, Broomfield Junction Box, Montrose-Dubton line.

Stoke Orchard, Cleev on the Birmingham-Bristol main line.

Stratford-on-Avon, Clifford Sidings, SMJ Stratford-on-Avon -Ettington.

Valley, Holyhead on the Bangor-Holyhead main line.

Woodvale, Freshfield Box on Liverpool Southport line, Formby- Freshfield.

Airfield mishaps were as follows -
1939.

On 2nd October, at 11.00, a plane crashed at Defford-Pirton Siding on the Birmingham-Bristol main line blocking the up line. The police refused to allow the plane to be moved until instructions were received from the Military, but no troops came. The plane was removed by crane at 16.50 up to which time Single Line Working had been in force since 12.30 with "Considerable upset to working"

1940.

On 21st March, at 15.45, an RAF plane crashed on the line at Henlow Camp on the Bedford-Hitchin line blocking both lines for four hours with buses substituted from Shefford to Hitchin.

On 10th June, at 15.45, a bomber from RAF Squires Gate struck a bridge at Squires Gate near Blackpool at 15.15 and crashed in a field blocking the lines for 30 minutes with the block telegraph lines interrupted for three hours.

On 24th July, at 11.50, an RAF plane crashed on the up goods line at Peartree and Normanton near Derby, blocking it for an hour.

On 7th September, at 17.40, the telecom to Selside box was put out of action at Horton-in-Ribblesdale,on the Settle-Carlisle main line following a crash by a plane bringing down the wires.

On 24th October, at 16.05 a crashing aircraft damaged power cables at Elstree, blocking the main lines.

On 9th November, at 00.30 an RAF Anson hit barrage

balloon cables and crashed on the Stechford-Marston Green line, bursting into flames with all five crew killed. All lines were blocked with the Bescot breakdown crane arriving at 02.20 with the up line cleared by 05.20 and the down line at 09.25.

1941.

On 16th May, at 12.25 a Hurricane on a training flight crashed between Frocester– Coaley, blocking both main lines for 4½ hours with some traffic diverted via Gloucester and Severn Tunnel Junction – the pilot had been blinded by smoke but was otherwise unhurt.

On 4th August, at 12.15, a British aircraft crashed on the Nailsworth-Woodchester line damaging 30 yards track that was repaired in four hours.

On 5th August, In the early hours, a crashing British aircraft did extensive damage to sheds at Whitgate Goods. Winsford CLC.

On 14th August, two aircraft engines from a crashing US Liberator, in which 22 passengers and crew died, fell on the track Auchcruive-Blackhouse Junction, blocking the up and down main Mauchline lines for six hours.

On 27th August, at 15.05, 1941, a disaster occurred at Blackpool Central following a collision between a Botha reconnaissance aircraft from RAF Squires Gate and a Defiant fighter. The Botha crashed on to the station roof and into the main booking hall bursting into flames. Five people were killed and 12 seriously injured. Traffic was diverted to the Excursion side of the station for 4½ hours.

On 26th December, at 15.15, both lines were blocked at Elmsthorpe-Croft near Leicester following a crash by a British bomber. Buses substituted until the lines were clear five hours later.

1942.

On 13th February 1942, a Wellington bomber overshot the runway and finished up on the SMJ line Stratford-on-Avon to Ettington line.

On 26th February, at 15.00, a Wellington crashed near Lichfield Trent Valley Station.

On 11th September, at 15.30, a crashing Wellington bomber blocked both Hixon-Weston (Ingestre) lines. The aircraft was only slightly damaged and normal working resumed in 1½ hours.

On 23rd September at 15.50 a USAAF fighter crashed near Berkhamstead on the WCML blocking all lines and cutting the telegraphs to Tring. Passenger and freight traffic was diverted or cancelled until the lines were successfully opened over the ensuing five hours. The Royal Train departure from Euston was delayed for two hours.

On 22nd November, at 19.00, an aircraft crashed and cut the telecom and block telegraph lines on the WCML, in both directions, at Armitage (Elmhurst Siding) – Lichfield Trent Valley, normal working was not resumed until 01.00 on 23rd.

1943.

On 13th May, the single Buxton-Ashbourne line through Alsop-en-le-Dale, was blocked by a plane crashing nearby,

disabling the telecom and block telegraph for 3½ hours.

On 2nd August, at 03.30, both lines Weston (Ingestre)- Hixon were again blocked for 6½ hours by a Wellington bomber that suffered failure of its hydraulics, overshooting the runway and bursting into flames.

On 10th December, at Bridge of Dun (Angus) a plane crash blocked both lines, cutting the block telegraph and telecom lines. Traffic was diverted and normal working resumed at 18.25.

1944.

On 22nd February, at 09.40, the line Irthlingborough-Ringstead & Addlington (Northants) was closed due to bombs exploding after two USAAF aircraft crashed nearby. Single line working was introduced at 13.15 and normal working some hours later.

On 11th March, at 11.40, a Curtis Tomahawk fighter crashed on take off at Weston (Ingestre)- Hixon line. The pilot was unhurt and there was little interference with traffic.

On 21st March at.15.30 an aircraft crashed on the up and down lines near Newark (Castle). Single line working commenced at 17.30 and normal working at 19.40.

On 27th March, around 21.30, an Oxford trainer taking off from RAF Wheaton, crashed on Gnosall-Haughton (Staffs) lines with normal working resumed after 90 minutes.

On 12th April, at 23.50, a British aircraft crashed, blocking both lines at Eastcroft Junction-Sandtoft on the LMS/LNE Axholme Light Railway, with normal working resumed at 10.00 the following day.

On 20th April, at 10.30, the Weston (Ingestre) line was again blocked by a Wellington bomber over-running the runway at RAF Hixon. Normal working was resumed at 13.05.

On 4th May at 02.50 the engine failed on a Whitley Bomber following take/off from Kinloss (Near Forres) and blocked the single line at Kinloss for 6 hours.

On 16th June, another Wellington bomber over-ran the runway at RAF Hixon at Weston (Ingestre) at 22.50, the crew were safe and there was no interference with traffic.

On 22nd June, at 02.50, a US plane crashed ½ mile from the St. Pancras main line near Leagrave. An airman reported that seven airmen had parachuted in the locality. All lines were searched and one airman was found injured on the line and taken by train to Luton, thence by the police to hospital. Parts of five parachutes were found but no airmen, traffic was held up while the search progressed.

On 29th Jun, at 17.20, an RAF plane exploded in mid-air with parts falling on the WCML Roade-Ashton Box. All lines were blocked for 25 minutes.

On 13th July, at 06.00, a training aircraft crashed on the down main and loop lines at Elford on the Derby-Birmingham main line with everything cleared in 45 minutes.

On 17th July, at 11.20, another crash occurred at Hixon when a crashed aircraft blocked both lines. **On 24th July,** there was a further crash at Hixon by an RAF plane 18 yards from the track that blocked both lines, with trains diverted via Norton Bridge until normal working resumed at 08.45.

On 11th August, at 15.20.Hixon again – when an aircraft

crashed, blocking both lines with traffic diverted via Stafford and Norton Bridge until normal working resumed after 6½ hours.

On 26th August, at 22.50, still at Hixon, a Wellington bomber over-ran the runway and crashed on the track Weston (Ingestre)-Colwich blocking both lines for 16 hours.

On 13th October, at 21.15, a British aircraft crashed blocking both lines Nuneaton-Stoke Golding, a goods line to Loughborough, for three hours with normal working resumed after 10 hours.

On 23rd October, at 18.30, the Kettering- Huntingdon line was blocked by an aircraft crash Kimbolton-Long Stow (Goods) for some hours.

On 27th October, an RAF Halifax crashed at Llandudno Junction, but as the LMS reported no incident the line was presumably not affected.

On 14th November, back to Hixon where, a plane crashed blocked both lines with passenger trains diverted for several hours.

On 28th December, at 22.05 a Wellington overshot the runway on landing and blocked the SMJ single line at Ettington, the SMJ commandeered a locomotive to investigate that collided with the aircraft.

On 18th December,, a US aircraft crashed damaging the Forfar-Brechin single line two miles from Justinhaugh Station, trains being diverted for two hours.

1945.

On 13th March, at 12.40 both main lines to Aberdeen were blocked for an hour when a British aircraft crashed at Cove Bay.

Disruptions due to Barrage Balloons and Cables on the LMS Railway.

On 20th August 1940 a storm caused barrage balloon cables to cut telephone lines on numerous important stretches of the LMS and LNER systems across the North West and Midlands for up to five hours – Timperley Junction-Broadheath CLC for 24 hours.

On 9th March 1942 a barrage balloon fouled the overhead electric wires of the MSJ&A Railway at Manchester (London Road) stopping all electric traffic. The electric service was run from Altrincham to Old Trafford with buses on to London Road. Normal working resumed after 13 hours.

Main line vehicles receiving attention from lady cleaners.

Hulton Getty Archive 80843368

11

STEAMERS, HOTELS, AIR SERVICES, RAILWAY WORKSHOPS AND ROLLING STOCK

To aid the War effort, various other LMS Railway activities and possessions such as steamers, aircraft, locomotives, cranes and hotels were requisitioned together with much of the workshops capability.

LMS Steamers

The LMS Shipping department was the responsibility of Captain Harris and before the war the LMS owned 66 vessels (3 jointly with the LNER) with a total gross tonnage of 67,360. Of this fleet 27 were large ships over 1000 tons and 49 of the vessels operated in three main areas - the Clyde Coast, the Irish Sea (of the five routes the LMS owned 3) and the North Sea from Goole to the Continent managed by Associated Humber lines. In addition there were others such as the Tilbury – Gravesend ferry (5 vessels), the lake steamers at Windermere and Coniston, and on Loch Lomond, Loch Tay and Loch Awe. Altogether 31 LMS ships were requisitioned for Government service for varying periods, made up of 28 passenger and cargo ships, two dredgers and one tug. All pleasure and lake steamers were suspended except on Loch Lomond (2 steamers jointly owned with LNER). The Goole to Denmark and Germany services were suspended in August 1939 but ships continued to sail from this port to Holland, Belgium and France up to the time of the invasion. The Board meeting on 25th June 1941 reported the cessation of Continental traffic sailings from the Humber, it is perhaps surprising that they had continued as long as they did. In September 1939 Clyde services were considerably restricted due to Admiralty requirements. Sailings from Ardrossan, Greenock (Princes Pier) and Glasgow (Bridge Wharf) were cancelled and Gourock services could not serve south of Dunoon because of a boom across the river. Prior to the war the LMS operated 21 vessels on the Clyde most of them being converted to minesweepers,

*Captain James Whyte Harris RNR was born in Glasgow in 1880 and served his apprenticeship in sailing ships before joining the Red Cross Line as 3rd Officer being transferred to the Booth Line in 1901. In 1904 he passed the BOT examination for extra master (Sail) becoming Chief Officer in the mail and passenger service of Booth Line, being appointed to command various ships from 1909 onwards. From 1913 to 1914 he was Assistant Marine Superintendent, Liverpool before joining the Royal Navy in 1914 serving as Lieut. Commander in the Grand Fleet and at the Dardanelles, following which he was demobilised for special service in New York from 1916 to 1918, where he acted as Marine Superintendent for the Booth and Blue Funnel Lines. In 1918 he returned to Liverpool as Marine Superintendent for Booth Lines. In 1927 he was promoted to Captain and in June 1931 he joined the LMSR as Chief Marine Superintendent, his salary being £1500.gradually increasing to £2750 in 1937 when his title was changed to Chief Marine Manager. By the time he retired on 31st July 1943 his salary was £3000. He was succeeded by **Capt William Laurie Sinclair (1943 to 1947)** who was born in Ayrshire in 1892 but did not come into railway service until 1st January 1935 as LMS Marine Superintendent and Harbour Master, Holyhead, his salary being £1000. He was appointed Assistant Marine Manager on 1st July 1937 before taking over from Captain Harris on 1st August 1943 with a salary of £2000, increased to £2500 on 1st November 1944. He later became Chief LMR and WR Marine Superintendent before retiring in 1952.*

LMS Magazine

three of which were sunk. Pre-war, 4,250,000 passengers were carried annually, that dropped to less than 2,000,000 in 1940. Gourock and Greenock were exceptionally busy ports when the Americans arrived, and many thousands of men and women in the Allied forces passed through those ports. The passenger terminal at Gourock was greatly enlarged to allow many small ships to disembark troops simultaneously. The LMS operated a fleet of 14 hired craft as tenders and had to make many trips when one of the Cunard White Star 'Queens' arrived with a whole American division. Large transport ships could not dock and the LMS was required to keep 3 vessels at Gourock to act as required by the Sea Transport Officer. Gourock Pier was also used for craft conveying dockers and stevedors to vessels discharging cargo in the river. From 1940, these activities came under the 'Clyde Anchorage Emergency Port' organisation.

When it became clear that invasion would not follow Dunkirk, Northern Ireland was brought into use for training troops and the short sea crossing Stranraer to Larne became of vital importance. The LMS had already provided (1938) a ramp to allow vehicles to drive onto the deck of steamers and this was strengthened for tanks. 'Princes Maud' (used at Dunkirk and St Valery, see below) was returned to the route and two SR Train Ferry ships transferred to the LMS operation – 'Shepperton Ferry' and 'Twickenham Ferry'. The difference in gauge with Ireland meant they could not be used as designed but they were fitted with travelling cranes which jutted out over the stern allowing heavy rolling stock to be lifted on/off easily. Other alterations included an entirely new port at Cairnryan on the seaward side of Stranraer, which allowed American transports to cut short their journey by discharging troops at Belfast. (the first arrived on January 26th,1942). In early 1944, once most troops were back in England for D-Day, 'Princess Margaret', the last LMS steamer in civilian service, was sent south from the Stranraer route to take part in the landings and

replaced by Thames pleasure steamer 'Royal Daffodil'. At the LMS shipping Committee meeting on 24th October 1945, the Chief marine Manager, Captain Sinclair, suggested a suitable plaque be installed on all the 31 ships that had been requisitioned that was approved. The last ships to be returned to the LMS following requisition were the 'Duke of Rothesay' on 16th September 1946 and the 'Duke of York' on 15th November in the same year.

Damage to LMS Vessels

The 'SS Mersey' of the LMS Associated Humber Lines, whilst on a passage from Antwerp to Goole, was mined off Ramsgate on 20th April 1940, the first marine loss for the LMSR in the war. Eleven men were lost including the master, three escaped uninjured and four others were taken to hospital in a serious condition one of which, the second officer, died. It was reported at the 30th May 1940 Board meeting, that M.V. 'Princess Victoria' (Stranraer – Larne), a new ship that was only brought into service on 7th July 1939 and specially built for motor traffic, but converted to a minelayer, was herself sunk by a mine off the east coast on18th May 1940 with the loss of 3 officers and 31 ratings, of whom 7 were LMSR staff. A replacement was authorised by the Scottish Local Committee on 13th March 1945 to be constructed by Wm. Denny & Bros. of Dumbarton. Minute 4105 on 27th June 1940 reported the loss of SS 'Scotia' and damage to SS 'Princess Maud' (Larne – Stranraer) by enemy shore batteries at the Dunkirk evacuation, and also the SS 'Duke of York'. The 'Scotia', an ex Irish Mail Steamer, captained by W. H. Hughes evacuated 3000 allied troops from Dunkirk to Dover and then returned to the coast of France. She was bombed on the way across and went into the port of Dunkirk where she embarked 2000 French troops but never got back to England as enemy bombers made a direct hit. Casualties were heavy but many were saved, and in the final list of awards Captain Hughes, who was the last

Left - Armaments being loaded on the train ferry at Stranraer harbour destined for Northern Ireland
British Rail

Opposite page - Both the "Hibernia" and "Cambria" were withdrawn and replaced with vessels of the same name. The picture shows the launching of the new "Hibernia" at the Harland and Wolff Shipyard, Belfast. The vessels are each 5200 tons gross and designed for both passenger and cargo carrying. The new vessels both operated on the Holyhead to Kingstown route.
LMS Magazine "Carry On".

to leave the ship, received the D.S.C., his bosun and two seamen the D.S.M. The *'Duke of York'* (ex Belfast – Heysham) was also involved in the evacuation from France. On leaving St. Valery-en-Caux she was shelled by German cliff top batteries and in the course of this action one shell landed on the deck and did not explode whereupon the Chief officer, Mr B. Williams, promptly picked it up and threw it overboard, an act for which he was decorated. The loss of 1897 vintage PS *'Kylemore'* was referred to in Board minute 4152 on 26th September 1940 was bombed off the Norfolk Coast on 21st August (and now a popular 'wreck-diving' spot). The SS *'Cambria'* was also attacked by enemy aircraft on 18th December 1940 whilst returning from Kingston to Holyhead. 3rd Officer W. S. Jones was killed and a lady passenger injured.

At the Scottish Local Committee meeting on 21st January the loss of the PS *'Mercury'* was reported. The *'Mercury'* was the newest of the Clyde paddle steamers, first in service on 4th March, 1934 and featuring enclosed paddle boxes. As Minesweeper J621, she struck a mine off the Irish Coast (all hands saved) and sank whilst under tow on Christmas Day 1940. (She was transferred to the Caledonian SP Co in December 1937; so was not technically an LMS vessel for compensation purposes). Goole steamer *'Rye'* was sunk off the east coast on 7th March 1941 with no survivors and Clyde paddle steamer *'Juno'* was reported at the same Board meeting on 27th March 1941. *'Juno'* was sunk by bombing on 20th February 1941 for which £80,000 was later received from the Ministry of Shipping with a further amount due when the vessel was replaced. It was reported to the Board that hopper barge *"F"* from Garston Dock was sunk by a mine near South Dingle Jetty on 13th May 1941 with six of the crew rescued and five missing.. The Board meeting on 29th May 1941 reported a settlement had been reached with the Ministry of Shipping in respect of four of the Company's vessels lost whilst on requisition. The amount received was £393,500 for the four vessels, (*'Scotia', 'Princess Victoria', 'Mercury'* and *'Kylemore'*), being the negotiated value as on 31st August 1939. A further amount of £98,375 (with interest) being the increased value of 25% of the value at the time of loss compared with that at the outbreak of the war that was to be paid when the vessels were replaced. The sinking of LMS grab dredger *'Rockford'* was reported to the Board meeting on 30th March 1944 but no details were given. Three LMS vessels were lost "during ordinary trading". This included Goole Steamer *'Ouse'* which sank on 5th August1940 after collision with sister ship *'Rye'* in the confusion following an E-Boat attack whilst in a convoy in the English Channel (all crew were rescued by *'Rye'*)

Twenty Six decorations were won by members on active service in the LMS Marine fleet thus -
 DSO x 1; DSC x 4; DCM x 1; DSM x 3; OBE & MBE x 7; BEM x 5; Meritorious Service Certificate x 1 and Mentioned in Despatches x 5.

The shortage of ships led to problems when a vessel suddenly became unavailable as happened on the 21st July 1945 when the SS *'Hibernia'* sprang a leak on the Irish, Holyhead to Kingston route. With no spare ship available, passengers were advised not to travel and make arrangements for a later date. A considerable number did however arrive at Holyhead and some days elapsed before they could sail due to the advance issue of tickets. The SS *'Cambria'* was withdrawn from the Heysham to Belfast service that was reduced to thrice weekly and sailings were again operated form Holyhead on 23rd July. The *'Hibernia'*, having been repaired, resumed normal service on 1st November 1945. Both vessels were later replaced, see below.

Docks

Railway investment in docks, harbours and wharves since 'grouping' amounted to some £72m and when the Government took control in 1939, it had a sufficient capacity to cope during the initial emergency. In peacetime the Board of Trade looked after all navigation matters and the Ministry of Transport was responsible on-shore. This split was at first continued with a new Ministry of Shipping but the two were combined in the Ministry of War Transport from 1941. Preparations began in July 1936 with the setting up of a Port Emergency Committee at each location, membership including representatives of all port users. Their remit was to "secure the efficient and rapid clearance of traffic through the ports". A good working system was therefore in place when Government officials took over. The LMS larger owned

docks suffered little enemy damage although Barrow and Garston had several major raids with much damage. Renfrew wharf (near Glasgow) was totally demolished in March 1941 and Poplar Dock on the Thames had been bombed out of action from December 1940 until May 1943. In addition to those improvements mentioned under 'Shipping' there were many improvements e.g. a new jetty and oil terminal was built at Heysham. The LMS expansion of Fleetwood in the 1930s was added to as it was handling double its pre-war tonnage of fish.

A challenge was to clear goods from dock quays and transit sheds as soon as possible. In 1941 the Ministry of War Transport decided to establish a number of inland sorting depots e.g. a huge depot (with two signal boxes) was established at Kirkby, about 6 miles from Liverpool. This continued to provide traffic to the LMS post-war and the various Dock improvements was a useful legacy.

Airways

Beginning in 1934 the LMS developed various air services that were operated by Companies in which the LMS had shares. The routes were over the west coast lines between London, Lancashire and Scotland and over sea routes to Northern Ireland, the Isle of Man, the Western Isles of Scotland, the Orkneys and Shetlands. The Government ordered all these to be suspended on the outbreak of the war. The aircraft and staff of the Railway Air Services Ltd. was placed at the disposal of the Air Ministry as recorded in Traffic Committee minute 6264 of May 1940. They helped to maintain communication with the British Expeditionary Force, largely by the transportation of staff officers and medical supplies. Some aircraft were actually in France when war broke out and within days brought back some of the first casualties. It was not long before some of the routes were reinstated for mail etc to the Western and Northern Islands of Scotland. With shipping at risk there was the tale of a crofter who refused to board a plane until he had first made his will. Other tales were of the 15 people who tried to climb aboard insisting that they did not mind if they had to stand all the way. Some journeys were humanitarian with 700 emergency cases involving accidents or maternity that took only a couple of hours against a day or more by ship. A difficult beach landing was made by a Scottish Airways plane to rescue six sailors who were driven ashore following their ship being torpedoed in the Atlantic, They had been in an open boat for several days. On occasions pilots found themselves in the middle of an aerial battle with German planes. During the whole of the war not one plane was lost, with over a million miles flown. In the spring of 1940, the Government decided that to transport service personnel and others engaged in the war effort it was essential to provide arrangements for more rapid communications between a number of important points, especially sea crossings. Under agreement with the Air Ministry the railway associated companies grouped themselves to form Associated Airways Joint Committee, with the routes as below. The Companies

still retained much of their pre-war status.

Company	Route
Railway Air Services, Ltd.	Liverpool-Belfast-Glasgow.
West Coast Air Services, Ltd.	Liverpool-Dublin.
Scottish Airways. Ltd.	Inverness-Orkneys-Shetlands.
Scottish Airways. Ltd.	Glasgow-Cambeltown-Islay.
Scottish Airways. Ltd.	Glasgow-Stornoway.
Scottish Airways. Ltd.	Glasgow-Tiree-Barra-Benbecula-North Uist.
Scottish Airways. Ltd.	Inter-Orkney Islands.
Isle of man Air Services Ltd.	Liverpool-Isle of Man.
Gt. Western and Southern Air Lines Ltd.	Lands End-Scilly Isles.

With the exception of the last Company, the LMS had a substantial interest in the others.

With the evacuation of Dunkirk these services were suspended on 17th May 1940 until June 3rd when operations were resumed. They were again suspended on June 15th with seven planes ordered to France. Four of these aircraft had to be abandoned at Bordeaux but all the crews returned safely. In another case one pilot took off almost under the eyes of the enemy, but with engine trouble over the channel was forced to land in Jersey. He then found a similar aircraft undergoing repairs and with the aid of his radio officer and flight engineer exchanged the engine for his own unserviceable one and then flew safely back to England. It was one of the last planes to leave Jersey before the German occupation. Services were again resumed on June 27th 1940 and continued with various alterations for the rest of the war. The routes still in being at the end of 1944 were:-

Railway Air Services, Ltd. – London to Liverpool; Liverpool to Belfast; Glasgow to Belfast.
Scottish Airways, Ltd – Glasgow to Western Isles of Scotland and the Hebrides; Inverness to Orkneys and Shetland *Isle of man Air Services, Ltd* – Liverpool to Isle of Man; *West Coast Air Services, Ltd* – Liverpool to Dublin; *Gt. Western and Southern Air Lines Ltd.*- Lands End to the Scilly Isles.

In addition special flights were made at government request. In the four years following June 1940 the air services flew 6,000,000 aircraft miles, conveyed 250,000 passengers and carried 6,000,000 pounds of freight, achieving 95% reliability on some routes and 100% on others, with some pilots having flown 1,000,000 miles. It should be noted the part played by Sir Harold Hartley in connection with Railway Air Services.

Hotels

In 1938 the LMS owned and operated 25 hotels, owned but did not operate three more and two thirds jointly owned a further hotel with the LNER that made the LMS Company the largest hotel owner in Europe. All these were the responsibility of Arthur Towle, who was also in charge of station catering and dining cars. Six Hotels were requisitioned by the Government namely, Gleneagles in

LMS Hotels Superintendent, Arthur Edward Towle CBE was born in Derby and went to Marlborough School and entered the hotel and catering industry in continental hotels such as The Majestic in New York City and the Grand Hotel in Rome. In 1898 he was appointed as Joint Assistant with his brother to his father Sir William Towle (who was at that time Manager of the Midland Railway catering business), assisting in bringing into being the Midland Hotel, Manchester that opened in 1903. He was appointed Joint Manager in 1913 during which year the re-built Midland Adelphi Hotel at Liverpool was nearing completion, and, on the retirement of his brother in 1920 was appointed as sole Manager. His experience was wide ranging having written a report on the reorganising of South African Railways catering in 1902. He was Director of the Ministry of Food in 1917 and Controller of the Hotels at the Peace Conference in 1919 and 1920. He also prepared a report on the catering at the Oxford and Cambridge Universities. Prior to the Amalgamations he was the Manager of the Midland Railway Hotels with a salary of £4000pa and remained so in 1923 under the LMS banner. By 1935 he was Controller of all 25 LMS hotels, refreshment rooms and dining car services, his salary being £9000 pa plus £1000 for expenses and taking into account that he lived in the hotels he ranked as virtually the highest paid employee. He retired on 1st January 1945 and was succeeded by Frank Hole. What is interesting is that his salary equalled that of the Chairman of the Company.

LMS Magazine.

Perthshire, Turnberrry in Ayrshire, Dornoch in Sutherlandshire, the Highland at Strathpeffer, the Midland at Morecombe and the Welcombe at Stratford-on-Avon. Rooms in various other hotels were also requisitioned such as Glasgow and Kyle of Lochalsh. A great number of staff went into the forces leaving a big problem with staffing that was partially overcome by transferring staff from hotels that had been requisitioned. The reduction and ultimate withdrawal of restaurant cars made travellers more reliant on the hotels and an even greater extent on railway refreshment rooms. In the 14 hotels where all or part was not requisitioned numbers rose from 330,000 in 1938 to 580,000 in 1943, an increase of 250,000.

As with other LMS property, hotels suffered considerable damage from air raids. Serious damage was caused to the Euston Hotel, the Midland in Manchester and Belfast, the Adelphi and the Exchange in Liverpool and the Queens Hotel in Birmingham. Others also received minor damage but in no case did any hotel cease business entirely even though considerable damage was done. The Midland in Manchester received showers of incendiary bombs, many of which landed in almost inaccessible parts of the roof but they were all extinguished by the hotel staff. The same hotel also lost 2,000 panes of glass in one night. The Adelphi Hotel in Liverpool was hit by a landmine with only a few casualties, but business continued and with the breakfast room damaged, breakfasts were served in the restaurant the following morning. A Board minute on 30th January 1941 approved an estimated expenditure of £40-50,000 for partial restoration. Euston was the victim of a direct hit that demolished a corner

of the west wing that left a long piece of stair carpet dangling from the third story. In Belfast the Hotel was burned out leaving only a few rooms at the rear.

The 'Hotel' Department was also responsible for the Company's refreshment rooms of which there were 227.and during the first two months of the war they were obliged to undertake the provision of meals for groups of servicemen and women travelling on duty. Eventually the demands under this heading became so great that an impossible situation arose to the extent that the Navy, Army and Air Force were appealed to, and in the fullest understanding other arrangements were made. It is easy to visualise refreshment rooms overwhelmed by service personnel with the travelling public unable to gain access. In order to ease the situation the LMS gave space at important stations for the establishment of canteens often run by the YMCA or other voluntary organisations. As with hotels, some refreshment rooms were damaged with those at Manchester Exchange, Barrow-in-Furness and Kensington destroyed with no casualties. In 1941, such was the shortage of food, representations were made to the Ministry of Food that were finally concluded with an increase in the supply of meat pies, cake and allied foodstuffs that could be easily handled and required no preparation. By arrangement with the NAAFI several LMS Buffet cars were put back into service and manned by NAAFI personnel for the convenience of members of the forces making long journeys, that gave both table accommodation as well as quick counter facilities with as many as 500 customers on a long journey. During 1944 it was estimated that 60 million persons were served with

breakfast, lunch, tea dinner, light snacks or cups of coffee and tea.

Railway Workshops

The LMS Railway, by virtue of the 1923 amalgamations, became a huge engineering organisation as befitted the biggest Company in the world. With works at Derby, Horwich, Crewe, Glasgow, London (Bow), Kilmarnock, Inverness, Wolverton and Earlestown it was in a great position to aid the Government's drive for the production of munitions. At the outbreak of the war there were 24,772 staff employed in the Company's workshops that increased to 29,920 during hostilities. Crewe alone employed 7,500 during the war. Derby works had manufactured 350 coaches and 10,000 wagons in a single year leaving no doubt as to its manufacturing capability. No definite approach was made to the Company until 1937 when it was asked to undertake the design of a medium tank. It was no small achievement for a group of specialists in steam locomotives to design a tank from scratch. These were the Mark V "Covenanters" cruiser tanks and were produced in numbers with Crewe producing 161 at the rate of 4 a week. Later in 1938 came orders to construct aeroplane wings for the Hawker Hurricane that were completed in time for the summer of 1940.

When war finally broke out building programmes for new locomotives was suspended, but it took until April 1940 before extensive Government orders were received, by which time a certain number of skilled men had been released to join the services or who had obtained more remunerative work. It took some time to agree with the various Government departments the type and quantity of work that could be undertaken in the workshops. The eventual outcome was more than satisfactory as by the end of 1943 no less than 4705 orders had been accepted for Government work, from simple machinery and castings to the complete assembly of tanks and aircraft. At the former Glasgow & South Western works at Barassie a complete repair service for damaged aircraft was established – including building a runway so that the aircraft could take-off under their own power following repair. All of this caused some Company concern as at the Board meeting on 26th June 1941 (minute 4311), the Chairman, Sir William Wood, stated "It is now becoming increasingly apparent that the LMS have reached, if they have not already surpassed, the limit of the Government work that can possibly be undertaken by them if they are to meet essential railway work requirements e.g. the locomotive building programme, repairing enemy damaged rolling stock etc". Over £18million was expended on this work - that is not a true figure as a large mass of material was provided free by various Government departments. Searchlights, driver's seats for tanks, wood parts for rifles and even conventional grocer's vans and builder lorries were transformed into what was known as 'Armadillos' for the defence of airfields. Between 3000 & 4000 pairs of wings were made for Hurricanes, Typhoons and Horsa gliders apart from many other aircraft parts. Later the workshops took on the repair of Lancasters, Spitfires, Hampden and Whitleys bombers. In addition to the "Covenanters" LMS tank production included the construction of "Matildas" and "A13 Cruisers" with hundreds built, the first in September 1939. Gun carriages, shells, steel railway bridges and trestles were constructed for the services. Naval work was also done with apparatus constructed to catapult aircraft from merchant ships and much secret work. Four million stampings were produced and 27,000 gun and aperture sights for American Lewis guns, built to an accuracy of less than a thousand parts of an inch. Over 8000 assault boats were built. To obtain every ounce of production the standard working week in the workshops was increased to 66 hours and it was not unusual to find men working up to 88 hours for long periods that involved seven days a week without a break. At Crewe, despite the huge workload, some 300 men were loaned to Rolls Royce to increase the production of Merlin engines for fighter aircraft. The role of women in wartime should not be forgotten and there were over a 1,000 at Crewe Works, many doing heavy jobs with steam hammers and drop stamps as well as undertaking highly skilled worked previously the domain of skilled tradesmen. The Company had also possessed steel-making plants that they had closed in 1932 but were re-opened for making ingots for ship-plates with tens of thousands of tons eventually produced. An interesting job was the breaking down of several hundreds of French designed covered goods wagons for packing for shipment and reassembly in Turkey and Egypt that required 740,000 feet of timber and 18 miles of hoop iron. Ambulances, armoured and breakdown trains were also constructed for the fighting services and it is not surprising that a backlog of repair work was beginning to establish itself meaning that a reduction in Government work became necessary. All this was a tremendous achievement, the downside of which would be the abnormal wear and tear on the Company's plant that would eventually require extensive maintenance or replacement at the end of hostilities.

LMS School of Transport, Derby, and the Melbourne Military Railway

It was reported at the Board meeting on 27th June 1940 that the school had been requisitioned by the Government. The school became the Railway Training Centre for the Royal Engineer's in conjunction with the nearby Melbourne Military Railway. The school was returned for LMS use on 1st November 1945, with Brigadier Manton re-

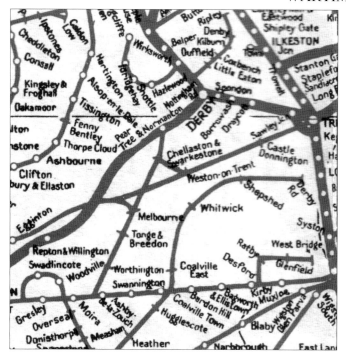

8F 2-8-0 8126 to 8175, 8301 to 8399, 8490 to 8493 – total **153.**
Diesel Shunting engines 0-6-0 7085 to 7123 – total **39.**
Giving a grand total of **345.**

At the beginning of hostilities in September 1939 the LMS had 7,597 locomotives that increased to 7866 in 1945. In addition American S160 class 2-8-0 locomotives began arriving in Britain in December 1942, 50 of which were loaned to the LMS Railway, see below. All 50 were recalled in September 1943 for shipment to Europe, the LMS mileage for these engines being 1,244,485

A total of 398 locos arrived and needed alterations to operate in this country. The LMS was tasked with arranging the alterations nationally and subsequent allocation of the locos for the REC.

As far as Motive Power Depots were concerned, a new depot at Carnforth (11A) was completed at the end of December 1944 that was originally authorised in April 1938 to replace the old LNWR, Midland and Furness sheds. The new shed was on the site of the old Furness shed, having a concrete roof and lit by electricity with six roads under cover, 150 ton coaling plant, 70 foot vacuum operated turntable, wheel and machine shop, new stores and offices including a canteen.

Throughout the war there was always a shortage of motive power for several reasons.:-

1. The Government were continually demanding locomotives for use abroad or for factories of ordnance depots.
2. The Railway workshops were making munitions and therefore the construction of new engines was severely curtailed
3. Likewise with engine repairs as the more intensive use had its effect on wear and tear.

In an attempt to ease the situation, engines that had been in the scrap roads were put back in service and the following measures introduced :-

1. Locomotive Examinations had the prescribed periods and specified mileages between overhauls of engines at Motive Power Depots extended in many cases.

commencing his duties as the Principal of the School. It was initially used to rehabilitate railway workers following their military action. The Melbourne Military Railway was on the LMS (former Midland) branch between Asbby-de-la Zouch, Leicestershire and Chellaston and Swarkestone in Derbyshire. The line was named after the principal station of Melbourne on the branch. The line was handed back to the LMS on 1st January 1945 who then submitted a bill of £25,265 to the War Department to restore the line that was finally closed on 21st May 1980.

Locomotives

From 3rd September 1939 to14th August 1945 the LMS built the following locomotives :-

4F 0-6-0 4587 to 4606 – total **20.**
7P 4-6-2 6238 to 6248 (streamlined) 6249 to 6252 (Non streamlined) - total **15.**
5P5F 4-6-0 5472 to 5499 and 4800 to 4889 – total **118.**

A Toton based USA Transportation Corps S160 2-8-0 2808 seen here on Willesden Shed. Fifty of these locomotives were loaned to the LMS prior to their movement overseas. No 2808 was built by the American Locomotive Company (Alco.) in 1943, works number 70963. It is believed that 2120 of these engines were built making it one of the worlds largest classes designed for use world –wide..
Real Photographs.

2. The time required for repairs in the workshops was speeded up. The stock of spare parts were increased at Motive Power Depots to minimise the time engines were awaiting materials to complete a repair.

3. Facilities at Motive Power Depots were increased by way of additional running lines, crossover roads, ashpits, watering points etc. particularly at depots where congestion was taking place. By the end of 1943, 46 such schemes had been authorised at an estimated cost of £53,823.

4. Engine requirements throughout the line were reviewed and engines reallocated to the best advantage having regard to the altered flows of traffic.

5. Greater utilisation of the smallest engines on train working enabled higher-powered engines to be released for more important duties. Inter use of motive Power Depots was instituted at contact points with other railways.

Examples – by removing the dining car, a smaller powered engine could be utilised or by substituting another carriage for the dining car more passengers could be accommodated. On the Tilbury section the class 3 LTS 4-4-2T engines were restored, thus making the class 4 2-6-4Ts available for freight work, albeit with an increase of three minutes to the journey time. The Euston to Birmingham expresses had the class 4 4-4-0 standard compound utilised with the load reduced, that nevertheless taxed them to the limit and also led to overcrowding, also articulated stock was used to help reduce the train weight Many more examples could be given.

According to the table below, one LMS locomotive was damaged by enemy action and withdrawn from service, but its identity has not been established.

The following table shows the engine miles run for all traction:-

Year	Miles	+ or – compared with 1938	+ or - %
1938	228,333,168		
1944	210,733,640	-17,509,528	-7.71
1945	205,450,860	-22,880,299	-10.02

LMS Locomotives Requisitioned by the War Department

When the various new Ordnance factories and their attendant sidings were authorised there was a failure to also order locomotives to carry out the necessary shunting etc that resulted in LMS 0-6-0 diesel shunting engines being requisitioned by the War Department, with a total of 52 being supplied that were either contractor or LMS built. A total of eight Standard LMS 3F 0-6-0T locomotives were requisitioned and sent to France in 1940. The LMS also contributed 51 8Fs of its own manufacture in addition to 240 ordered directly by the WD from the North British Locomotive Company and Beyer Peacock Ltd. The Ministry of Supply also ordered further 8Fs that were built by the GWR, LNER and Southern Railways that were used by the home railways. Locomotives were also loaned to collieries, traders and other railways.

Locomotive Coal

The policy regarding coal was, that the LMS always kept good reserves of at least four weeks supply that they had at the commencement of WW2. This ensured, that should there be any interruption in supply due to such things as weather or strikes, the difficult period could be negotiated without the need to reduce or discontinue services. There were, however, times during the war when supplies became the source of much anxiety. In the Spring of 1940 stocks fell to less than 2½ weeks supply when strong representations had

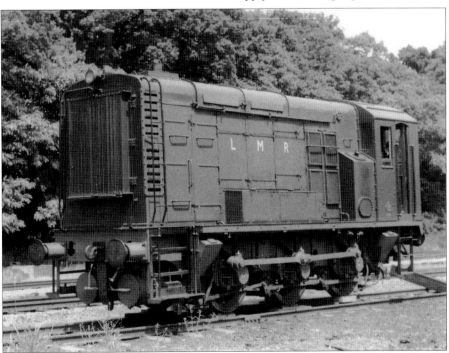

An unidentified LMS 1944/5 Derby built twin motor diesel electric locomotive on the Longmoor Military Railway. Between 1945 and 1969, four of these locomotives were employed at Longmoor, the first being WD 70273, which was there from April to December 1945 before departing and eventually serving with both the Dutch and Danish state railways. In June and July 1945 WD 70271 and 70272 went to Longmoor where they were locally renumbered 43 and 44. In 1952 they officially became WD 877 and 878. In 1956 No. 43/877 was scrapped following a head-on collision with an 8F and was replaced by WD 876 (ex-70270). This was the last of the LMS diesel-electric shunters to serve at Longmoor, being withdrawn and scrapped in 1969.
Courtesy - David Hunt collection.

Stanier 8F WD70387 constructed by the North British Locomotive Company, works number 24695, in 1941 as WD No 387. Initially it went to Iran, where 143 of this class saw service from February 1942, as Iran Railways No, 41.155 and was allocated to Tehran shed. The engine had been converted to use oil fuel and had a ventilated cab as fitted to engines working in a hot climate. In March 1946 the engine was transferred to the Middle East Forces and went to Egypt, seen here with nine others and renumbered as 70387. The engine later became Egyptian State Railways No. 834.
Courtesy - David Hunt collection.

to be made to the Government that did bear fruit, as by the end of November there was 6½ weeks supply. This ideal did not last long as a similar situation arose in 1941 with a fall in the spring and an increase in the autumn. The year 1942 was worse with a very serious decline when stocks fell to just over two weeks supply due to the collieries being unable to honour railway contracts due to – labour shortages at the pits – absenteeism – reduction in output per man. In addition the priority was to supply the Admiralty for bunkering purposes, and the munition factories on the direction of the Ministry of Fuel and Power. Briquettes were introduced at the beginning of 1942 for steam raising and for engine duties of a local character and proved satisfactory for such workings. Later it was found that a mixture of 50% briquettes and 50% best quality coal was satisfactory on express passenger trains The situation eased in 1943 due to the extended use of household coal, opencast coal, briquettes and coke. The quality was also a little better as the tonnage of better grades supplied increased. The year 1943 had opened with a little over two weeks supply and finished with nearly five weeks requirements. The economical use of fuel was paramount and the diet of locomotives varied with household coal, opencast coal, briquettes and coal salvaged from the line, marshalling yards and sidings. Gas coke, totalling 22,000 tons was also utilised on engines employed on local workings, the ratio being one of coke to four of coal. The rate of coal consumption per mile rose slightly due to the heavier loading of trains and increased freight train mileage. The smoke-box char produced by locomotives was also supplied to LMS power stations, notably Derby and approximately 10,000 tons was collected from running sheds during the year and mixed with coal that reduced coal consumption. A further way of easing the coal situation was to use waste wood from the Company's workshops that was mixed with coal for engine steam raising instead of only using coal. A total of 17,000 tons was used during the year

with 12,000 tons purchased from outside contractors and 5,000 tons coming out of the workshops. This resulted in a saving of approximately 8,500 tons of coal. In an endeavour to counteract the inferior quality of coal, contracts were given to South Wales collieries for delivery by ship to the west coast ports in both England and Scotland. This coal proved to be dusty and small and with some coalmen refusing to handle it resulting in its use only at sheds with coaling plants that restricted its use. Time was often lost by engines using this coal due to the fireman's inexperience in its use, accordingly it was only used in the lowest class of work. Locomotive fuel economy also suffered due to the release of men for the armed forces. In order to ease the situation 17-year-old youths were sent out on firing duties having had only a short time in the sheds. To counteract their inexperience additional Firing Inspectors were appointed in an attempt to conserve fuel. The use of shed staff as firemen so quickly following their recruitment, led to engines not being cleaned. To counteract this paid voluntary part time workers were recruited in July 1943 to clean engines at weekends with the Ministry of Labour also providing workers. The experiment proved successful and was extended throughout the system. During a 28week period, mainly at weekends, 47,687 volunteers worked 373,991 hours and cleaned an equivalent of 21,592 locomotives. The average equivalent days per week worked were 1,670 and the number of engines cleaned weekly averaged 771. With a stock of 7,801 engines, these figures equated to each engine being cleaned every ten weeks that later reduced to eight weeks as more volunteers were recruited.

Breakdown Cranes.

Railway cranes were vital for the rapid clearance and re-instatement of bomb damaged track, bridges etc. and accordingly a review was made of railway cranes, the result

The LMS designed 30ton crane of which eleven were built, the first in 1941 and the remaining ten in 1942 and 1943. Cowans and Ransome & Rapier each constructing five.

BR, LMR Courtesy Collection of Peter Tatlow

being as follows with regard to cranes of 15tons capacity and upwards. The LMS possessed 31, GWR - 13, LNER – 29, SR – 12 and the LPTB 2, making a total of 87. This was considered insufficient and the Government sanctioned 12 additional cranes with a lifting capacity of 45 tons each. The LMS was well supplied with cranes including five of 50 tons capacity, the most powerful in the country, accordingly the new cranes went equitably to the other three main companies. Crane re-distribution was made to ensure the country was covered for any emergency that involved inter-Company use if required. As with other phases of development and modernisation, the LMS had developed a new 30ton steam crane that had been designed and was in the course of manufacture when war broke out, being delivered in 1941. The design proved so successful that ten further cranes of the same type were constructed together with the required runner wagons, riding and tool vans that replaced older obsolete lower capacity cranes. Four were delivered in 1942 and the remaining six in 1943 that were allocated to Wakefield, Hurlford, Perth, Carnforth, Llandudno Junction, Wellingborough, Plaistow, Edge Hill, Chester and Polmadie.

Coaching Stock and Ambulance Trains

When war broke out the LMS owned about 17,500 passenger coaches with virtually no new construction during the war apart from corridor brake vans and open carriage trucks. In the first few months 3,300 of these vehicles were not required due to the reduction in passenger train services, but by 1943 passenger travel had increased by over 7% with a decrease of 1,350 carriages due to enemy action and the provision of ambulance trains. The War Office required the railway companies to provide four ambulance trains for overseas and eight for home use. Those for abroad consisted of 16 vehicles and those for home use nine, later increased to eleven, all 136 vehicles being converted from existing stock. Further requisitions were made later with nine sent to France

that were all lost. In September 1942, the War Office wanted 27 more ambulance trains for overseas use to be provided by all four Companies pro rata, the LMS requirement was therefore 14 trains. The LMS had already provided 64 coaches in four trains in 1940 that were destined for France but never sent   The new trains were of the "Austerity" type consisting of 14 vehicles, so that by withdrawing 2 ward cars from each of the trains already supplied the LMS needed to supply stock for the additional 9½ trains. The "Austerity" ward cars comprised of brake vans with brackets to convey stretchers. In addition 17 casualty trains were provided by the LMS out of a total of 36 supplied by all four companies to remove the air raid injured from blitzed areas, being stationed near to the larger cities. In February 1945, an urgent request was received from the Ministry of War Transport for the Railways to provide 150 passenger coaches for use in France for the movement of troops. Of this number the LMS provided 75 making up five trains. This provision was authorised on 15th February and consisted of old non-corridor stock that had been stabled and required a visit to the workshops in the first instance to fit them for running long distances. In spite of the work required, the first LMS train arrived in France on 28th February and the last on 7th March, all 75 coaches being sold to the Government. In June 1945, a further request was made for an additional 10 trains for use on the Continent to consist of thirteen passenger coaches and a corridor brake van of which the LMS provided three trains that were put through the works and shipped on the 9th, 25th, and 25th. July. The 42 vehicles were loaned to the Government and returned on 8th 9th. and 14th November 1945. These figures do not include the 144 lost in France in 1940. At the end of the war in Europe, LMS coaching stock comprising of evacuation trains and home ambulance trains were released, the first being returned on 2nd June. The first LMS vehicles to be returned from overseas arrived back in this country on 28th November

1945. At the end of the war 475 passenger carrying vehicles and brake vans were on loan with 204 having been released by the end of December 1945.

Ambulance trains carried 361,480 sick and wounded during the last year of the war from D-Day to the final unconditional German surrender.

Wagons

At the outbreak of the war virtually all the wagons of the four railways were pooled, along with requisitioned privately owned wagons as below:-

	No. of wagons	No. of wagons	Totals
At outbreak of war	All railways Railway owned 649,373*	Privately owned Requisitioned 583,789	1,233,162
At end of 1945	658,304	585,194	1,243,498

*Figure includes 3,150 20ton GWR wagons on redemption hire to traders that was reduced to nil by the end of 1944. The tonnage handled at LMS goods terminals increased form 21,395,329 tons in 1938 to 26,467,456 tons in 1945 with the largest figure, being as to be expected, in 1944 when the tonnage was a record 29,126,517 tons, an increase of 23.71% over the 1938 figure.

The vast majority of railway wagon stock comprised of the basic one to five plank wagon, often sheeted when carrying merchandise. Special wagons were built for the meat and refrigerated traffic, oil and petrol, pipe vans, shock absorbing wagons and bogie wagons etc. Bogie bolster wagons were vital for the movement of vehicles and tanks etc and to this end the entire stock of such wagons owned by the railways were pooled amounting to 4,250 approx. These were classified into four groups - A, length over headstocks of 33, 34 and 35 feet. B-over 40 feet. C–45,46 and 47½ feet and D –50 and 52 feet. To cater for the immense number of armoured fighting vehicles the war Department, Air Ministry and the USA authorities constructed additional special wagons of both flat and well types that were loaned to and controlled by the railways. By the end of 1943 the number authorised for railway control was – 160 Warflats, 364 Warwells, 50 USA Flats and 23 Parrots (for the conveyance of aeroplane wings and parts). Plate Wagons belonging to all railways totalled 750 on 1st October 1941 and Fish vans 3,200 in July 1942. By the end of 1943 the number of containers owned by all the railways totalled 14,274.

War conditions demanded further designs for large castings, propellers, boilers, guns and tanks etc. Innovation was also required, as when a large consignment of long steel and iron billets exceeded the supply of bolster wagons. To deal with the problem twin bolster wagons were improvised by linking two end door wagons together. Aircraft imported from the USA arrived in boxes such that only a few railway owned

vehicles could accommodate them, requiring a number of special wagons to be built, code named "Parrot" that were for convenience controlled by the LMS. As with locomotives, a backlog of wagon maintenance occurred due to the shortage of labour, and by the late summer of 1943 the number of wagons awaiting attention rose to 5.4% as against the acceptable 3%. It was then suggested by T. W. Royle, the Operating Manager, that, as with locomotive cleaning, volunteer labour should be recruited for weekend work. Initially the idea was tried at Derby that was so successful that an immediate extension was made through out the system where circumstances permitted. Between the 8th August and the 17th October 1943, 373 volunteers repaired about 10,000 wagons. Repairs were achieved with CME staff marking suitable cripples that were shunted out during the week and worked to selected depots before each weekend. During that period 5,500 wagons were conveyed by 110 special trains. Such was the success of this scheme that the other railways were furnished with details of the scheme and the method of working. From 1939 to 1943 inclusive, 18,317 new wagons were built- this coupled with 11,589 wagons that under normal times would have been broken up gave a grand total of 294,804.

Rolling stock destroyed or damaged

The table below lists the number of locomotives, coaches and wagons destroyed during the war for all the Main Line Companies and the London Passenger Transport Board as taken from the Book – "War Damage on Railways" by B. W. L. Brooksbank.

	Locos	Passenger Stock	Wagons Railway Owned	Wagons Requisitioned
GWR	2	18	109	54
LMS	1	169	1096	143
LNER	4	278	1035	370
SR	1	153	169	69
LPTB	-	19	6	-
Totals	8	637	2685	636

In addition, as far as the LMS was concerned - 71 Locomotives, 2,986 passenger vehicles, 7,089 railway-owned wagons and 1796 requisitioned wagons were damaged. These figures vary slightly from the following statistics given in the Book "The LMS at War" by Nash.

	Destroyed	Damaged
Locomotives	1	73
Steam, electric and other coaches	254	2973
Wagons (railway owned)	1230	7093
Motors	37	264
Motor trailers	46	99
Drays	493	557
Horses	34	75 (injured)

12
THE CIVIL DEPARTMENT – MATERIALS AND LABOUR AND THE STORES DEPARTMENT

General

During the concentrated bombing attacks, the Railway had been kept operational by the application of "First Aid" that had been achieved by diverting a large number of the diminishing strength of the Department from their normal tasks. In some cases it therefore proved desirable to obtain assistance from demolition contractors. Military labour had also been used in clearing the lines during the exceptionally bad winter of 1939/40, and as such a well established liaison was set up that proved very useful during the raids and later in providing work checking and agreeing the accounts for services rendered. Demolition Contractors were paid on a "Cost Plus" basis, the urgency and nature of the work making the tender of competitive or lump sum tenders impossible.

The decline of bombing to negligible proportions after June 1941 allowed attention to be given to less urgent but nevertheless serious problems arising from the raids. Many repairs to essential services were only temporary, important goods sheds had either been destroyed, or had received much damage, seriously impairing their usefulness, meaning that there was a vast amount of work required to restore facilities to their former condition. The problem was a national one of restoring damage with an ever-reducing labour force, not to mention material shortages, as works required for the war effort were the obvious priority. Many of the damaged or destroyed structures were old, obsolete in design, and unsuitable for modern daily railway working, one such warehouse had been an eighteenth century prison. The irony was that the German Air Force may well have helped the railway by eventually enabling schemes to keep it at the forefront of transport undertakings. This meant that the early rebuilding of stations, goods sheds, warehouses and depots on a wholesale scale was neither practical nor desirable, with the consequence that only in a few case were structures of this nature reinstated. In general rebuilding was kept to a minimum to enable essential functions to be carried out until post-war requirements could be considered, and labour and materials readily available. Nevertheless in one month alone 34 contracts were let for the making good of air raid damage, over and above the work done by LMS Company's staff. It goes without saying that ordinary maintenance work suffered from the movement of staff to the task of dealing with air raid damage, but the department did succeed in laying 390 miles of track during 1941 in spite of the heavy demands for track laying for the war-time schemes dealt with in Chapter 3.

The table on page 99 shows the weekly total of incidents from August 1940 to July 1941 with the weekly totals for the two areas, London and Liverpool that were subjected to the heaviest bombing. The total number of recorded incidents (i.e. damage caused within a local site by one or more bombs) up to May 1941 was 2,800 of which 607 were within the London area and 487 in the Liverpool area. The cost incurred in making good the damage caused up to May 1941, as far as structures and permanent way was concerned, was estimated to be £4million, the most costly of which are listed below in date order.

September 1940.
London.
7/9/1940   Poplar "A" Warehouse and Goods Shed.
                                             £250,000
9/8/1940   Haydon Square Warehouse.
                                             £ 80,000
Liverpool.
21/9/1940 Alexandra Dock Warehouse.
                                             £190,000
25/9/1940 Brunswick Goods Shed
                                             £ 40,000
26/9/1940 South Docks Warehouse Shed and offices
                                             £ 35,000

October 1940.
London
8/10/1940   Poplar B Warehouse and Dock wall.
                                             £ 80,000
Birmingham
15/10/1940 Curzon Street Warehouse
                                             £ 20,000
26/10/1940 Birmingham Central Goods Station and
                   Grain Warehouse   £ 40,000
November 1940
London.
1/11/1940   Commercial Road Warehouse.
                                             £ 25,000
Bristol
24/11/1940 St. Phillips Goods Shed and Warehouse.
                                             £ 40,000
December 1940
Liverpool
20/12/1940 Sandhills Viaduct
                                             £ 50,000
20/12/1940 Canada Dock Warehouse.
                                             £190,000
20/12/1940 North Mersey Goods dock Warehouse
                                             £ 50,000

WARTIME LMS

20/12/1940 Park Lane Warehouse
£ 33,000

20/12/1940 Bankfields Goods Station.
£ 30,000

Manchester.
22/12/1940 Victoria & Exchange Station.
£220,000

22/12/1940 Oldham Road Goods Shed
£157,000

22/12/1940 Salford – Bailey Street Goods Warehouse
and offices   £ 70,000

22/12/1940 Central (CLC) Goods Warehouse.
£ 50,000

22/12/1940 M.S.J. A. Castlefield Viaduct.
£ 50,000

London
19/12/1940 Whitecross Street Depot
£ 40,000

May 1941.
Liverpool
4/5/1941   Exchange Station.
£250,000

4.5.1941   Waterloo Dock Warehouse.
£ 20,000

4/5/1941   Huskisson CLC Warehouse.
£100,000

London
11/5/1941   St Pancras Station.
£ 10,000

As can be seen the damage and destruction was impressive in monetary terms but if the aim of the Luftwaffe had been to stop the flow of men and materials and to bring the railways to a standstill, then it failed. In September 1940 the daylight raids were supplemented and later superseded by night bombing, and for three months London was the main target during which there were only twelve nights on which the LMS was free from bombing incidents and only one night during September and October, meaning that damage could be said to be continuous. The London campaign began on October 7th 1940 with a massive daylight raid on the dock area with extensive damage caused to permanent way and structures. Poplar "A" Warehouse was completely destroyed by incendiaries and a high explosive bomb with the partial destruction of the station and Plaistow engine shed. This gave a taste of what was to follow with 23 incidents to LMS property occurring on the night of 15th/16th October 1940 alone. From August 24th to November 1940 inclusive the LMS Railway was affected by air raids on 95 of the 99 days, the raids being heavy on 53 of those days. Referring to the tables given in the previous chapters, the number of incidents and the area in which bombs fell is not a particularly good guide to the damage caused to railway communications or railway property in any area for any period. The strain on the staff and organisation of certain of the Engineering Districts was intense but there were relatively few occasions when the enemy succeeded in closing a line for more than a few days

and very few in which limited operation was not resumed within a few hours. Even when unexploded bombs or extensive damage occurred to delay the restoration of traffic, there were usually alternative arrangements that solved the problem

Labour, Materials and New Works

The main problem for the department was the shortage of labour and material together with the external and internal control measures to deal with that shortage. The stock position when war broke out was good and initially the increased demand for war-time works was offset by deferring New Works schemes that had been authorised before the war. However the demands of the war on national production, the heavy loss of imported material during the U-boat campaign, and the repair of air raid damage, had the inevitable effect on the railway's resources as the war progressed. Materials had to be used to the best advantage so it was inevitable that the Government would eventually intervene with control arrangements. March 1940 saw the Ministry of War Transport set up a Committee made up of representatives of Government Departments and the Railway Companies to allocate the available supplies of track for war-time schemes which later dealt with the allocation of track for all the railway Companies for all purposes. For other materials the external control was more complex. and was primarily a matter for the Stores Department and set up by the Ministry of Supply. The intervention of Government Departments was not, however, restricted to the supply of materials for the carrying out of work, as under Defence Regulation 56A, the authority of the Ministry of War Transport was required for schemes, except for maintenance and renewal work, estimated to cost more than £100. This control was later extended to include maintenance and renewal works estimated to cost £10,000 and over. The authorisation of works by the Ministry of Transport was not sufficient in itself to ensure that the labour and material would be available to carry it out, and, as the labour shortage became worse, a procedure was set up whereby the consent of the Ministry of Works, acting in conjunction with the Ministry of Labour was also necessary to enable the Contractor to obtain and retain his labour. The Department pre-war freedom of action in dealing with contract work was still further curtailed by the Essential Works Order that contained the following gem of legislative drafting. –

"Provided that a branch, department, or part of an organisation shall not, except where the organisation is that of a local authority or is a public utility undertaking, be treated for purposes of this Order as a building undertaking or a civil engineering contracting undertaking unless it is wholly or mainly devoted to the carrying on of any of the said activities for persons, other than the persons controlling the organisation of which it forms part, entering into contracts with it or with that organisation".

With this series of enveloping movements, Government Departments were in a position to exercise overriding authority on new Works from start to finish. Needless to say Forms made appearance in bulk, and that references to B.P.2, W.B.A. and other selections from the alphabet fell easily from the tongue in Departmental chat. New works schemes lost their individuality being disguised under such titles as M.T.(R) 0843(L). The passion for initials penetrated the internal organisation of the railway, and esteemed railway officials were addressed as the E.M, the C.O.P (Chief of Police) and even the C.O.L.&E., while Assistant Stores Superintendent narrowly escaped being described as A.S.S. A typical instruction was as follows –

"The plan and estimate will be sent by the Divisional Officer of the technical department to his Chief Officer at Headquarters advising the C.O.S. when he has done so, and Chief Officer, when satisfied, will pass the plan and estimate to the C.O.M. and/or C.C.M The C.O.M and/or C.C.M. will then sign (also where necessary, obtaining the signature of the C.O.L.&E.) and return the plan, if approved, to the C.O.S. who will forward the proposal to the C.O.N.W. for action under the existing procedure".

Permanent Way

It should be noted on the question of control, the Government had not so far intervened directly in the normal maintenance and renewal work of the Civil Department carried out by railway staff. Indirectly Government Departments were able to exercise considerable influence on maintenance and renewal work via the various controls that were set up to regulate the supply and use of materials, reference already having been made to the allocation of track. The amount allocated to the LMS was not sufficient to maintain the pre-war extent of relaying and several modifications were required to make the best use of the quantity and type of material supplied. In 1940 rails were put back on 95 miles of new sleepers due to new rails being unavailable, with the re-railing carried out the following year. Home grown timber was used extensively for sleepers as Baltic Pine was no longer available and imports of Douglas Fir from Canada were seriously reduced. The reconditioning and re-use of switches, crossings and fasteners was resorted to. Nothing was sent to the scrap bin that had remotely any life left in it. Taking relaying in new materials for comparative purposes, the figures are as follows –

1938.........619 miles
1939.........578 miles
1940.........370 miles
1941.........370 miles
1942.........346 miles

The home produced supply of rails were supplemented by imports from America that were rolled to the British Standard 95 lb per yard for bullhead rail, but in 39 foot lengths as opposed to the usual 60 foot standard used by the LMS. When used in tunnels and on long bridges these rails were welded together to form lengths of 78 or 117 feet. Up to October 1943, 285 miles of track were laid using American rails. With timber in short supply, attention turned to the use of concrete as an alternative, the advantage being that they could be manufactured in the UK. In 1943 the use of concrete sleepers had still to be established and as such they were restricted to sidings, where they were extensively used in the various Government siding schemes as dealt with in Chapter 3.

Building Materials

The position regarding structure maintenance was much more involved. "Controls" had been set up early in the war for material for which there was certain to be a large demand and a diminishing supply. The best example was timber, which was stringently controlled. Other shortages developed and appropriate controls established or strengthened with cement being one example due the enormous demand for roadblocks and pillboxes etc at a time when invasion looked extremely likely. When Malaya fell a strict control of rubber was introduced and the demand for wall boarding as a substitute for timber resulted in the imposition of controls on that material. As far as the railway was concerned the method adopted was to allocate a supply of the controlled material and to provide for exceptional approved demands as they arose. The Department had taken steps to ensure, as far as possible, that supplies of material for maintenance and renewal of railway structures should be used for that purpose, and that any used for special works for Government Departments would be approved and made good by "control". More important still was the effective control of the available material by the department following supply to ensure that it was used to the best advantage. The peacetime organisation was tightened up to such an extent, that in the case of timber, each issue of new and second hand material from the District stocks required the personal authorisation of the District Engineer, and subsequently reported to Headquarters for review and record. Using these records, Headquarters had a detailed knowledge of the class, size and quantity of timber on each District at any time and could meet deficiencies or special requirements in one District by calling on another to supply, or failing that, by taking special steps with Timber Control through the Stores Department. Timber and off-cuts that would have normally been relegated to the scrap heap or firewood was retained for use with the nails removed, a procedure considered uneconomical in pre-war days. Reinforced concrete was a material then came to the forefront during the war due to there being a plentiful supply of the materials for concrete, apart from the short period referred to earlier. In consequence, the Newton Heath concrete works was very busy manufacturing beams, slabs, posts etc. that would earlier have been made of timber or steel. Several MPDs were re-roofed with reinforced concrete, even to the glazing bars. Paint was another item for which controls applied, the railway being restricted to one

Top - *A wartime canteen constructed at St. Phillips – Bristol.*
Bottom - *The interior of a wartime canteen built at Willesden.*

Both British Rail

Civil Staff

The shortage of labour for maintenance and renewal work was less of a problem to the railway and less subject to unexpected developments than the shortage of materials, as railways were classified as "essential" undertakings. This meant that the call on staff for the armed services was restricted and resignations were subject to the approval of the Ministry of Labour. When war was declared the Civil Department employed 32,700 staff. In 1943 there were 2,458 in the forces, of which 75 had lost their lives, 50 were prisoners of war and 21 were missing. The current staffing was 27,380 of which 1,120 were women. The position would have been much worse but for the retention of staff beyond their retiring age, and the re-engagement of retired staff who volunteered to return to fill gaps caused by enlistment and natural causes.

Staff Amenities

The Civil Department was not exclusively concerned with the never-ending task of avoiding deterioration to permanent way and structures. Many of the New Works listed earlier were still under construction in 1942/3 with some additions. These were classified under the general heading of "Staff Amenities" and did provide much work for the Civil Department. One such activity was the provision of Canteens and Mess Rooms for employees that was covered by emergency legislation, and actively encouraged by Government Departments. Four mobile container type canteens located in London, Birmingham, Liverpool and Glasgow were provided to supply food to emergency repair gangs of the Chief Engineer's and Signal and Telegraph Departments. The object of the canteen programme was to provide hot meals for railwaymen throughout the system at points convenient to their work. This was achieved by establishing canteens with self-contained kitchens, or, where a number of feeding points were required in a town, by the provision of a cooking centre from which food could be sent out in containers to the subsidiary service canteens. For those preferring to bring their own meals, cooking, hot water, and sink facilities were provided. Although there were site difficulties in congested areas, planning and methods of construction were devised in order to obtain the maximum speed of erection, economy of materials, simple buildings with pleasant well-lit interiors. Up to October 1943 about 170 canteens were programmed, each providing from 100 to 300 meals daily.

As far as the Operational staff were concerned, 118 staff canteens were in use up to December 1945. Of these 17 were

third of the amount normally used. In consequence, all decorative painting was out and only important structures such as girder bridges remained a priority, stations were only "patch" painted and for interiors only distemper or water paint was used. Air raid damage led to the exposing of interiors to the elements, aggravated by the removal of glass in station roofs carried out as an ARP measure. The time taken to repair a roof was greatly affected by the material shortage. In one case the design of a large roof to a stable was altered three times due to the fluctuations in the materials permissible and available, the result was the horses had to be housed a considerable distance away for several months. An important and serious problem was, that the damage caused by the air attacks of 1940/1, had not in many cases been permanently repaired, with no prospects of being made good as long as the war lasted.

Sandham John Symes OBE, MIME, MILoco.E, was born in County Wicklow, Eire on 25th February 1877 and in 1894 entered his apprenticeship as a Fitter and Draughtsman at Inchicore Works on the Great Southern and Western Railway, Dublin. He later transferred to the North British Locomotive Company, Glasgow as a draughtsman in 1903. In 1904 he entered the service of the Midland railway and in 1913 he was promoted to Chief Draughtsman and to Works Superintendent of the Midland Division of the LMS in 1923, his salary being £1,200. On 1st May 1928 he became Personal Assistant the CME at Derby on £1,750. In January 1931 he was transferred to Euston in the same capacity before becoming Chief Stores Superintendent on 1st July 1933 when his salary was £3,000pa later increased to £4,000. For a brief period he was CME when Stanier was in India and during the War, from 1943 he was loaned to Ministry of Production and the Board of Trade at which time R. A. Riddles succeeded him, he retired on 30th April 1947.

LMS Magazine

coach body snack-bars with 37 more under construction. A further 41 were planned of which only nine were eventually approved. The total cost being £422,500.

The withdrawal of meals and refreshments from trains, and the congestion at stations led to the demand for quick service of food to passengers, that was met by the provision of "Railbars" of which there were two types. The large type constructed at terminal stations such as Euston and St. Pancras, and the smaller type serving counters at selected intermediate stations placed at intervals along the platforms. The latter were pre-fabricated and delivered on site, with erection completed in six hours.

In more remote areas or other circumstances where loss of time occurred due to travelling to and from lodgings, or the maximum number of men on site was essential. To ensure this mobile sleeping and mess accommodation was provided, composing of a third class sleeping car, a kitchen car and a third class vestibule coach located at strategic points ready for use as required. Dormitory units comprising of a third class sleeping car and a third class dining car were also stabled at suitable points within easy reach of the inner cities subject to air attack

The Stores Department

The Stores came under the umbrella to the Chief Commercial Manager as did the Hotels and Research Departments. The Stores Department was the responsibility of Sandam John Symes that did most of the Company's buying that included 250,000 items from coal to LMS buttons and selling things that are of no further use to the Company such as old sleepers, rail, timber, wagon sheeting and scrap metal etc. In one year the following were sold for scrap – 80,000 tons of steel rails, 18,000 tons of firewood, 94,000 tons of iron and

scrap steel and 230,000 sleepers. With the war imminent huge sums of money was spent on bridge and permanent way materials as referred to in Chapter 2, these together with signal and telegraph and locomotive spares. Quantities ran into half millions and even millions for ARP materials. The de-centralisation of the stores meant that only £14,900 worth of stores was lost due to enemy action. In 1942 quantities of new materials had to be purchased by the Stores Department to appropriate Government specifications that amounted to £2,000,000, exclusive of aircraft stores, which amounted to 28,000 items. Stationery was a major item, the annual peacetime requirements being - 1,305,648 pencils; 33,000,000 envelopes; 560,880 pen nibs; 40,000,000 wagon labels and 6,048,950 sheets of carbon paper. In 1938 3,200 tons of paper were used for advertising, operating publications, stationery and sundries. Paper was an enormous problem as up to the middle of 1943 no less than 60 control orders were issued requiring an extremely close scrutiny in the use of paper. The LMS managed to reduce usage by over 1000 tons as compared with the pre-war amount, which was roughly one third. Every single item of paperwork was reviewed amounting to 18,194 items of which 4,524 were permanently cancelled and 3,390 temporarily suspended, with most of the rest reduced in size. The LMS set up the first stationery reclamation depot in the country, where all used paper and envelopes were dealt with at a rate of 100,000,000 items per annum. From this two manufacturers produced envelopes and wrappers from certain of the Company's old account forms, and amongst other thing, these were used to send shareholders a copy of the accounts. One recipient found an outstanding bill for 2s.4d on the other side of the wrapper and promptly sent the amount to the secretary, who returned it with an explanation. The Stores Department also controlled mills for horse provender, shops for rope making and maintaining ropes and wagon sheets and a watch and clock repair shop, also a factory where one third of the LMS uniforms were made.

Research Department

In 1930, Lord Stamp saw the need for a research department, when an advisory committee was formed of scientists for guidance and planning. Many successful investigations took place, including train heating, fuel economy, water softening, paint, wear and tear on rails and tyres etc.

With the advent of war attention turned to such matters as chemical warfare, paint, motor headlamp masks, the penetration of rifle bullets and such interesting things as an emulsifying agent for rendering petrol useless at wayside stations. Substitutes for rubber and new fibres for manufacturing wagon sheets and pigments for paint manufacture were all on the agenda. The chief chemist and his staff gave advice on the transportation of unusual, and sometimes dangerous, traffic, the fight against insect pests and advice on drinking water supplies. Also work on tanks, gun axles, gun barrels, aircraft searchlights and special paints. The Company was also involved in the development of F.I.D.O – a method of dispersing fog on aerodrome's runways.

Light and shade at St Pancras. 22 March 1943.

Hulton Getty Archive 3350302

13

ARMED SERVICE REQUIREMENTS, FREIGHT TRAFFIC AND 'D' DAY

As stated the public were discouraged from travelling, as the requirements of the military were always an unknown factor. There was no ebb and flow and the railways could be called upon to move personnel or equipment urgently and at any time. These varied from a small contingent in an ordinary passenger train to huge concentrations requiring 300 specials and from a single wagonload to 50 trains loaded with tanks or similar. Such trains varied from east to west movements or from camps in the South of England to training areas in the far north utilising single track lines where stations were ill equipped to handle such traffic. After the collapse of France, British, Colonial and other Allied forces and later American personnel were assembled all over the country to continue their training and preparation for 'D' Day. During 1939 naval mobilisation went on gradually, invariably using only the ordinary passenger service, but mobilisation of the Army and Air force was a different proposition. Commencing on Saturday 2nd September, at a time when the evacuation of children was at its peak – and spread over 14 days, that involved the running of 164 LMS special trains, over and above these movements, two expeditionary forces were proceeding to the continent and both within the province of the LMS Railway. The first ran to Glasgow for embarkation and the second to the same port, ran between September 7th and October 7th. When the expeditionary force was sent to Norway, 202 trains were required running mainly from Glasgow to Leith and included three trainloads of French troops from one end of the country to the other.

The year 1943 saw large contingents of troops arriving from overseas that not only included long serving men from India etc but vast numbers from Canada and the USA destined to take up their positions in the common task. Arrivals by escorted liners usually required about 35 trains to disperse and had to be carried out in daylight hours in one day. The first large convoy arrived in July 1943 when 86 trains were required to clear the personnel in three days. The largest convoy arrived in October 1943 when 203 trains were required of which 86 were worked from the Clyde, 82 from the Mersey and 35 from the Bristol Channel. November 1943 was a particularly busy month for movements by special trains on behalf of the services. From 31st October to 6th November 580 passenger trains and 319 freight trains were run requiring 1,133 locomotives, 1,385 sets of enginemen and 1,362 guards and these figures do not include those required for empty stock working. A great many more instances could be quoted but prisoners of war had also to be dealt with as when the North African campaign came to a

satisfactory conclusion in May 1943 when 36 special; trains arrived at the ports in five batches. In July a larger contingent arrived requiring 42 trains in three days from the Clyde and Mersey. These trains ran to camps in Scotland, Northumberland and Lancashire. Five special trains were required to return the escorts back to the ports. With regard to traffic other than from London, following the resumption of services leave, the railway was allowed to run relief trains to convey members of the services who would otherwise be left behind, and also members of the general public but these trains would not be advertised or put in any timetable. The railways were also allowed to run additional trains from London to convey troops on leave for distances over 25miles provided they were relief trains and not Service specials. From Sunday 2nd July to Sunday 1st October 1944, 776 such trains were run from St. Pancras and Euston. The number of Naval, Military and Air Force special personnel and freight trains run by the LMS between the out-break of the war to the end of 1945 to meet the requirements of the fighting services were 105,213 for personnel, 99,542 for freight giving a total of 204,755 trains. The year 1944 saw the highest total of 57,605 with 1945 having 45,991 such trains. In addition to special trains run, large numbers of parties of services personnel were catered for on ordinary trains :-

Year	Number of parties
1939	1,972
1940	14,675
1941	21,839
1942	38,075
1943	51,392
1944	70,517
1945	64,598

The longest run with an LMS Troop train was made on 24th March 1945 when four officers, 144 men and 15tons of baggage of an army unit was moved from Thurso to Stanford-le-Hope, a distance of 773 miles requiring eight different engines and six sets of enginemen and guards, the time taken being 26½ hours.

Freight Traffic.

With Great Britain building up forces to eventually move back into Europe, not only were trains required to move the troops but freight trains were equally required to keep them fed with munitions, armour and not the least food. Everything from shells, guns, beer, building materials, saucepans and toilet rolls, not to mention his porridge. Initially only a few trains were required each week when the

special vehicles and so high sided wagons were converted by the removal of the four centre wooden planks enabling one arm of the propeller to be dropped into the aperture with the other two arms supported by the means of wooden cradles, a practice later adopted by the other companies.

Congestion often occurred at docks, when, due to the lack of shipping space, materials could not be taken aboard, at which time they would be returned to the Ordnance depot without being removed from the wagon. When Germany declared war on Russia in June 1941, Britain immediately announced full material support would be given to our new allies with the result that two months later, between August and November many specials were despatched by the LMS. An LMS Operating Department report referred to a consignment of 34 wagons from Woolwich to Glasgow that consisted of a heavy naval gun with its component parts that would be leaving a depot on the outskirts of London for exchange to the LMS at the nearest junction. From there it was to be worked to Clydeside to arrive within 38 hours. The train included nine wagons of a special type that could not be run at high speed. The train was exchanged four hours later than expected, meaning that the LMS now had 29 hours to make the 400 mile trip that was achieved in 24 hours, leaving five hours to spare. In most cases movement of material from factories could be planned although much cross haulage took place that could have been eased if the factories or depots nearest to the ports had been used. Whilst this could not always be done, representations were made to the War Office in 1942 in an attempt to find a solution. The volume of freight traffic grew and as an example, in 1943, 400 special trains were run in one week. Apart from items one might expect such as the conveyance of bombs, grenades, shells and explosives there was barbed wire and, up to June 1942 the LMS ran 760 special trains that conveyed 5,000,000 coils of barbed wire from just a single factory in the North West area. As far as petrol was concerned, in August and September 1943, at the time our bombing reached its height, and before pipelines were laid, 200 special trains were run weekly conveying well over 20,000,000 gallons of fuel. This was largely from ports in the west to airfields in the east, from the Mersey and Severn to bomber bases in Lincoln and East Anglia. A further problem in 1943 was absenteeism due to sickness in November that at first only affected the London, Rugby, Nuneaton and Manchester areas before affecting practically every area of the country. With the arrival of the Americans, the vast requirements of the American forces and the welcome lease lend products began to flow into Britain. This material began to arrive in quantity in August 1942 and its growth was rapid and from September to December 1942, 22,956 wagonloads were forwarded from LMS ports, but in the same four months in 1943 the total rose to 36,914 loads. Care was eventually taken to endeavour to ensure that ships that arrived in convoy from the USA were loaded as far as possible and destined to the port nearest to where they were required. To achieve this railway personnel were sent to America to advise as to how this may be

forces were in France, but as Allied forces were built up in the Middle East the task became much greater. For the most part the various services kept their supplies in depots of which there were hundreds in all parts of the country as a result stocks were continually increasing and with the transfer of stocks from factory to depot and depot to the docks meant there was plenty of work for the railway. The movement of tanks could be particularly difficult as designs were frequently modified that did not always take into account what dimensions should be adhered to. This resulted in "out of Gauge" loads, that not only restricted the speed of a train but also the route that could be taken. Such a problem arose when sand shields were fitted to tanks sent to the Libyan desert that fouled the loading gauge thus requiring a much slower and circuitous route to be made. Later in 1943, with the countries' factories now in full war production, the situation got much worse with over 10,000 "out of gauge" loads that included transformers, guns and ship parts.

A particularly notable movement was the joint LNER/LMS consignment of a stator weighing 130 tons from Newcastle to Coleshill via Eggington, that could only be run on Sundays, eventually taking five weeks Arrangements were made to move the load transversely 12" from the centre to either side to clear lineside structures. The movement of war material often called for the modification of wagons. One item of equipment that caused such a problem was aircraft propellers having exceptional dimensions. As the movement of these increased it became impossible to provide the number of

War time traffic, left: tanks, right: propellers for the Air Force.

achieved in order to avoid unnecessary cross hauling after unloading had taken place at our ports. One problem as far as convoys were concerned was the need for radio silence meaning that it was not known until a few hours before the first train was due to leave the port whether the movement could take place according to plan. Gales or fog could cause delays and trains of empty carriages had to be concentrated in port areas and train crews had to be found.

The following figures will give the reader an idea of the enormous achievement carried out on behalf of the services by the LMS Operating Department up to the 8th May 1945 (VE Day). *Passenger Trains Run* – special trains 89,926. Officers conveyed 949,084, other ranks 25,552,183, baggage, tons 531,099 and horses 47,225. *Freight Trains Run* – *Equipment and Stores*, special trains 49,141, wagons conveyed 1,758,947. *Ammunition,* special trains 11,253, number of wagons 396,411. *Petrol,* special trains 27,043, tank wagons conveyed 747,558, gallons (approx) 2,704,300,000. *Forces mail,* special trains 2,621, wagons conveyed 42,612. Of particular note is the fact that most of the War Department Depots were situated on the western side of the country meaning that the LMS was called upon to bear a large percentage of the rail transport involved. During the exceptionally bad winter of 1939/40, which included dense fog in December, the deep freeze in January/February and heavy snowstorms at the end of January, coastal shipping was disrupted and further hampered by enemy attacks. In February 1940, in the midst of exceptionally bad weather, the Mines Department submitted plans to switch an additional 10million tons a year to rail in 'convoy' trains of 50 wagons of 12ton capacity. These were initially centred on the North East with 140 trains to London per week. With the LNER mainly using hoppers, open wagons had to be brought in, mainly from the Southern Railway, a move that caused further problems as the wagons supplied were not used to running such long distances. The scheme was then extended to include the Midlands, Lancashire, Scotland etc. In 1941, 10,034 Convoy trains ran, equating to more than 200 trains most weeks. Three of these trains were equal to five normal

'goods trains' and required very careful planning as they could not be accommodated in many of the loops en-route.

The transportation of coal brought problems as pre-war, a large proportion of coal went by sea from one coast port to another, but this was suspended as the route around the east and south coasts of England became a very dangerous proposition due to attacks by enemy E-boats and aircraft. This in itself led to further problems at the London end where much of the coal had to pass via the railway Companies' wharves due to the end customers being only able to accept delivery by river. In January 1940 the London Coal Tipping Control was established with representatives from the Port of London Authority, Lighterage Executive, Mines Department and the railways that two months later became the London Port Emergency Committee. This was formed to ensure coal supplies were maintained to public utilities and other firms by prompt turn-round of barges that were pooled rather than working for individual customers. The railways were eventually carrying 4,000,000 tons weekly, the LMS share being 1,450,000 tons. Such became the need for coal that miners who had enlisted were returned back to the collieries to ensure that war factories did not run short. The cutting of Scottish timber rose to such an extent that 1,513,785 tons had been carried in 1943 with the LMS conveying the major share. An interesting statistic revealed that 43% of all loaded wagons forwarded by the railways originated on the LMS. Certain types of wagons had been pooled in the years up to the war to reduce the running of empty trains. This arrangement was extended to cover special vehicles for carrying meat and other perishable traffic as was wagon sheets and ropes. Additionally 600,000 privately owned wagons belonging to 4000 owners were requisitioned by the Government on September 12th 1939.with the Central Wagon Control keeping contact via stationmasters and railway officials. Such was the increase in the bombing of German cities and towns from airfields in England, the Air Ministry, in 1943, initiated an extensive programme of re-surfacing and extending the runways. With most of the aerodromes situated in the Great Eastern Section of the LNER immense quantities of material such as tarmacadam, stone, chippings and cement were moved from firms served by the LMS. A programme of 36 trains of tarmacadam and 55 cement trains per week were scheduled and timed paths given. In the 52 weeks of 1943 the total tonnage handled at Goods Sheds was 28,934,804 tons, being the highest since 1924 and 35.2% higher than in 1938. The Transport of Flowers Directive issued by the MWT in March 1943 remained in force in 1944 and the extent to which plants were conveyed by rail was limited according to the demands made on the available rail facilities by perishable foodstuffs and other essential traffics. Economies in the use of rail transport were sought wherever possible as with the case of the distribution of white fish. The country was divided into zones with supplies of fish to these zones being based on specific landing ports requiring the shortest haul. The scheme was introduced on 17th October 1942 and during the first four weeks a saving of 6003 train miles was achieved across all four main line companies, the LMS saving being 2,551 miles. A year later a similar review revealed that 10,610 miles had been saved, the LMS amount being 5,122 miles. In 1944 circumstances required the fishing fleet to move from the west coast to the east coast ports, the result of which was to increase the weekly rail mileage for fish distribution by 1,529 miles, the LMS figure being 957 miles.

The Build-up to D-Day.

Initially there were many internal movements as large forces were sent to Northern Ireland to strengthen the garrison there. LMS steamers and trains took a big part in this, with all civilian passenger sailings cancelled. Whole army divisions were also often moved from one area to another. The construction of new RAF air bases called for transport and the Navy also made calls for transportation. The largest repositioning of troops took place in February and March 1941 when again the LMS had a big share of the rail traffic. In May 1942 there was a large movement of troops, Bren-gun carriers, bridging materials, guns, tractors and baggage from remote parts of Scotland to the Isle of Wight, and three weeks later they were all returned to their original starting points. Minute planning was required such as allowing Indian troops to break a long journey one hour every four hours to enable them to prepare food and perform religious rituals. Special trains conveying 10 to 18 tanks plus personnel would travel from the south of England to training grounds in the north of Scotland. The majority of troop movements were, however, made up of small groups of 20 or more, and in 1943 the LMS provided accommodation for as many as 51,392 such parties. The Middle East situation required a constant build up of forces with the pace quickening in May 1942 culminating in the most extensive draft ever dealt with up to that time in November of that year when 339 trains were run in 13 days. The effect of this eventually brought victory when the Germans and Italians were overthrown in Tunisia the following year. Large-scale military manoeuvres also brought problems to the LMS as attacking and defending forces had to be taken to their initial battle stations with the return of the combatants often a complex affair. On one occasion 221 trains were required in one week. Leave required more trains with 71 special trains required on one day alone.

Prisoners of war also required special trains, the first being in September 1939 when the crew of a captured 'U' boat ran from Thurso. In June 1940 nine such specials were run following the Governments decision to transfer prisoners to the Dominions. In July 1941 the decision was made to transfer Italian prisoners from the Middle East for agricultural work. When the North African campaign ended, many specials were required to transport POW to camps in Scotland, Northumberland, Leicestershire and Gloucestershire. On the more pleasing side, in October 1943, the railways for the first time, brought repatriated British prisoners home from Germany via Sweden when they landed at Leith and at Liverpool with the LNER involved in the major work although several ambulance trains were worked by the LMS.

Then there was the arrival of troops from the empire, the first being a contingent of Canadians who landed in the West of Scotland in December 1939. From 1940 to 1943 a great many large and small contingents arrived that included a large number of airmen trained under the vast Empire Training Scheme in Canada and the USA. The Clyde was the port initially used the most but later Liverpool was made use of, both ports largely served by the LMS. The LMS handled 3,000,000 service personnel in and out of Glasgow from 1939 to 1943. On 6th January 1943, President Roosevelt of the USA announced that American forces would come into the war. On the same day US forces arrived in the British Isles with a substantial number disembarking in Northern Ireland. When the main body of US forces arrived they were dealt with largely by the LMS with hundreds of trains running to all parts of the land. The first huge convoy arrived in July 1943 requiring 86 trains in order to clear it, this was followed by an even bigger requirement in September when 148 trains ran, but the largest lot came in October when no less than 203 specials were run on six consecutive days, these being the peak movements. *The author was twelve at this time and armed with his Ian Allan two shilling LMS reference book, spent all the 1943 summer school holiday train spotting between Northfield Station and Longbridge Junction on the Birmingham to Bristol main line. There were many American troop specials, which, to our delight, frequently threw candy bars, chocolate and even cigarettes out of the carriage windows.* In November 1943 two convoys arrived in port in quick succession and the total number of trains running from the west coast for that month was 496. The service authorities did insist on daylight disembarkation that resulted in the loss of many thousands of train hours and for every special train there would doubtless be an empty stock working. The 1943 Christmas mail for the American forces amounted to 168,613 bags.

D-Day

When Dunkirk was evacuated, D-Day seemed a very long way away, but as we have seen the British forces, together with those from our Dominions and later the Americans gradually assembled and trained for the final offensive requiring the invasion of France that took place on 6th June 1944. Shortly before D-Day, Field Marshall Montgomery honoured 400 railwaymen by addressing them in the shareholders' meeting room at Euston. He paid a very handsome tribute to their work, expressing his confidence in their support for the task that lay ahead. In 1940 just less than 15,000 special Government trains had run on the LMS that rose to 39,000 in 1943, reaching an amazing total of 58,000 in the D-Day year of 1944, in addition to which civilian traffic was also maintained. The earlier experience gained from the Expeditionary Force to North Africa proved invaluable making it clear that huge quantities of stores, equipment and supplies would be needed, and, following a landing rehearsal on the south coast of Wales in the summer of 1943, invaluable experience was gained in the manner in which ships would have to be loaded.

Under the strictest secrecy, senior officials of the four mainline companies began to formulate plans, with nothing left to chance. The official date for the beginning of the large-scale operation was March 26th, and it was on that day that the Operating Manager was advised that the railway's greatest test had arrived and the waiting days were over. From then on, the whole of the south of England became a huge concentration area with the build-up of Allied Forces from as far away as the Highlands of Scotland. Not everything came by rail as personnel also came by road in their own transport, but virtually all tracked vehicles and tanks were conveyed by rail. As far as the LMS was concerned the largest group of trains were worked from Scotland with journeys of over 500 miles with tank transport causing a considerable strain on line capacity. In the 11 weeks from March 26th to June 24[th,] 1944 the LMS ran 13,729 trains, with the highest weekly total being 1,585, a figure that did not include the thousands of wagons sent by ordinary freight trains. Once the beachhead had been established the traffic flow increased to maintain supplies for the invading forces. From D-Day until 31st December 1944 the War Office stated that 14,763 special invasion trains had been run on British railways. Within the same time scale the LMS calculated that it had run 7,281 trains, meaning that the LMS had worked some 50% of those trains for at least part of the journey. As the war progressed, the use of ports

further up the French and Belgium coasts required the shipping pattern to change requiring amendment to rail routing. As the war moved into Holland an urgent request came from the Government for rubber boots. Part of the order required 17 wagons to be loaded up in Stirling and run at express speed, stopping only in Leeds to attach 15 further wagons to be later loaded on a steamer bound for Antwerp. The following gives an idea of some of the requirements of the Allies to keep the armed forces supplied – ambulance trains, motor cars and lorries, breakdown cranes, tanks and fighting vehicles, steam and diesel locomotives, mobile workshops, fuel, oil and petrol, foodstuffs, bridging material and pontoons, guns and ammunition, railway wagons, often full of coal etc. Whilst the above called for a tremendous effort by the Operating Department the contribution by the LMS Shipping Department must never be overlooked. LMS steamers were involved when the *Duke of Argyle* anchored off Courselles at 06.05 on D-Day to successfully discharge assault troops, the Second Battalion Canadian Scottish Rifles, the following day she was back embarking US troops en route to Utah Beach in the American sector. The *Duke of Lancaster* was refitted as a hospital ship and arrived off the French coast on D-Day-plus-2, utilising her ambulance boats to run a steady service to and from the ship before returning home. Sometime later in the autumn the *Lancaster* operated from the re-captured ports of Ostend, Dieppe and Cherbourg. The *Duke of Rothesay,* also on D-Day-plus-2, was instructed to contact a guard-ship stationed off the Normandy coast to be directed to "Mulberry" harbour where several of the crew were wounded by shell splinters following heavy aerial activity. She also collected casualties from merchant and navy vessels anchored offshore. Eventually a more direct contact was made with the land forces at the Juno beachhead and the synthetic port of Arromanches, where she took the wounded from the shore either in her own craft or from army "ducks". The *Lancaster* also saw service at the ports of Ostend, Dieppe and Cherbourg, and up to 10th, March 1945 carried 23,950 Allied casualties, steaming 12,697 miles making 62 trips to France or Belgium. The *Princess Maud* sailed from Weymouth with an American task force before D-Day, later being the first cross-channel troopship to enter Ostend. The *Princess Margaret* carried commandos and the *S. S. Dearne* stores and other cargoes. It is doubtful if the world will ever see such a massive transportation feat that was so brilliantly carried out by the railways of Britain, with the LMS right there in the forefront.

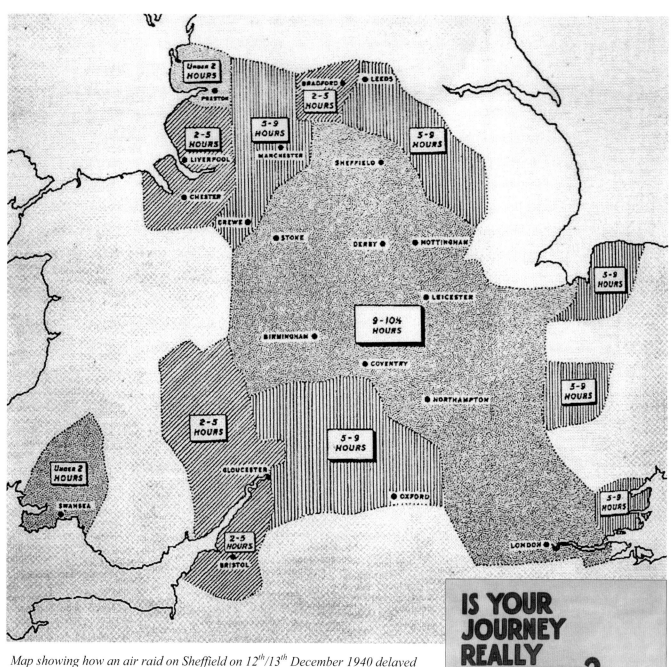

Map showing how an air raid on Sheffield on 12th/13th December 1940 delayed trains over virtually the whole of the LMS system in England.

14

THE OPERATIONAL PROBLEMS - 1939 TO 1945. TIMETABLES, CIVILIAN TRAINS AND PEACE RETURNS

The pre-war train situation.

In the summer of 1931 no passenger trains were scheduled at a booked average speed of 60mph and over, but in the summer of 1939 there were 67 such trains that covered 6,882 miles daily. The acceleration of passenger trains can be seen by the number of trains affected, and the total amount of acceleration. In the eight years from 1931 to 1938 alterations were made to the timings of passenger trains in 16,267 instances, thus saving` 886 hours daily. Also a close review was made to obtain accelerated point-to-point timings, where possible of all freight trains, so as to secure the best possible performances from the modern motive power stock in relation to the traffic to be moved and to maximise track usage/track occupation. In the seven years 1932 to 1938 accelerations to freight trains numbered 691, saving 384 hours. At the end of 1931 there were only 173 freight trains composed wholly or partially of wagons fitted with the vacuum brake, whereas at the end of 1938 the number of such trains had risen to 339, an increase of 96%, with a total daily reduction in journey time of 150 hours.

The effect of air raids on time-tabled trains

When war commenced the timed speeds of freight trains was not altered except that certain of the "fitted" (vacuum braked) and partially fitted trains were reduced in classification. Express passenger trains that, during pre-war years had been accelerated, and running at high speeds were decelerated at the outbreak of the war, and at the time of air raids were booked to run at speeds not exceeding 60 miles per hour at any point. Even with this reduction in booked speed of trains, the dislocation to the pre-arranged plan that occurred under air raid warning conditions when the trains had to be brought to a stand, the drivers warned and the speed reduced to 15mph in the case of passenger trains and 10mph in the case of freight trains, and subsequently stopped again for the warning to be cancelled will readily be appreciated. Additionally, passenger trains had to make a stop at the next station after receipt of a warning to enable the passengers to be advised so that those who desired to do so could alight. When the night bombing started in earnest in September 1940, air raid warnings occurred mostly during the blackout hours and extended for many hours, frequently continuously throughout the night, and were having such a strangulating effect on the railways that it became necessary to take some steps to ameliorate the onerous conditions imposed on the speed of trains. With the authority of the Ministry of

Transport the speed during raids, commencing on 11th November1940, was revised to allow passenger and fitted freight trains to run at 25mph during non- blackout hours, 15mph during blackout hours, and all other trains at 15 mph under both conditions. The extent to which train operation was retarded will be gathered from the map opposite which portrays the areas that were under "Red" warnings and the approximate length of time that warnings were in force. During the night of a typical raid on Sheffield on the night of 12th/13th December 1940, it will be observed that practically the whole of the LMS as far north as Lancaster was working at greatly reduced speed for prolonged periods, with all "Exempted" lighting extinguished.

To give an example, the 19.20 Euston to Perth was subject to a 15mph limit from the start, and the loss of time on this basis compared with the booked timing was sufficient to account for a delay of 12 hours in reaching Lancaster. In practice the train would not sustain delay to that extent as its progress would be so slow that the raid would have terminated before the train had reached Lancaster. It would, however, be some seven or eight hours late at the end of the raid even if the running was not interfered with by damage to the railway. Similar conditions applied to all other trains, both passenger and freight, proceeding north, south, east and west, and so planned working was entirely destroyed. It is not surprising that in the light of experience a further relaxation in the speed restriction was made on 17th February 1941 when all classes of train were permitted to run at normal speeds in non-blackout hours (this removed the necessity to stop trains to warn drivers and again to withdraw the warning during daylight). The speed restriction was increased to 30mph during blackout hours. The stop to advise passengers was also abandoned as in practice only a few passengers availed themselves of the opportunity to alight. The air raids followed one another with such frequency and were of such long duration that recovery from one could not be made before another attack commenced. Thus the effect was cumulative and the Operating Officers were faced with a constant struggle to over come the seemingly almost impossible task of moving passengers, goods and coal, essential to the war effort and the life of the nation.

Other effects of the raids on trains

Previous chapters have described the effect of air raids and an attempt follows by means of a few concrete facts and figures to convey the extent to which railway working was held up, apart from the physical damage sustained.

During the six darkest months of the year – October 1940 to March 1941 the average rate of movement over LMS lines in England and Wales fell by 5% for passenger trains and 20% for freight trains, and by 14% for both classes together, compared with the same months the previous winter, when the railway was already working under war conditions. Similar figures for the months of October, November and December 1940 were even worse, being 8% for passenger and 27% for freight, and 19% for all trains. To that extent each train on the average took longer, to pass over the line. The effect on freight traffic in and around the London region is demonstrated by the figures for wagon miles worked in the Willesden and Kentish Town Control Areas that included the LMS lines approaching London from the north and in London over which traffic to and from London and via London to and from the South-east and Southern counties

	Wagon Miles	
	Willesden Control Area	Kentish Town Control Area
11 weeks ended 25 November 1939	13,597,355	9,126,672
11 weeks ended 25 November 1940	7,736,192	5,993,174
Decrease - number	5,861,263	3,133,498
%	43	34

normally passes.

It is reasonable to assume that, but for the blitz, the traffic flowing via London would at least have been equal to that passing during the corresponding period of the previous year, yet it was reduced by 43% in the Willesden area and 34% in the Kentish Town area.

A further example in the Liverpool District, where in the final two weeks of May 1941, when Liverpool was suffering from the effect of seven consecutive night raids at the beginning of the month, the movement of freight decreased by 47%, compared with the corresponding weeks in the previous year. But the goods got through, if not by one route, then by another. And all the traffic proffered for conveyance by the railway was carried. The extent to which shunting operations were retarded is exemplified by the results taken in a large traffic yard on the

		No. of wagons shunted	
'A'	No 'Red' warning	502	No physical damage in any instance
'B'	'Red' warning in operation the whole time	344	
'C'	'Red' warning the whole time. A.A. guns very active	140	

The loss under condition 'B' was 31%, under 'C' 70%.

night shift under three conditions.

Heavy demands were made on the Company's recourses of locomotives owing to slower running, it being necessary to turn out additional locomotives to complete jobs and to take up return workings, the engines for which had not arrived. This created shortages, and engines of the correct types were not always available for trains. The servicing schedules could not be maintained. During the height of the blitz each locomotive was in use between 7% and 9% longer than at the corresponding time of the previous year. The raids caused the most extravagant wastage of man-power, and a great burden was thrown upon the staff, particularly trainmen, who were called upon to work exceptionally long hours. Owing to the slow progress over the line a train that would normally occupy a set of trainmen only a portion of the day, frequently required three sets of men to man it before it reached its destination, at a time when manpower was at a premium. Such requirements created shortages that reacted on the number of hours worked, the effect of which is seen in the average weekly figures of the number of cases of Engine Drivers on responsible duty over 10 hours in comparable periods of 1939 and at the height of the blitz in 1940, that rose from 2,997 a week to 15,780, whilst Engine Drivers turns of responsible duty exceeding 14 hours in length, increased from 16 to 2,341. A similar state of affairs existed with regard to firemen, and the figures for guards rose from 2,230 per week to 12,096 (over 10 hours) and from 16 to 2,018 (over 14 hours). Trainmen, shunters and goods shed workers were also required to take duty on practically every Sunday to keep pace with the work. It is a well-known fact that drivers, firemen and guards are called out from their homes to work special trains, and in emergencies. The conditions prevailing naturally created a greater number of emergencies owing to the appropriate men not arriving to take up their return workings. Frequently men off duty could not be located during air raids by reason of the fact that they were in air raid shelters. No blame attaches to them in this respect as they were acting in accordance with the public policy. Others were bombed out of their homes, sometimes for a second or even third time. The tonnage of merchandise traffic handled at Goods Sheds in London during the three months September, October and November 1940, compared with the preceding three months, decreased by nearly 305,000 tons or 38%. Whilst for the most part cartage operations ceased during the hours of darkness, the results of enemy action reduced their efficiency. In London and other cities, considerable additional mileage and time was involved in making detours necessitated by the closing of roads, following air raids, and further time was lost in locating tenants of bombed premises or bringing goods back to the station as undeliverable.

Road Transport and Cartage

During 1943 the LMS road transport department conveyed the highest tonnage ever recorded, being 18,150,107 tons, an increase of 38.05% compared with 1938. As far as cartage was concerned, the 1943 figure was 14,599,515 tons conveyed, an increase of 18.89% compared with 1938. On the other hand, 1943 parcel traffic decreased by 46.48% compared with 1938. At the end of 1943 there were 3,579 LMS motor vehicles, 301 more than pre-war and 17,009 horse drawn vehicles that was 1,497 more than the pre-war total. Considerable economy in mileage reduction was made in the London with the LMS and LNER co-operating in order to save overlapping of cartage units. There was also a scheme involving all four main line railways in the London Postal District. Up to 1943 the number of LMS horses dropped by 631 to 5819 being due to the inability to obtain horses. Also there was a shortage of carters due to their call-up requiring female carters to be trained of which there were 229 at the end of 1943.

Civilian Traffic

Early in 1939 the railway companies had to face the task of endeavouring to foresee the effect the war would have to passenger timetables with air raids, and the requirements of the armed forces a major consideration. This resulted with the paring down of ordinary peacetime trains, the possible suspension of dining cars and sleepers and also for the reduction in train speeds as a safety measure in order to keep within the maximum average speed between stations of 45 mph. These war timetables had been completed in July 1939 and on Monday 11th September were brought into force. Generally speaking it worked well, but some adjustments were made and services augmented. All but 28 restaurant cars were withdrawn in May 1942, and even these came off in April 1944. At the same time sleeping car accommodation on certain heavy trains was taken over by the Ministry of War Transport and limited, so that the first call on sleeping berths was given to passengers travelling on urgent Government business. The cessation of Summer Time, in the first war winter with the earlier blackout made many businesses change their hours of work to enable staff to reach home before dark. This obviously resulted in the evening rush hour starting and finishing an hour earlier, with the result the morning peak period reduced from two to one and a half hours. Workmen's trains also featured in the altered conditions as factories sprang up throughout the country, often away from towns involving more and more trains. As an example, on the LMS at Chorley, 222,500 journeys were made each week by factory workers alone.

The blackout caused the late running of trains as passengers had difficulty in finding seats when blinds were down and soldiers with kitbags etc made movement through corridors slow and difficult with the loading and unloading taking more time in the restricted lighting. Also, with railway staff having been 'called up', their replacements were less skilled and less able bodied to handle heavy and bulky packages as their predecessors.

Holiday traffic was a further problem, as referred to later 73 trains were required on one day alone for servicemen's leave. This was on 21st December 1939, and the total extra trains to run on the last 13 days of that month for the forces totalled

385, but for civilians during the same period no less than 2,693 were required with the peak being on the 23rd when 644 trains were required. Such effort could not be expected to continue and the services were appealed to for help and the public requested not to travel unless it was absolutely essential, hence the wartime phrase "Is your journey really necessary". At Christmas 1940 it was made clear by the REC that there would be no additional services or cheap travel. The summer of 1941 saw the public requested to take holidays without travelling. Traffic remained heavy and the same appeals were made in 1942 with little or no effect as the months from May to September saw traffic rise to new heights exceeding the 1938 figures by 74%. The appeals to the public were not therefore very successful as doubtless the strain of war years meant that a reasonable summer holiday was more necessary than ever and folk felt justified in visiting family or taking a holiday. In March 1943 the Ministry of War Production again called for staggered holidays but similar levels as in 1942 still prevailed. To give an example of the disregard to "stay at home" the flow of traffic to Blackpool during the period May to September was as follows – 1936 – 2,426,248; 1942 – 2,068,682; 1943 – 2,598,600.

The following table shows the number of tickets, including season tickets, issued during the war years in comparison

Year	Number	Increase/decrease	+ or - %
1938	410,911,329		
1939	372,189,765	- 38,721,564	- 9.42
1940	326,655,468	- 84,255,861	-20.50
1941	363,931,496	- 46,979,833	-11.43
1942	418,851,453	+ 7,940,124	+ 1.93
1943	440,906,167	+29,994,838	+ 7.30
1944	437,267,369	+26,356,040	+ 6.41
1945	426,177,730	+15,266,401	+ 3.72

with 1938:-

The numbers of originating passenger journeys do not tell the full story as they do not include through journeys commencing on other railways, e.g. troop movements and leave journeys starting in the southern counties that pass over the LMS railway possibly for distances of 400 miles or more. These figures are the only measure available of the increase in the volume of passenger traffic that show that the peak passenger travel was in 1943. It should also be noted that comparing 1945 with 1938, 3.72% more passengers were carried, with a reduced passenger train mileage of 29.54% that indicates a much heavier loading of trains. The decline in the number of originating passenger journeys in 1945 was due to a marked decrease in the number of workman's journeys and in local travel. Long distance traffic continued at a high level exceeding that in 1944 and pre-war.

The number of passengers who commenced their journey on the LMS increased enormously when comparing the year 1938 with 1945. In 1938 the figure was 32,485,726 and in

1945 it was 199,327,333 that includes monthly return, period excursion, tourist, trades, contract, other reduced tickets, and services travel with warrants, both duty and leave.

The train miles run in 1945 and 1944 compared with 1938 were:-

Year	Miles	Increase/decrease Compared with 1938	+ or - %
Coaching			
1938	103,668,285		
1944	70,457,214	-33,211,071	-32.04
1945	73,040,435	-30,627,850	-29.54
Freight			
1938	55,577,730		
1944	63,980,878	+8,403,148	+15.12
1945	59,733877	+4,156,147	+ 7.48
Total			
1938	159,246,015		
1944	134,438,092	-24,807,923	-15.58
1945	132,774,312	-26,471,703	-16.62

Whilst the 1945 coaching train mileage showed an increase over the previous year being 3.07% greater than in 1944, it was 29.54% less than in 1938. The increase over 1944 was due to relief trains to cater for traffic that could not be dealt with by the booked services, and to additional trains run for Whitsuntide and August Bank Holiday as far as stock, available staff and essential traffic permitted. The decrease in freight train mileage in 1945 was due to the sharp decline in traffic following Victory in Europe, whilst after April coal traffic was lower than in 1944 and mineral traffic less than any time during the war years.

Apart from the Easter holidays, when The Ministry of War Transport placed limits on the number of long distance trains that could be run, no such directions were issued for the remaining bank holiday periods and so the LMS ran as many trains as possible in line with the available staff.. Needless to say all trains were loaded to capacity and there were instances of passengers not being accommodated at originating stations and junction points. Various interesting Government directives were issued, one of which was in October 1941 which stated that all 1st class accommodation be withdrawn from trains commencing and terminating in the London Passenger Transport area. The situation became farcical, as, after the order came into use, there was a rush for the 1st class seats that resulted in people standing in them whilst other parts of the train were fairly empty. Referred to earlier was the curtailment of sleeping coaches, and a further attempt was made in 1941 to increase capacity, when arm rests in all 3rd class compartments of modern design were screwed back. The situation was summed up by the Chairman of the Company, Lord Royden, remarking at the 1944 General Meeting that "*Railway travel now places a considerable strain on one's physical powers of endurance,*

A typical wartime picture that could have been taken on almost any main line station in Britain. British Rail

not to speak of one's power of resistance to irritation". As in the 1st World War petty theft increased with the LMS losing 400,000 hand towels in1941 alone, what was worse was the slashing of upholstery and the breakage of windows and fittings that reached disturbing proportions. Also of interest was that limitations had been placed on the number of times that parents could visit their evacuated children. The Minister, in 1945, felt that this was no longer justified provided they did not visit more than once per month. In November 1945, the rationing scheme for the concession travel for the wives of servicemen was cancelled for journeys over 30 miles. On 12th October the President intimated that he had agreed informally with the Minister of War Transport to additional trains, that were the strengthening of regular services, could be run for particular parties, or where the additional traffic arising in connection with special events could not be dealt with on regular services provided that - any such trains were available to the general public and no special accommodation was reserved. Cheap day tickets,

A photograph that could have been taken at any one of the many marshalling yards in the country. Coal was the life-blood of the country as the power stations depended on it, as did the gas industry and almost every house in the kingdom relied on a coal fire for heating the home. The LMS required some 6million tons in 1939 for its steam engine fleet that increased by 12% during the war.

British Rail

excursion and other reduced fare facilities withdrawn in the early part of the war were not reinstated and this continued to have a limiting effect on passenger travel, although during the summer months trains were seriously overcrowded with people intent on enjoying a holiday, in many cases for the first time in six years, and with forces personnel on ordinary and demobilisation leave. The 1945 Christmas traffic was exceptional with the number of passengers for the three weeks ending on 7th January 1945 totalling 2,665,000. Cases occurred when passengers could not be handled on the trains for which they had presented themselves, that were however cleared by subsequent services or the running of additional trains. In all 707 additional passenger trains were run between 20th and 27th December.

Such was the effort required by the staff that many showed the strain, whilst sickness amongst train crews and yard staff was heavy and in addition, a number of men simply failed to turn up for duty.

During the five days from 27th to 31st December 1944, absent staff totalled 6,515 or 13.10% of the total staff at the depots concerned situated in the Western, Midland and Central Divisions.

Sporting Events

The programme for the 1944 Flat Racing Season approved by the Government was similar in regard to venues and the number of days as in 1943. Whilst the railway Companies had authority to convey race horses by rail in connection with certain "Open" events at Newmarket in 1943 the Ministry of War Transport imposed a total embargo on the acceptance of horses for transport during the 1944 season. In both 1943 and 1944 no special trains were allowed for race-

goers to or from meetings. The MWT approved a limited resumption of steeple-chasing for the 1944/45 season subject to there being no rail movement of horses or spectators.

Rail facilities were granted by the MWT for racing pigeons in 1943 and 1944 with 30 special trains run by the LMS. .

Mail Trains

The LMS Railway had an agreement with the General Post Office dated 10th December 1930 for the conveyance of mails and a number of trains were specified to run at certain times on specified days of the week. Some trains were able to throw out and collect mails at speed but the prohibition of external lighting caused this practice to be discontinued early in the war that was not re-introduced until 1st October 1945.

Royal Trains and Special Trains for Important Personages

The LMS Royal Train was stored at Wolverton and used for tours by their Majesties the King and Queen, and up to the end of the war the LMS ran 151 tours on the Company's system, covering 35,690 miles. Tours could last for several days while they visited Army, Navy and Air Force bases. Care was taken as to where the train was stabled, and where possible near a tunnel to enable the train to be drawn into it should an air raid occur. The LMS train was also loaned to other companies – LNER, 55 tours; GWR, 15 tours; and SR, 7 tours. The Prime Minister, The Rt. Hon. Winston Churchill, also had a special train known as the "Rugged" train, comprising of a 1st class brake, two saloons, a 1st class vestibule, 1st class dining car and sleeping cars with one saloon specially adapted for the Prime Minister's use. This train was first used in September 1941 with a total of 36 journeys made during the war period that totalled 16,000 miles. In September 1945 the Rt. Hon. C. R. Atlee expressed a wish that the special coaches forming the "Rugged" not suitable for general purposes should be kept for his disposal and arrangements were made to hold the corridor brake first, saloons 803 and 804 and the vestibule first, the remainder to return to general service. A train known as the "Alive" train for the Commander-in-Chief, American Forces in Europe was supplied by the GWR. This train did 41,022 miles on the LMS rails and was shipped across to Europe on 14th December 1944. Finally a further train known as the "Rapier" train was formed for the Commander-in-Chief, Home Forces. This train was provided by the LNER and ran until 11th July 1945 by which time it had travelled 26,689 miles on the LMS metals.

1945 - Peace Returns

The cessation of hostilities brought no let up for the LMS with thousands still travelling with hundreds of special trains. Combat troops were returning on leave being replaced by reinforcement personnel. Prisoners of war and internees were returned home, Soviet Nationals were repatriated, Belgian, Dutch, Polish and Canadian servicemen were returned home and all the time servicemen were arriving from the Far East by ship. American servicemen were returning to the USA at the rate of 15,000 at a time on the Liners *Queen Mary* and *Queen Elizabeth*. From 'VE Day' to August these departed from the Clyde requiring 37 special trains each time from the Salisbury area.

The situation was eased when the ports of Tilbury and Southampton could again be used thus taking the pressure off the Mersey and the Clyde that had been the only ports used for the previous five years, both served by the LMS. As far as demobilisation was concerned, that commenced on 18th June 1945, the army had nine centres for troops serving at home. For army overseas personnel a place was allocated to each arrival port as follows – Carlisle (from the Clyde), Strensall near York (from the Mersey), Shorncliffe (from Folkestone), Reading and Oxford (from Southampton and the Bristol Channel). The RAF had its own plan with demobilisation centres at Hednesford (Staffs), Cardington (Beds), and Kirkham (Lancs). The Navy had given no indication as to its plans and demobilisation was carried out direct from the various Naval barracks. Special trains were planned, but with few using them they were withdrawn, with block reservations on ordinary trains being utilised. Extreme pressure was experienced at some of the demobilisation centres and so others were opened such as at Aldershot and Woking. A centre was opened at Prestatyn for Pioneer Corps personnel. Following documentation these men were transferred to Stalybridge where they were passed out of the army with a special train being run each day from 4th September to 1st October.

From June 18th to 31st December 1945, 410 special trains were run in connection with demobilisation. Obtaining the exact arrival time of ships was often a problem, resulting in

valuable empty stock trains waiting their arrival. It was a common occurrence for ships to arrive earlier or later than planned. A good example was when the *S.S."Georgic"* arrived at Liverpool with 5,000 personnel. Considerable difficulty was experienced in obtaining from the Captain the ship's expected time of arrival. This matter was taken up with the Ministry of War Transport with a view to obtaining definite arrival times of ships.

There were thousands of prisoners of war in the country that required special trains for their movement, an example being 14 trains to move 12,400 to Northern Ireland early in 1945. At the same time 2,500 were moved to the Isle of Man requiring five special trains, some of which later returned to help with the 1945 harvest. With POWs arriving at Southampton from the continent in large numbers, frustration was experienced with what was expected from the railways. As an example prisoners were being loaded into two trains at Southampton before advice was received by the LMS that the destination was Forres in the North of Scotland, a journey of 585 miles. In the event engines and men were provided at London Junctions within six hours, but the War Office was notified that such long distance hauls could not be undertaken in future unless ample notice was given. The number of POWs increased to such an extent it was necessary for a re-distribution in March 1945 when 29 special trains were run in a three-day period. Prisoners were also carried on ordinary passenger trains with instructions issued by the War Office as below following complaints from the public that they were standing whilst POWs were comfortably seated.

> No reserved accommodation to be provided for parties of less than 20.
> Parties for whom no reservations were made must not occupy seats if ordinary passengers are standing.
> Parties of 20 or more to be given reserved accommodation at the rate of eight to a corridor compartment and 12 to non-corridor compartment.
> Ordinary passengers must not be removed from a compartment to make room for a POW.

A camp in the Windermere District was occupied by high-ranking German Generals from where parties of these individuals travelled to London by ordinary train for interrogation. In October evidence was being gathered for the Nazi Nuremberg War trials when a party of 42 travelled from London to Windermere in first class accommodation at the request of the War Office.

It goes without saying that the allied forces were often in a sorry plight once the camps they occupied were overrun by the allies and ambulance trains were often required at urgent notice to get them to treatment centres or hospitals. A total of 83 special trains conveying 26,592 ex prisoners of war were run between 10th April and 1st June 1945 with numerous small parties being conveyed by ordinary passenger train. It was not until 12th October that the first ex prisoners of war returned from the Far East and from that date until 10th November 26 special trains were run from the Mersey

Christmas leave for the forces in 1945 provided problems as little restriction was imposed by the Service Departments. WD Depots and Establishments closed for the holiday with 335 special trains worked over the LMS between 20th and 28th December. In some cases special trains that had been programmed were either lightly loaded or cancelled, as the number of personnel did not reach expectations. To quote a couple of instances – eight trains were booked to convey RAF personnel from Kirkham to Glasgow, York, Manchester, Birmingham, Cardiff and London on Sunday morning 23rd December. Two of these trains were cancelled and the remaining 6 conveyed only 25 to 50% of the numbers anticipated. It later transpired that the men had been released at noon on Saturday 22nd December and consequently 4000 personnel had made their own way home thus contributing to the overcrowding. A further instance concerning the conveyance of US servicemen from London to Lytham found that only 120 passengers were on the train instead of the 500 expected, the train was terminated at Preston.

A scheme was devised by the Ministry of Health for parties of Dutch children to come to this country for recuperation lasting two to three months. The first batch of 500 accompanied by 100 adults arrived at Tilbury on 11th February, with a special train provided to take them to Coventry. Other groups followed and the first party returned to Holland in May.

The Liberation of Europe also brought problems to the LMS in that stores already en route had to be cancelled, on the other hand the liberation of the Channel Isles on 10th May required large quantities of food and civilian supplies to be sent with all possible speed. Liberation also led to the disposing of large quantities of ammunition in the sea off the Mull of Galloway. Almost a train a day was sent from various W.D Depots to ports on the North Coast such as Cairneyan, Silloth and Workington from the middle of June to the end of December. A quantity was also sent to the South Coast for dumping in the sea. A total of 270 special trains were run by the LMS for this purpose. Eighteen special trains ran from the USA Depot at Kimbolton carrying bombs in 720 wagons to South Wales for shipment to the Pacific front and following this, a further 15 special trains were run to Swansea for shipment back to the USA.

With many Ordnance Depots being closed at the end of the war it was necessary to transfer stocks and supplies to those depots of a more permanent nature that required special trains as the following examples show –

Thirteen special trains from Lytham, (USA Depot) to Manchester and Southampton for shipping back to America. Fifty-five special trains of petrol and oil were run from Grangemouth, Birkenhead District and Carnforth to various other depots. Fourteen trains of armoured vehicles from Salisbury to Redditch. One hundred and twenty two trains from Ashchurch to Southampton, South Wales and Birkenhead returning stores and supplies back to the USA. Twenty trains of armoured vehicles from Winchester to Leicester and Gateshead. Thirty-five trains of heavy tanks from Rainford, near Wigan, to Histon, near Cambridge and thirty-four trains of armoured vehicles from Coventry and Stechford to Hereford.

There were other more peaceful requirements the LMS had to deal with such as the resumption of banana traffic, the first consignment of which arrived at Avonmouth on 31st December 1945. This traffic used special vans fitted with steam heating to ripen the bananas en route to their destination. The problem was that all these vehicles had been used during the war for the transport of meat and other commodities and required the steam heating apparatus to be restored with 1500 vehicles completed in time for the first consignment. New housing became a Government priority as the war neared its end with pre-fabricated houses being imported from the USA. Each house was shipped in eight packages weighing 7.3 tons and 30,000 were programmed of which 8,600 had been received up to the end of November 1945

A great many further instances could be given detailing the efforts made by the LMS Railway and its staff rose to every occasion in the movement of just about everything.

Cars and Sleeping Coaches for Staff

Due to the shortage of footplate staff and guards in 1944, provision was made at Bletchley, Northampton and Nuneaton to accommodate staff transferred from other centres. With lodgings difficult to find camping coaches, sleeping and kitchen cars were utilised to provide sleeping accommodation and meals. Games, wireless, magazines and darts were also provided for which the men concerned paid 28/0d per week, (£1.40 today). Similar arrangements were made at Rugby and Cricklewood in the early months of 1945. Facilities for lodging were also provided at Gloucester for men booking off away from home due the difficulty of the men obtaining private lodgings. The recruitment of staff from Ireland and Eire caused an accommodation problem that was solved with the temporary use of a British Sugar Corporation Hostel at Nottingham.

Operating Staff

The total number of staff employed in the Operating Department in all grades, clerical, supervisory and wages including shed staff in 1938 was 118,367 and at the four weeks ending on 31st December 1945 it was – Goods and Traffic – 88,801 and Motive Power – 47,696 making a grand total of 136,497. Such was the shortage of staff, that commencing in February 1944, the loan of troops from Royal Engineers, Railway Operating Companies was utilised to ease the situation. The LMS share was 351, being Firemen,

S. H. Fisher was educated at Repton School before entering the service of the LNWR in March 1904, in the Goods and Traffic Departments. He was then appointed Outdoor Assistant to the Superintendent of the Line in 1910 and in November 1912 he was appointed Assistant to the District Superintendent at Euston for the Southern District of the LNWR. In May 1919 he was made Assistant District Superintendent at Liverpool for the Northern District. In March 1922, the Crewe District Goods Manager's District was converted into a Traffic Superintendent's District, and Mr Fisher was appointed District Traffic Superintendent, Crewe. In March 1925 he was appointed Operating Assistant at Crewe to the Chief General Superintendent. On 1st January 1932 he was appointed Operating Assistant to the Chief General Superintendent, Derby on £1550pa. On 1st October 1932 he was Operating Superintendent, Euston on £2000. On 1st May 1934 he was appointed Assistant Chief Operating Manager, Euston on £2250. By the 1st January 1944 his salary had risen to £3000, when on that date he was appointed Deputy Chief Operating Manager on £3250 before becoming Chief Operating Manager on 1st August 1944 when T. W. Royle became an LMS Vice President, his salary being £4000, increased to £5000 just prior to nationalisation. It was S. H. Fisher who wrote the final wartime reports dealing with the Operating Department for 1944 and 1945 – TNA references Rail 418/199 & 200 respectively.

LMS Magazine

Shunters and Shed Staff, all of which were withdrawn on Monday 28th August 1944. At the end of 1945 the number of Operating Staff still serving with the forces and who were expected to resume with the LMS was 19,808. The number of staff already demobilised and had resumed duty by that date was 1,380 whist casualties and resignations totalled 1,225. During the same period the number of women employed in male wages positions was 12,776 or 9.1% of the total wages staff, at the end of December 1944 it was 15,262 or 11.5% of the wages staff. At the end of 1944 the number of women employed as Signalmen, Porter Signalmen, Passenger Guards and Porter Guards was 1006.

The Measure of success achieved

Figures have been quoted to demonstrate the effect of the blitz on railway operation, but what may be even more surprising is a measure of the extent of the success that attended the efforts to circumvent and surmount the unprecedented handicaps. In the nine months September 1938 to May 1939 inclusive, under peacetime conditions when there was no black-out, the number of passengers in the long distance category was 20,231,064, whereas in the corresponding months of 1940 and 1941 – the period of the blitz- the total was 29,125,124, the increase amounting to the remarkable figure of 8,894,060, or 44%. The demand for short distance travel was consistently less than in peacetime, so that comparisons are not relevant. On the freight side, the loaded wagon miles – that are the truest means of effective operating work performed – increased in the same period by 207,440,750 wagon miles, or 21%. The quantity of freight handled in goods sheds rose by 2,876,800 tons (17%) and the volume of freight carted by LMS vehicles by 763,700 tons. Assuredly, the Chief Operating Manager, Mr T. W. Royle, together with his operating staff, accomplished superhuman feats in the face of the greatest upheaval of railway working of all time. It should be mentioned that the Operating Manager T. W. Royle was appointed a Vice President of the LMS on 1st September 1944 when S. H. Fisher succeeded him and who wrote the war report for the final wartime years.

15

DISRUPTION DUE TO WEATHER CONDITIONS

Railway operations are always at the mercy of the weather and in Britain the weather is always unpredictable and can easily present conditions that overcome the precise order of railway traffic, whereas roads have the benefit of a much wider network. The winter of 1939-40 was exceptionally severe at a time before the enemy began to interfere with railway operations.

In January and February 1940 the lowest temperatures and heaviest snowfalls in living memory were experienced and the following two winters were also exceptional. On the plus side, cold winters usually reduce the incidence of fog. During the first winter of the war December was a particularly foggy month and was followed by heavy falls of snow succeeded by prolonged frost to reach a climax between *27th* and *28th January*, when snowstorms and blizzards swept across the country to an unbelievable extent.

On the LMS there were 313 blockages up to twenty feet deep with many trains stuck fast in various parts of the system.

This also affected communications with 250 telegraph poles blown down and 500 miles of telegraph and telephone wires out of action. Points froze and brake gear on freight trains was frozen solid, signal wires jammed or snapped, engine injectors froze and grease in axle boxes solidified, couplings required to be hammered apart and locomotive water supplies froze. In an attempt to overcome these difficulties, various ideas were adopted such as – supplies of hot water maintained on platforms to assist the staff to detach engines and coaches – the staff had to protect themselves by wearing gloves, or by wrapping their hands in cloths, when handling metal couplings – the stone sets in the 4' 0" way between the rails in certain engine sheds had to be taken up as they were not clear of the water scoops on the engines owing to the

The weather in full control.   *British Rail*

frost having raised them. – Oil lamps were used for illumination as the gas pipes froze – and snow ploughs were employed to keep the lines clear of snow, engines without ploughs were also utilized for patrolling the lines for a similar purpose.

During January 1940 the number of engine hours specially worked in this way totalled 2,975. Goods stations could not be cleared and marshalling yards ceased operation. With the roads also frozen goods station freight could not be cleared. This meant coal could not be delivered, apart from the fact that it had to be hacked out of the wagon with a pick that also caused difficulties at engine sheds when coal had to be tipped from the wagon into the coal hopper. Steamers were delayed, passengers were stranded and hotels were short of food. Traffic movements over some 1,000 miles of line were either brought to a standstill or considerably delayed. On the main lines where eight trains would pass every hour, there were no through expresses for seven days. A train left Glasgow on the first of those seven days, a Saturday, and did not get to London until Tuesday, and three express trains that left the same terminus a little later came to a stand near Beattock summit with some passengers having to shelter in the neighbouring villages for five days. A block between Lancaster and Preston took an army of workers four days to clear, and on occasions rescue trains themselves became stuck. An aftermath of snow is the thaw that follows causing landslides and blocking lines again. At one place 10,000 tons of rock and soil required 26 days to remove before traffic could again resume. A further problem was that during February 9% of the engine-men and 13% of guards were on the sick list mainly with influenza.

Whilst being no-where near so severe, the following 1940/1 winter was again abnormal with heavy snowstorms occurring in many parts of the country between January 18th and 30th, and in Lancashire, Yorkshire and the north of Scotland up to 8th February. Lines were blocked in 76 places with trains again stuck. The LMS were assisted by 5000 troops in clearing the lines. The single line to Thurso was particularly affected as reported in LMS 'Carry On' Staff magazine.

"In the vicinity of Forsinard and Altnabreac, about 130 miles north of Inverness (a region noted for severe snow blockages in the past), two freight trains were completely snowed up for three days. A snow plough sent from Wick to clear the line became itself snowed up at Altnabreac, and the PW Inspector and 52 men who had gone to clear the line were isolated. Flying across snowy wastes under appalling weather conditions an aeroplane (RAF) succeeded in dropping supplies of food for the marooned men, who were fortunately able to get their train out soon afterwards, being assisted by a "relief" from Inverness carrying fresh men and equipment".

A similar situation required an RAF plane to drop food for 90 passengers and 60 permanent way staff isolated at three separate places in the same district. A further occasion saw a loaded restaurant car sent to feed passengers and crew until they could proceed with their journey. It did not help when the third wartime winter, 1941/2 was not a great deal better. Lines were again blocked and freight and passenger trains stuck. On the section between Birmingham and Glasgow very fine powdery snow sealed the points solid, and as fast as they were released they froze again. At such places as Crewe there were over 200 sets of points that had to be located, covered by up to three feet of snow.

Although so many passenger trains were held up in drifts, no passengers were injured and it was always possible to find them food or accommodation in the vicinity. The worst case occurred between Kinbrace and Forsinard, when the 11.46 military special train from Keith to Wick was stuck in a drift early on the morning of January 25th 1941, and was not cleared until the afternoon of 27th. Food was again dropped by plane with the men released on 28th. Needless to say the Press had plenty to say, having no real idea of the situation in the north of Great Britain due to the rigorous censorship on weather reports.

It would need many pages to list the weather problems the LMS faced during the whole of the war and so to give the reader an idea of what the Operating Department had to deal with only the major problems in the winter of 1939/40 will be listed in detail.

Widespread and dense fog, particularly around Christmas, caused much trouble on the railways. The Christmas passenger traffic, and very heavy Service Leave traffic led to some arrears of freight traffic. These arrears would not have been serious but for the heavy falls of snow that was accompanied by prolonged frosts more severe than anything seen during that century. Snow began to fall in the northwest on *17th January*, and then spread until a climax was reached during the weekend of *27-29th January* when intense snowstorms and blizzards were encountered. Until the air raids began later in 1940 the staff slithered about in sidings with snow and ice underfoot. Couplings, axle boxes and the like were frozen and there was widespread chaos due to failures of the block signalling system and the freezing of points, water troughs, water columns, locomotive injectors and carriage heating pipes and even brake blocks. During the blizzards, snow ploughs had to be run over hundreds of miles of track and often failed to prevent drifts from blocking the lines. Engines failed due to freezing of water and lubricants. Derailments were common. Snow and freezing rain interfered with the running of third rail electric trains as on Merseyside and steam engines were used to head electric trains. These problems were especially serious under war conditions with the blackout also to contend with. At terminals, traffic could not be cleared owing to the bad state of the roads. Where coal and other rough traffic had to be handled, it had to be hacked out the wagons being frozen solid. The clearance of wagons was heavily delayed and shunting drastically slowed as for example in hump yards where wagons could be passed over the hump at only 50 per

A snowplough near Beattock summit.   *British Rail*

hour instead of the usual 200.

On **19th January** at 17.00 the 15.45 ordinary passenger train from Bangor to Amlwych, with seven passengers, became snowbound between Llanerchymedd and Amlwch, with communications with the mainland still cut, a relief train did not arrive until 03.55 with the original train eventually arriving at Amlwch at 19.50 the following day, 27 hours late. On **24th January** snow ploughs were out on the WCML at Shap and on the Cockermouth, Keswick and Penrith line and on **26th January** they were out on the Settle to Carlisle and Stranraer lines, and on the **27th** at Denby Dale. On **25th January** on the Cheshire lines at Castlefield Junction, a special heavy gun train Ardwick to Ordsall Lane was derailed, demolishing the signal box and cutting power cables, thus requiring Altrincham electric trains to be substituted by steam. Starting around noon on **27th January** and continuing during the following day, snowstorms and blizzards fell heavily over practically the whole of the country, especially southwards from Scotland. The storms were particularly severe between the English Midlands and the Forth – Clyde Valley and there were few railways south of Glasgow where working was unaffected.

The March 1940 issue of the Railway Magazine stated:- "*In the last days of January there was an exceptionally heavy snowfall nearly all over Great Britain, and snowdrifts were* responsible for putting 1500 miles of line out of service. Such drifts 10 –15 feet deep were encountered in places as far apart as Buntingford and Beattock, Fakenham and Garsdale. Over 300 snowploughs were used to clear the lines, and in some cases four engines had to be used to drive them through the frozen snow. Scores of trains were snowed up. One of the districts worst affected was the neighbourhood of Beattock, on the LMSR WCML, where six passenger and two freight trains and a newspaper train were blocked for many hours. On the Midland Division lines in the Peak, 13 goods and passenger trains and seven engines were held up; trains were also blocked on the Settle/Carlisle and Galloway lines of the LMSR*". "Many hundreds of miles of telegraph and telephone wires were brought down in various parts of the country. On the Somerset and Dorset line between Bath and Bournemouth, accumulations of snow and ice caused the wires along considerable sections of the line to collapse, bringing down some 200 telegraph poles and disorganising the working of the block system between Midsomer Norton and Evercreech. In consequence, a series of emergency posts was established and permissive working at five-minute intervals was introduced. Weights of trains were reduced to give locomotives a greater margin of power. As a temporary measure an emergency telephone system was installed. The freezing of the points necessitated longer runs by the bank engines assisting goods trains over the summit of the line* *near Masbury, where the Mendip Hills are crossed, before a workable crossover could be reached" "During the thaw that followed there were further difficulties from slips in cuttings. Just north of Watford Tunnel, on the LMS, a slip occurred just as a Northampton – Euston train on the Up Slow line was passing. The engine and four coaches were derailed and one passenger lost her life".*

On the LMSR traffic movements over approximately 1000 miles of line were brought either to a complete standstill or were considerably delayed. Over 500 miles of line the blockages continued for three days or more, the situation in Lancashire being extremely serious. LMS lines were blocked at 313 places (Western Division 146, Central Division 100, Midland 49 and Northern 18) these included long stretches of main lines and complete branch lines, in some instances snowdrifts 20'0" deep. On the LMS 90 passenger trains and 88 freight trains (some conveying livestock), and 40 light engines were snowbound or held up by drifts. Over 80 marshalling Yards were either completely or partially blocked. A considerable number of goods and coal yards and carriage sidings, including colliery and private sidings and dock lines, were also blocked. Miles of block telegraph and telephone lines were damaged, particularly south of Carlisle, signals and points, and other signalling apparatus, were either put out of order or obstructed by snow. There were no express passenger trains to Scotland from Euston after to 10.00 to Glasgow on Sunday *28th January* until 23.05 on Saturday *3rd February*. In the other direction there were no express passenger trains after the 10.00 from Glasgow on Sunday *28th January* (that did not reach Euston until 00.10 on *30th January)*, until the 17.40 from Glasgow on *3rd February.*

The passenger services St. Pancras to Manchester operated from St. Pancras to Derby only, and the first trains to make the full journey after the storm ran on *3rd February*. Services from Liverpool Exchange to Manchester Victoria were suspended on *28th January until 7th February.* During the week ending *3rd February*, when the weather conditions were at their worst, little over half of the normal freight train mileage was run; on the Central Division where the line blockages were the most pronounced, only a third could be worked. All traffic via Normanton and via Burton–on-Trent had ceased, ie the greater part of the Midland Division. *On 30th January* the WCML was blocked by snow at Brock and frequently by deep drifts at Golborne, with single line working in operation at several points in Cheshire. The chief dislocations by snowdrifts were in SW Scotland, including Stranraer – Newton Street, Maybole – Girvan, Old Cumnock – New Cumnock, the Kirkcudbright, Portpatrick and Wigtown Branches, Lanark – Muirkirk – Auchinleck, Muirkirk – Ayr and Symington – Elvanfoot. At 18.00 no trains were running north from Hellifield and it was still snowing in Yorkshire. The main lines Chinley – Millers Dale – Matlock, and Totley Tunnel were blocked – the latter for only 24 hours, the Peak line until *3rd February*. In the

Birmingham area a number of stretches were blocked and Washwood Heath Yard was completely out of action. There were no freight services on the Central Division until after 12.00 on *31st January*, but coal was still reaching London on the Western and Midland Divisions. Also on *31st January* the Up WCML was blocked Crawford – Elvanfoot, but at least some freight was run on the London- Preston stretch. The WCML was now completely blocked at Brock and on the Up side at Scorton. Overnight *31st January/1st February* there was a complete blockage by snow of the WCML via Carstairs again, also on the G&SW main line was blocked Old Cumnock – New Cumnock. Western Division lines/ places blocked by snow included – Cockermouth – Penrith (CK&P) for 11 days. (The line was subject to a serious accident at Blencow on this line on the afternoon of *31st January* when two workmen and one soldier were killed and four other men were injured. A locomotive and three coaches left Penrith at 15.50 with two doctors and ambulance men, returning with the injured to Carlisle at 17.15.). Ingleton and Bickershaw Branches, Whelley, Market Bosworth, Colwich – Stone, Market Drayton and several other NSR lines, Buxton, High Peak, Ashbourne, Wigan – Widnes Branch at Farnworth, Rainhill – St. Helens Junction, Norton Bridge – Stone, Aldridge – Brownhills, Soho Loop (Birmingham), also several other lines were partially blocked, with only one line open.

The Settle & Carlisle line was snowbound and blocked by a derailment at Dent. There were blockages on the Burton-on-Trent to Leicester line and on the main line at Oakley (near Bedford), Liverpool – Wigan was blocked at Ditton Brook; Liverpool – Bolton/Blackburn at Walton Junction; Blackburn – Chorley. Scottish lines, in addition to those on *31st January* included – Moniaive Branch; Largs line; Girvan – Stranraer; Uplawmoor – Lugton East; Castle Douglas – Newton Stewart.

On *1st February* the WCML was opened for freight at Brock and the G&SWR main line was opened. Most Scottish branches remained blocked overnight, and Dumfries – Castle Douglas was now blocked, although the Kirkcudbright Branch and Lanark – Muirkirk lines were now open. At Dore and Totley, the 07.00 ordinary passenger train from Sheffield became stuck in a snowdrift; one line was open through Millers Dale; the Burton – Leicester line was blocked at Bardon Hill. The WCML Down line was now open at Brock, but was occupied by snow clearance wagons. Blockages by snowdrifts remained at – Whalley Bridge – Buxton, Colwich – Stone, Blackburn – Wigan, Barrow-in-Furness – Ravenglass, Market Drayton Branch, Bolton – Rochdale at Bradley Fold, Ormskirk, Skelmersdale – Rainford Junction, Bolton - Liverpool at Crow Nest Junction (Hindley), Ramsbottom – Accrington, Bolton and Blackburn lines at Walton Junction. However, in general, freight traffic was much better and the 10.00 express from St. Pancras – Glasgow and two Expresses St. Pancras – Manchester were run. By *2nd February* things improved and Postal trains were

An ex Midland railway 3F snowbound near Colne in February 1940.   *British Rail*

now running. In Scotland there was little change overnight. Single Line Working was in operation at Dent and at Millers Dale, and continued at Brock, otherwise blockages were much as before. On the CLC in Liverpool, 1000 troops were assisting with snow clearance. On *3rd February* the LMS reported little change. On *4th February* the Settle and Carlisle line was blocked by the Civil Engineer's to allow repairs, and freight trains were diverted via Carnforth and the WCML that was now clear north of Preston. The Perth - Inverness main line was completely blocked by two freight trains stuck in snow at Dalwhinnie, and traffic was diverted via the LNER and Aberdeen. The Glasgow – Stranraer line remained blocked for a further two days, and Branches still blocked were Moniaive, Largs, Portpatrick and Whithorn. However the Whalley Bridge – Buxton, Poynton – Adlington (Staffs), Derby – Peak Forest, Skipton – Colne and Dumfries – Stranraer were now clear.

When the thaw finally set in the troubles were by no means at an end as many landslides and floods occurred. Between *4th and 8th February* there were ten cases of landslides or floods causing lines to be blocked. At one place between Workington and Whitehaven the lines were obstructed for 26 days with around 10,000 tons of rock and spoil having to be removed. On *4th February* a landslip blocked the Slow line at Watford Tunnel North Box, and the 09.14 ordinary passenger train from Northampton to Euston ran into it, referred to in Chapter 16. The obstruction was not cleared for over four days. Landslides in the same place on *11th & 13th November* blocked the Slow lines again for about 16 hours, but no trains ran into them on these occasions. By *5th February* the Settle & Carlisle and several other LMS lines were now clear, but overnight a further snow block occurred at Dalwhinnie (for 36 hours), also Girvan – Dunragit again. On *7th February* further blockages by landslips or floods occurred at Parton – Harrington, Waverton (Crewe-Chester for 36 hours) and Walsall for three days.

Fortunately when the worst of the air raids of 1940 were taking place the weather was kind. As stated the winters of 1941/2 and 42/3 were almost as bad, but the foregoing is sufficient to give a good idea of the problems faced by the Civil Engineer's and the Operating and S&T Departments.

16

SERIOUS ACCIDENTS ON THE LMS RAILWAY - NOT DUE TO ENEMY ACTION

There were hundreds of railway accidents during the war and only the more serious are referred to here. There were many freight train collisions and derailments due to defective wagons, snow, track defects or careless shunting, generally without injuries. In addition, due to the lack of maintenance, locomotive failures became common with big end failures, coupling rods and other main components breaking that would result line blockages with breakdown gangs required.

1939.

Willesden Junction High Level – 27th September. At 16.30 three coaches of an LMS (NLR) train were derailed by an unknown cause on an embankment blocking both lines. Five passengers suffered from shock and the line was not fully cleared for two days.

Hartford – 12th October. At 23.05 the 21.30 freight from Edge Hill to Nottingham was derailed in dense fog and the engine overturned. Both WCML tracks were blocked for 15 hours.

Bletchley – 13th October. At 20.53 the 19.50 Euston Stranraer double-headed express collided head-on at 30-40 mph with a locomotive shunting a van on to the rear of the 19.37 express from Euston to Inverness that had been standing on the Down Fast Platform 3 for nearly 10 minutes. The heavy impact caused the ex LNWR 0-8-0, with its brakes on, to mount the platform demolishing the refreshment room and waiting rooms, (where most of the

casualties occurred), as well as the van and two other brake vans at the rear of the Inverness express. The leading locomotive of the Stranraer Express was badly damaged. The driver of the shunting engine was killed together with four other people and seven seriously injured with 26 less so. The Stranraer express was also scheduled to stop at Bletchley, but was running down from Tring at 70 mph (in spite of the wartime limit of 60) – and was doing 40 – 50 mph when the accident happened and would have overrun the station in any event. The disaster was attributed to the failure of the relatively inexperienced driver of the leading engine (primarily responsible for observing signals) – or the driver of the train engine – to observe the signals over the two miles after Stoke Hammond Signal box. The conditions were bad at the time with driving rain, the blackout coupled with the inexperience of the pilot engine driver. Driver Haines of the leading engine was brought before the Buckingham Assizes on a charge of manslaughter but was acquitted. Considerable damage was done to the station and the 0-8-0 and the up and down main lines were blocked for 36 hours, with traffic running on the slow lines or possibly diverted to the Midland Division of the ECML.

Winwick Junction – 16th October. At 21.50 a light engine ran into a freight train on the Down Slow line fouling the Down Fast. This was followed with the 16.50 express from Euston to Heysham running into the wreckage with one person injured. All lines were blocked for almost 24 hours with most of the traffic diverted via Manchester. Through

Opposite and right - Wembley. Patriot Class 4-6-0 No. 5529 following derailment, having hit a platform barrow that had fallen on to Up Fast line on 12th October 1940. The engine was unnamed at this time having previously been 'Sir Herbert Walker KCB' to be later named 'Stephenson'

British Rail

the night the Up Slow was cleared for the passage of a few trains in the vicinity but it was not until 18.05 the following day that normal working was resumed.

Inverness – 20th October. The 19.15 Euston to Thurso special collided at 01.35 with wagons being shunted at Welsh Bridge but only a few passengers were hurt.

Liverpool Central – 22nd October. At 10.30 the station was isolated for eight hours following an outgoing train being derailed in a shunting accident.

Liverpool Exchange – 23rd October. A passenger was injured when a light engine collided with a passenger train.

Hindley – 31st October. At 05.00 the Horwich Fire Train of three vehicles propelled by a 2-4-2T was returning to Horwich from a fire at Ince Moss refuse tip when it ran at 25 mph into the buffers of the Up Loop between Nos. 1 and 2 Signal boxes, striking an abutment beyond. The leading van conveying the fire brigade was wrecked with the guard, who was the Fire Brigade Captain, being trapped and killed. Nine other members of the team were injured, five seriously. The driver had mistaken a signal and the line he was running on, but complete line blockage was brief.

1940.

Stretford – 10th January. Following a misunderstanding by a signalman at 17.15, in darkness, on a busy line devoid of track circuits the 17.01 MSJ&A EMU Altrincham to Manchester train was allowed to enter a section occupied by the stationary 16.55 EMU from Altrincham, also by a steam train from Warrington. The electric trains collided heavily at 25mph resulting in telescoping and extensive damage to both trains. One passenger was killed with 22 passengers and 3 staff injured.

Above and opposite -
Accident at Bletchley on Friday 13th October 1939 when the 19.50 Euston – Stranraer express headed by class 5P5F 5025 and Royal Scot 6130 "The West Yorkshire Regiment", ran head-on into and ex LNWR 0-8-0 shunting in the station.

Left - Winwick Junction on 16th September 1939 when un-named Patriot 5544 ran into the wreckage of a slightly earlier mishap when light engine 4F 0-6-0 4059 ran into a freight train blocking both lines.
Both British Rail

Kyle of Lochalsh Line, Achterneed – 13th January. Around 09.30, the 08.45 freight train from Dingwall to Kyle of Lochalsh, comprising of two passenger vans, 22 wagons and a brake was nearing the summit of the long 1-in-50 incline at Raven's Rock when a coupling broke between the two vans. Being on an incline the guard was unable to stop the rest of the train from careering back down through Achterneed Station to be derailed violently at catch points, but the guard did manage to jump from the train. The signalman at Achterneed had already accepted another train from Dingwall, thus a far worse disaster was avoided.

Watford Tunnel North Box – 4th February. Melting snow caused a severe landslip in the deep cutting when, at 11.20, the 09.14 ordinary passenger train from Northampton to Euston ran into it. The locomotives and six coaches were derailed with one person killed, ten passengers, a driver, fireman and guard injured. The Up and Down Slow lines were blocked for 4½ days.

Slochd Siding Signal Box – 5th March. At 20.21 Signalman Ferguson at Slochd Siding Box stopped the 13.30 double-headed (5160 & 5017) freight from Perth to Inverness, and then allowed it into the Down Loop with the intention of

allowing it to proceed towards Inverness while he held an Up train in the Up Loop. Unfortunately, as the Down train was passing his box at 20.26 he noticed – which the enginemen had not – that it had divided! Ferguson wrongly assumed that the rear portion was still standing at the Home signal and had just telephoned as much to signalman Carter at Carr Bridge, but five minutes later the latter reported that the runaway was passing him. A jerk had broken the wrought iron coupling on an old private owner wagon when the train at Slocht had moved forward. Carter had already accepted the 14.45 double-headed freight from Perth to Inverness from Aviemore and was in the booking office (from where the exchange of tablets would be made) and therefore was not in his North Box, from which he could have reversed the points to divert the runaway. It was too late, the rear 21 of the 30 loaded wagons and brake van ran back for 9¼ miles, through Carr Bridge on the single line at high speed, colliding with the 14.45 train at 20.36 about two miles north of Aviemore. The train was travelling at 35mph causing the leading engine of the 14.45 to be thrown on its side at right angles, killing the driver and fireman instantly, with about nine wagons being totally wrecked or damaged, but remarkably the train

Sudbury Junction, Wembley, 13th October 1940, a year to the day after the Bletchley accident.

Hulton Getty Archive 80928352

engine was not derailed. The guard of the runaway jumped, having realised he had lost control, receiving minor injuries, but the guard of the Down train was also injured. The blame was placed on Signalman Ferguson for his unjustified assumption and to a lesser extent the guard was blamed, who was too late in realising that he was running backwards in his van (with no sanders). The permanent way remained intact and the line was cleared in 27 ½ hours.

Strawfrank Junction (Carstairs) – 15th June. At 14.30 the leading engine of a double headed empty wagon train was derailed, the driver and guard were injured and all lines at the Junction were blocked for nine hours.

Stanmore – 4th August. The 16.52 auto train from Harrow and Wealdstone ran into the buffers with three people injured and the service suspended until the following day.

Coppenhall Junction (Crewe) – 5th September. At 00.05, the 22.10 ordinary passenger train from Liverpool to Crewe ran into the rear of the 19.00 Fish train from Fleetwood resulting in seven railwaymen badly injured and all lines blocked.

Carstairs 10th September. Five miles before Carstairs, the firebox crown of Coronation class 6224 'Princess Alexandra' collapsed when working the 10.00 express from Glasgow to

Euston. The driver and fireman were badly scalded with the driver later dying. Both men were of limited experience who had been booked on at the last minute in lieu of the regular crew. The fireman had failed to maintain an adequate fire on the heavy climb up from Uddingtston (with a stop at Motherwell) to Craigenhill summit and the train came to a standstill from the lack of vacuum. Then on the downgrade past Cleghorn the boiler water level had been allowed to fall dangerously, resulting in the collapse.

Pollockshields East – 20th September. At 20.50 a Glasgow Central to Uplawmoor ordinary passenger train overran a signal and ran into the rear of a Cathcart Circle train that was stationary at a home signal with 18 passengers injured, one dying later.

Sudbury Junction (Wembley) – 12th October. At 19.15 the engine and seven coaches of the 11.50 express from Liverpool to Euston, hauled by un-named Patriot 5529, running at 55 mph derailed and overturned when it struck the complex point-work, after hitting a barrow at the north end of Wembley Station. The barrow was unnecessarily heavily laden and had overcome three men trying to push it up a ramp onto the platform. They slipped and allowed the barrow to run back onto the Up fast – the Up Home signal was off and there was no time to warn the signalman at Sudbury Junction. The express ran on for 200 yards after hitting the barrow and began derailing south of the station, eventually coming to rest after 375 yards. Most of the damage was done to the engine, its boiler pierced from end to end by a rail, and to the leading three coaches. The driver had evidently tried to stop the train, but he, his fireman and nine passengers were killed with four more seriously injured. All four steam lines were blocked and Euston Station was closed for steam services. Although the customary London air raid had commenced soon after the accident, casualties were removed within 50 minutes and clearance began using hand lamps. In 5½ hours the Up Slow to Up Loop connection was brought into use for perishable traffic but most clearance work was delayed until daylight. WCML trains were terminated at Watford or diverted into St. Pancras, until the Down Fast was cleared after 24 hours. The Up Fast was cleared in 46 hours with the remaining lines taking 3 to 8 days.

Between Bedford and Wellingborough – 19th October. At 16.50 the 13.24 express from Nottingham to St. Pancras was passing the 14.45 St. Pancras to Derby, when an obstruction hit the latter and a number of passengers were injured in both trains. No further information was given.

Perth General Station – 25th October. An ordinary passenger train hauled by a class 5, collided with an LNER, NB 4-4-0 Station pilot that was shunting a carriage. Both engines were derailed and a shunter badly injured.

Clifton Down Tunnel (GW and LMS Joint) – 30th October. At 18.35 the 14.55 freight from Avonmouth to Bristol East Depot derailed blocking both lines on this important route. Passenger services were suspended Clifton Down – Shirehampton and shuttles put on from Stapleton Road to

At Holmes Chapel on 14th September 1941, the 00.45 train from Crewe to Leeds was struck in the rear by the 00.55 express from Crewe to Manchester. The first three coaches of the Leeds train were derailed and 2-6-4T No.2395 overturned
British Rail

Clifton Down and Shirehampton to Avonmouth, with buses from Clifton Down to Sea Mills – Avonmouth Dock. LMS freight traffic was diverted via Henbury or suspended. The lines Clifton Down – Shirehampton were re-opened after a week, but for freight and overnight only, the Tunnel was re-opened for freight at 17.50 on 10th November and for passengers the following day.

Gretna Junction – 5th November. In darkness and heavy rain, at 18.09, the 10.05 express from Euston to Perth, running under clear signals, collided at 45 mph with the 08.55 freight train from Shawfield to Carlisle crossing its path, having run through signals. The signals had at first been cleared and then set back to danger too late. With the evidence of the crew of the freight train being in total conflict with that of the Gretna Junction signalman the conclusion of the MOT Inspector placed the blame on the latter. The engine (Compound 4-4-0 1141) and five leading coaches of the express, the tender of the freight engine (Ex CR 4-6-0 14650) and 15 wagons were derailed and badly damaged. The driver of the express and two passengers were killed, one fireman and 41 passengers were injured and detained in hospital. Both the Caledonian and G&SW main lines were damaged and blocked but were cleared in 18 – 24 hours, with passenger trains diverted via the Waverley route and freight brought to a standstill.

1941.

Ratcliffe Junction – Kegworth – 12th January. The driver and fireman of a Garratt engine were scalded to death by the explosion of a boiler tube

Wallneuk Junction, Paisley - 21st January. The engine, (8F 8247), and two wagons of the 15.30 freight train St. Rollox to

Greenock de-railed. The wagons were re-railed in a few hours but the engine had fallen broadside down a walled embankment, blocking the Up and Down Fast Lines. Three heavy cranes were needed to recover the engine requiring a much longer time.

Garsdale – 6th March. At 05.30, the 23.35 Freight Carlisle to Birmingham passed an adverse signal at Ais Gill and collided with the rear of the 19.09 freight train Carlisle to Leeds, the guard of which was killed. Both lines were blocked and several wagons fell down the bank. Traffic was diverted to the Western Division via Ingleton, until the lines were cleared after 15 hours.

Glossop – 15th May. At 15.35, the 15.27 push and pull from Dinting overran the buffers and the first vehicle was propelled into the street, with some passengers suffering minor injuries.

Dukinfield - Ashton-under-Lyme – 16th May. At 01.35 a derailment of a tank wagon in the 21.45 freight from Copley Hill to Shrewsbury led to nine other wagons being derailed causing extensive damage to the permanent way and two bridges. The 22.40 express from Liverpool Lime Street to Huddersfield ran into the obstruction and the engine and first coach were derailed but with no injuries. The lines were blocked for 20½ hours, followed by single line working for two days.

Hanwood (LMS & GW Joint) – 23rd June. At 19.30, the 18.35 freight from Shrewsbury (Coleham) to Welshpool ran into the 16.45 goods from Minsterley, that had been crossed over for the 19.15 ordinary passenger train from Minsterley to Shrewsbury. Nobody was hurt but both engines were damaged and one wagon of the Minsterley goods smashed into a Shropshire & Montgomery (WD) train that was stabled in the Down Loop. The Down line was blocked Sutton Bridge Junction – Cruckmeole Junction and single line working was applied over the Up line until normal working resumed at 12.55 the following day.

Carlisle 7ᵗʰ July. At 19.25 an LNER pilot engine ran into the rear of the 13.00 express from Euston to Glasgow. Three passengers were injured, but with little damage as all lines were clear within an hour.

Holmes Chapel – 14ᵗʰ September. A serious accident occurred at 01.25 due to lapses by the signalman of routine Block working in the small Bradwell Signal Box. The 00.55 Express form Crewe to Manchester, hauled by Patriot class 5514 'Holyhead', ran into the rear of the 00.35 express from Crewe to Leeds that was just moving away from a signal stop at Holmes Chapel, hauled by 2-6-4T 2395. Three coaches of the latter were telescoped and smashed and three coaches of the Manchester train were damaged, the engine of which overturned and was damaged, but the crew were scarcely hurt. Six passengers (one a goods Guard off duty) were killed and 44 injured, 20 seriously so), with three dying later in hospital. Both lines were blocked for 15½ hours with passenger trains diverted via Warrington and Earlestown.

Rearsby – Syston – 16ᵗʰ October. The 07.03 ordinary passenger train from Melton Mowbray to Leicester ran into a lorry on the crossing Rearsby-Syston pushing it into the path of a freight on the Down line. The first vehicle was derailed and the lorry driver injured. Both lines were blocked for 4 hours

Lansdown Junction – 26ᵗʰ October. A collision occurred at 04.35 between the 11.37 mineral train from Toton to Gloucester and a GW freight. The Up and Down LMS lines were blocked, but as it was a Sunday it was practical to divert LMS traffic to and from the West over the GWR via Worcester, Ledbury and Gloucester – with enormous delay. Both lines were cleared within 8 hours.

Glasgow Central – 12ᵗʰ November. At 18.15 a light engine ran into the rear of the 18.12 ordinary passenger train to Kirkhill. The driver of the light engine, 15 passengers and a guard were injured.

Heaton Norris – 14ᵗʰ November. In dense fog at 22.25, a signalman allowed the second part of the 22.40 express from Euston to Manchester to leave before the first part was out of section, so there was a collision and one coach was damaged with twelve people receiving minor injuries. The Down Fast was blocked for one hour.

Sandhills – 17ᵗʰ November. An EMU from Southport ran into the rear of an EMU from Aintree at 07.20. Three coaches were damaged, the Southport motorman was killed and one guard injured together with 15 passengers. All lines were blocked and buses ran between Liverpool – Sandhills and Bank Hall – Kirkdale. Normal working was resumed by 11.45.

Templecombe 20ᵗʰ November. A special troop train from Wickwar to Bideford arrived at Templecombe off the S&D at 12.10 with one coach on fire. The vehicle was gutted but there were no casualties.

Hallaton 9ᵗʰ December (LMS/LNER Joint). At 15.20 a collision occurred between the11.10 freight from Colwick to Welham Sidings and a ballast train blocking both lines, with one driver injured. The lines were blocked for 36 hours.

Wigan NW – 14ᵗʰ December. At 07.15 the 06.35 ordinary passenger train from Wigan to Preston took the wrong line and collided with the empty stock in a carriage siding. One empty coach was pushed through a brick wall, to overhang all the L&Y lines below. The latter were blocked for five hours, but the power signalling was cut and all freight had to be diverted until normal working resumed at 03.40 the next day.

Eccles – 30ᵗʰ December. At 08.20, in fog, the 06.54 ordinary passenger train from Rochdale to Pennington, running at 35mph on the Down Slow passed two adverse signals and collided side long into the 06.53 ordinary passenger train Kenyon Junction to Manchester that was crossing from the Up Slow to the Up fast across the Down Slow. Three crowded coaches were wrecked in one train and one in the other, with 23 passengers, including three staff, being killed and 56 passengers and the driver of the Pennington train injured. All four lines were blocked, the wreckage being such that the last of the injured was not extracted until 13.30. The Slow lines were cleared in 20 hours and the main lines in 33 hours. The fog was extremely dense and obscured signals and it lasted over 12 hours, requiring fog men to be relieved. Nine fog men were thought to be on duty, but owing to a misunderstanding one was not. As well as the driver of the Pennington train going too fast and missing the signals protecting the crossover, mistakes made by the Eccles Station Box Signalman, together with the general confusion under very difficult conditions caused the disaster.

The wrecked coaches at Eccles on 30ᵗʰ December 1941 when a Rochdale to Pennington train collided sidelong into the Kenyon Junction to Manchester train, hauled by Fowler 2-6-4T No. 2406 and Stanier 2-6-2T No. 207 respectively.

British Rail

1942.
Farnley Junction – 10ᵗʰ January. At 23.00 the Ward's

Siding Box signalman was unaware that the 12.20 freight from Birkenhead to Copley Hill had divided before it passed him, thus allowing the following 20.20 ordinary passenger train from Manchester to Leeds, hauled by Jubilee class 5706 'Express' to run into the rear of it. A petrol tanker in the freight train caught fire and two passenger coaches were burnt out. The guard of the freight was killed and two passengers were seriously injured, with six others less so. The track was extensively damaged and all lines blocked. Services were terminated at Morley and buses ran from Morley to Leeds from 09.00. Freight for the Midland Division and LNER (NE Area) via Leeds was diverted via Normanton. Normal working resumed at 05.45 on 12th January after 30 hours delay.

Falkirk Tunnel – 16th June. At 11.55 a Down Military Special ran over an Engineer's squad working in the tunnel. Three length men were killed and one injured. The gang were hurrying out for dinner and had just been passed by an Up train and were unaware of the oncoming Down train.

Todmorden East Junction – 4th September. At 22.00 Fowler 4F 4541 and several wagons of a westbound coal train derailed and fell down an embankment. The driver and fireman were buried under coal and were badly injured. Up Main and Up Loop lines were blocked. The Up Main was Time Interval Worked until 04.05 and Normal working in 14 hours.

Stafford – 21st October. The 22.45 Parcels from Willesden to Crewe ran into the rear of the 23.35 express from Euston to Crewe at 04.45. There were no injuries although a loaded coach was derailed, two horse- boxes telescoped and an engine was damaged. Most Down lines were affected, but the Down fast was clear in an hour and normal working resumed in 6 hours.

Castleton North Junction - Heywood – 22nd November. Due to irregular working of the Block telegraph, a Rochdale to Blackpool ordinary passenger train ran into the rear of the Manchester Victoria to Bacup ordinary passenger held at signals. The guard of the Bacup train was killed and several passengers received minor injuries.

Wigan NW – 19th December. In thick fog at 18.20, the 17.58 ordinary passenger train from Wigan to Blackburn ran into the 17.05 ordinary passenger from Manchester Exchange that had just arrived. The guard of the stationary train was injured and six passengers suffered minor injuries and shock. Normal working resumed at 22.10.

1943.

Kirkcowan – 16th January. At 06.05 a light engine collided with the 02.37 express from Carlisle to Stranraer, blocking the Up and Down loops on the single main line. Both engines were damaged and five passengers and two staff received minor injuries. Normal working resumed after four hours.

Alness – 9th June. At 00.15 ten coaches of the 20.00 Military Special express from Thurso to Perth were derailed, blocking the single line with one passenger injured. The passengers were transferred to an empty train sent from

Inverness. Until the Down Loop was cleared at 08.20, allowing through working, passenger services were worked to either side. Normal working was resumed at 18.00 the following day.

Glasgow Queen Street Low Level- 26th August. At 08.55 the 07.45 ordinary passenger train Bathgate Upper to Partick collided with the 08.33 ordinary passenger train from Springburn to Hyndland. Two coaches of the Bathgate train telescoped and one derailed. Casualties were reported as 24 shocked or injured with four staff injured. Down lines 'A' & 'B' were blocked. Normal working resumed on the 'B' lines in 3½ hours and over the 'A' lines at 04.05 the following day.

Steeton & Silsden – 10th October. The 21.50 express from St. Pancras to Edinburgh collided with the 01.54 freight train from Leeds to Carnforth at 04.55. The express engine, Jubilee 5582 'Bihar and Orissa', seven coaches and ten wagons were derailed blocking both lines. Three staff and one passenger were injured. The Up line was not clear until 48 hours later, then single line working was employed Kildwick & Crosshills, until normal working was resumed at 11.20 on 12th October.

Audlem –Nantwich – 3rd December.. At Hack Green Crossing at 09.30 in fog, a freight train was allowed to collide with the second of two buses conveying RAF personnel, two airmen were killed and 14 injured. The inexperienced crossing keeper had not checked his 'Train-on-Line' indicator or set his signals to danger. The Up line was blocked for seven hours.

Ditton Junction – 13th December. At 06.40 the 05.45 ordinary passenger train from Chester to Liverpool Lime Street ran into the 06.25 auto train from Ditton Junction to Timperley. Both engines were derailed and both Fast lines were blocked. One person was killed and several injured. Traffic was worked over the Slow lines for eleven hours.

1944.

Brinnington Junction (Stockport) – 30th January. At 21.20 a petrol train from Helsby to Gunness was being shunted onto the branch line towards Reddish Junction to allow a double headed troop train to pass, but the latter train collided with the brake van of the petrol train. The brake and five petrol wagons were derailed and the leading locomotive of the troop train fell on its side with two coaches derailed. Only the fireman was injured and traffic was diverted. The Down line was cleared in 8 hours and the Up line in 42 hours with normal working resumed at 17.35 on 2nd February.

Preston – 12th February. At 09.20 a Down express to Stranraer collided at No.2A signal box with a Down express to Blackpool. The Up and Down Trough and Down Slow lines were blocked for 10 hours.

Henstridge (S&D) – 13th March. At 14.35 near Henstridge, a USA Army lorry with trailer on the main A30 road veered off and crashed through the parapet of a hump backed bridge over the single track S&D line. At that same moment a delayed double-headed southbound troop train had just reached the bridge, with the result that the trailer landed between the two engines, but mainly on the tender of the leading engine (an SR 4-4-0). The engine broke away from its tender and continued on, still on the rails, until the shocked but otherwise unhurt crew brought it to a halt not far from the station. The train engine, (an LMS 0-6-0), and the five leading coaches were derailed. Five passengers were seriously hurt and nine less so, with the engine crews suffering severe shock. The motor section of the vehicle fell onto the line-side, the driver being killed and the other occupant sustaining severe injuries. The single line was blocked for 24 hours.

Mossband Box (Floriston – Gretna Junction). At 03.15, a serious accident occurred on the extremely busy two-track section of the WCML north of Carlisle. Coronation, 6225 'Duchess of Gloucester' and ten coaches of the twelve, five of which were sleeping cars of the 20.40 express from Euston the Glasgow (St. Enoch) derailed at about 55mph, blocking both lines. The leading coach turned round and was crushed against the tender and the second coach was badly damaged. The driver and fireman were thrown down and badly shaken. Their detonators had been thrown out of the cab and lost, but the lines had to be protected urgently, so Fireman Graham scrambled with a torch all 1½ miles ahead to Gretna Junction Box to inform the signalman – taking only 19 minutes. Meanwhile the guard – also thrown off his feet by the crash, hurried back to inform Floriston Box (Mossband Box – cut out anyway at the time, had been wrecked). Three passengers were killed – and not discovered for 15 hours, nine were injured and one passenger slept through it all. The cause of the accident was allowing heavy trains to pass at normal speed over a stretch of track that had been re-ballasted only hours before, with some difficulty over wet clay subsoil. It appeared that some trains had passed through earlier and reported exceptional lurches and one preceding the express had already stopped at Beattock to report this. The lines were badly damaged and a rail had been thrown up destroying Mossband Box. Through passenger trains were diverted via the LNER with freight traffic held back. Both lines were cleared in 26 hours - with a five mph speed restriction.

Dumfries – 12ᵗʰ June. At 21.35, an empty stock train hauled by Jubilee 5660 'Rooke', running from Leeds to Kilmarnock, ran into a rail-motor (1P 2-4-2T 6635) near No.1 Box at the west end of the station. Not booked to stop at the station, the stock passed three distant signals, that, owing to a defect, accidentally failed in the Clear position, so, in spite of the Down Platform Starting signal being at danger, the driver overran it at speed. His train nearly derailed on the crossings at the junction of the Stranraer and Lockerbie lines, where it crashed into the rail-motor. The driver was instantly killed and the severely injured fireman died in hospital. The guard was also injured. The engine of the rail-motor was at its far end and the fireman unhurt, but the driver in the driving compartment also died. Serious damage was done to the locomotive of the empty stock train and the end coach of the rail-motor that was propelled back 160 yards with minor

damage to other coaches. The main lines, and also the Up Lockerbie Branch, were blocked for 10 hours with buses provided from Dunfries – Powfoot ROF and Dumfries – Southwick.

Hellifield – 19ᵗʰ July. At 03.45, a train of loaded petrol wagons divided whilst being shunted. The guard was killed and four vehicles derailed blocking the main lines until 06.35 when Single Line working was introduced from Long Preston began. Normal working was not restored until 09.30 on 20ᵗʰ July.

Hartford – 5ᵗʰ October. The 21.25 express from Euston to Glasgow fell on its side at 02.00 when it collided with the rear of a freight train. Two coaches were derailed, also the brake van and two wagons of the freight train. There were no injuries to passengers, but the guard of the freight train was injured. All traffic was diverted via Chester or Manchester as necessary and a number of freight trains were stabled during the ensuing 48 hours or so.

Northampton (Castle) – 21ˢᵗ December. At 18.45 the 16.15 express from Wolverhampton to Euston was turned into No.2 (Market Harborough) bay in error. The engine derailed and the stop blocks were demolished. Several minor injuries occurred and one person was taken to hospital. Normal working returned in 5½ hours.

Birmingham New Street – 22ⁿᵈ December. At 15.30 the 11.30 express from Euston to Wolverhampton ran into the rear of the 14.07 empty stock from Coventry standing at the end of the platform. Twelve passengers in the express were seriously hurt.

Derby (London Road) Junction – 24ᵗʰ December. At 13.50 in dense fog a collision occurred between a light engine and a freight train. Both engines and two wagons were derailed, blocking all Main lines to the south and west. The driver and fireman of the freight engine and the fireman of the light engine were seriously injured. North – south passenger trains were run via Chaddesden, reversing at Derby. West of England services ran via the Down and Up goods lines, reversing at Derby North Junction. From 18.00 on Christmas day platform lines 1, 2 and 3 were available, but normal working did not resume until 19.30 on Boxing Day.

1945.

Wakefield Road (Leeds) – 9ᵗʰ January. At 22.45, a collision occurred between Troop and Government Stores trains blocking the Up and Down Main lines. Two coaches derailed and were taken out of service, but the remaining occupants (including three injured soldiers) went forward. Several wagons were also derailed and damaged, with normal working resumed 16 hours later

Bootle – 22ⁿᵈ March. A serious explosion occurred at about 22.15. The following description is quoted from the gallantry citation. "The 19.10 freight from Workington to Bankfield (Liverpool), consisted of 57 wagons and a brake van with the leading seven wagons loaded with depth charges from Camerton Admiralty Depot, headed by 3F 0-6-0 3579. When passing Bootle Station, Fireman Stubbs noticed in the station windows a reflection of fire coming from his train.

Signalman Southward in Bootle box had already noticed the fire and warned the signalman ahead and in rear. Driver Goodall at once stopped the train (running at 24 mph) and Stubbs jumped off the engine before it stopped, and ran back to find flames coming from the sixth wagon from the front. He at once unhooked at the rear of the burning wagon and then raced back to the engine, telling the driver to draw ahead. After 80 yards Stubbs again left the engine before it stopped so as to be opposite the burning wagon, got down again, stooped underneath the flames and uncouple it from the other five wagons attached to the engine. By this time flames were coming out like gas jets, at the top and through the bottom round the draw gear, so he ran considerable risk of being severely burned, quite apart from the great danger from the contents of the wagon. Stubbs then ran back to the engine for a supply of detonators to protect the opposite line, and, having correctly placed the first detonator he was thrown to the opposite side of the line by the explosion of the burning wagon, but he at once proceeded to place four more detonators. Returning to the scene of the explosion, Stubbs was met by the guard who informed him that the driver had been killed – and he owed his life to him having been well ahead placing detonators at the time. The alertness of Stubbs in so, promptly detecting the fire and his action in acting so quickly isolating the burning wagon undoubtedly prevented a far more serious accident, and his subsequent promptness in protecting staff coming forward on the opposite line is deserving of the highest commendation". Fireman Stubbs was awarded a George Medal. A verdict of accidental death was retuned at the inquest of Driver Goodall. The explosion was undoubtedly caused by a spark coming from the engine setting fire to a defective wagon sheet. It made a vast crater 105 x 50 feet deep, demolishing about 60 yards of both the Up and Down running lines, hurling masses of ballast, rails and other debris a considerable distance that damaged buildings 1,500 yards away. However, neither the engine or any of the remaining wagons were derailed or seriously damaged. A single line was restored in 45 hours and normal working, under Special regulations, were restored in 68 hours. Buses were provided from Bootle to Silecroft.

Kirkby, Lancs. – 19th April. At 09.35 a serious accident occurred near Dale Lane Box. With one signalman oversleeping, there was a misunderstanding between the others responsible for working the other boxes that controlled the two exits from the Kirkby Ordnance factory. In consequence the 06.15 express from Bradford Exchange to Liverpool Exchange was allowed to run at 60mph into an engine (ex L&Y 0-6-0 12117) and brake van carrying out a crossing movement. The resulting violent smash killed not only the regular drivers of both engines but also two extra drivers on the express engine who were learning the road and a shunter. The leading coaches of the express were damaged and 33 passengers injured, eight seriously. The main lines were blocked, taking 24 hours to clear

Euston – 24th April. An empty stock train crashed into the coaches for the 13.15 to Blackpool that was standing in Platform 14 awaiting its engine. Several coaches were badly damaged, and, as many passengers had already settled in, 26 were injured, six seriously so. Platforms 12 – 15 were blocked, but Nos. 12 and 13 were cleared in 40 minutes, the rest in 8½ hours

The War in Europe ended on 7th May 1945, with one further serious accident occurring before Victory over Japan was declared on 14th August.

Ecclefechan – 21st July. At 15.07 the 13.00 express from Glasgow to Euston hauled by Coronation 6231 'Duchess of Atholl' passed two home signals at danger and collided sidelong at 60 mph into the fourth wagon of a freight train that was setting back into the Up refuge siding to clear the line for the express. The express engine and tender overturned. instantly killing the driver and the fireman died of injuries the following day. The van behind the engine was swept aside against the station footbridge and wrecked. The remaining 12 coaches remained upright although five derailed with one penetrated by a displaced rail. Damage to the coaches was relatively minor and passenger casualties comprised of 31 hospital cases and 19 with minor injuries. The freight engine (4F 4324) was driven forward for 110 yards and derailed but remained upright, the tender was crushed and the first three wagons wrecked with the fourth badly damaged, the remaining 41 wagons and brake van were unaffected. Both tracks through the station were destroyed, together with much of each platform face, the signal box and equipment were also badly damaged. In spite of the isolation, ambulances and doctors arrived in 18 minutes and an American Army surgeon travelling on the express gave valuable assistance. Carlisle Control was informed at once and a Junior Operating Manager travelling on the express summoned heavy-breakdown cranes from Carlisle, Motherwell, Hurlford and Polmadie, with the result that clearance was effected by 13.10 on 22nd July. In the interim services were diverted via Dumfries and over the LNER line from Carlisle with much freight held back The cause was attributed to the inattention by the deceased driver of the express, as no other explanation could be found.

As with the incidents of severe weather, the above list is only a fraction of those that occurred and mainly deals with those where injury or death took place. There were something in the order of 35 to 40 incidents across the big four per month that roughly averaged five locomotive derailments or serious failures in traffic, eight passenger train collisions or derailments, ten freight train collisions or derailments, three level crossing accidents, fires and various miscellaneous incidents. Other common incidents connected with freight trains were derailments due to defective wagons, track defects or careless shunting. Coaching stock incidents were less frequent but derailments and occasional collisions due to defective couplings were fairly common. As maintenance suffered there were many locomotive failures due to big-ends, coupling rods or other major components failing which, on occasions, could damage the track. Finally traffic could also be interrupted by fatalities due to trespass or suicide.

17

THE PRESS

The travelling public could have little idea of what was happening on the railway, all they knew was that services were altered or diverted frequently at short notice, and many gained the impression that the railways were deteriorating and were unable to stand up to the demands of war. In fact, the railways were subject to much unfair, unwarranted and unjustifiable criticism at the time, both by the public and the press. It is almost a prerogative of Englishmen to grumble, or "grouse" as it was called in wartime. Frequently the grousing was done merely to relieve pent up feelings, but in this case it went much deeper, and some of the newspapers joined the ranks, probably owing to the fact the writers of the articles had themselves been placed to some inconvenience, and by reason of their profession were able to make their views and impressions more widely known than other members of the public. A large body of users of the railway displayed commendable qualities of patience and understanding, but others, and as it is usually the case with grumblers, they were the more vociferous, voiced their opinions whenever the service that the railway was able to afford was not as efficient at that to which they were accustomed. It will be well, therefore, to analyse the origin of the complaints in order to demonstrate how they were due to lack of thought, to lack of knowledge and to a great extent, to the selfishness of the individual. Every reader must be impressed by the catalogue of events just recorded, but he must appreciate that little of it was known outside a strictly limited circle of officials and could not possibly be passed on to the public. Posters everywhere told us "Careless talk costs lives". Information that would have been of the utmost value to the enemy is contained in this account and could not be divulged, and it was national policy, for security reasons, not to announce anything that could be utilised by the enemy. This policy seemed at times to be carried to extreme limits although doubtless for good reasons, for frequently, with much truth, the German wireless announced that a certain British town had been bombed long before any official British confirmation was forthcoming. Whilst current information necessary to enable the local railway officials and staff to perform their duties to the public was disseminated as speedily as communications would permit, even they were not supplied with information that they did not need, and in any event railwaymen played their part in the suppression of careless chatter by generally limiting their replies to enquiries to the actual requirements. Thus, the travelling public could only be aware of what came to their immediate notice. When travelling by road, the effects of enemy bombs were clearly evident as signs were put up blocking the roads or areas that had been damaged and traffic was diverted using alternative routes. On the railway it was frequently impossible for the traveller to see the reason for the dislocation to the train working and he could not be told that the reason for the curtailment of travelling facilities or the diversion of his train was due to the fact that bombs had dropped on a certain portion of line. No matter what the experience of the individual had been overnight - and he may have heard scores of bombs falling and exploding – when he arrived at the station in the morning he expected, or hoped, to find his usual train to the city, whereas there may have been a variety of reasons why that train could not be available. The carriage shed may have been bombed or set on fire, the engine shed may have been hit or the coaling plant or water installations put out of action. A bomb may have fallen on the exit roads from the engine shed, thus blocking all the engines. A signal box may have been put out of action or the line may have been severed out in the suburbs so preventing the service being run as usual. If the train did arrive at or near its booked time, its journey to the city maybe interrupted by a break in the track or severe damage to a bridge or viaduct, and the terminus itself might be completely out of action.

The public did not understand the far-reaching reaction of incidents that geographically, may be miles away. How, for instance could a passenger joining a train in Scotland realise that his train was late due to a bomb falling on say Berkhamsted in Hertfordshire? Yet such may have been the case, but it was not possible or permissible to tell him exactly why his train was late. Consider the passenger making a journey from a provincial town served by a main line express such as Rugby or Leicester to London. He would select the train from the timetable and arrive at the station at the appointed time, and may have found that he had a long wait for the train. He would probably be aware that air raids had taken place somewhere in the country by reason of the fact that sirens had been sounded in the area in which he lived, but he would have no knowledge of the place raided, or the severity of the raid. There may have been a most intensive raid on Manchester or Liverpool from either of which cities the train by which the passenger had elected to travel was booked to start, and delays were inevitable.

An extract from the Operating Managers Report for the period to 1943

"Whilst the conduct of the staff merited and received the highest praise from the Management, it is regrettable that railwaymen were at the time subjected to so much vilification by public and Press. The conditions of secrecy imposed made it impossible for railways to defend themselves, and there was no championship of their cause, when it was most

required, by the Minister of Transport, so that they had to suffer in silence. At a late stage the railways were permitted to issue advertisements demonstrating, within prescribed limits, some of the conditions with which they had to contend, and eventually statements were made in the House of Commons, the wireless, and in the Press, praising the railwaymen and the railways. It is hoped that by these means the harm done in those trying days will have been undone, as comparatively few will ever know the facts set out in this book. It was gratifying that one contributor to the newspapers at least was imbued with a sense of awareness, as was Lord Castlerosse when he wrote – "England expected the railways not only to do their duty, but also the impossible"."

This then leads on to two examples of main line journeys upon which delays were encountered and which received much publicity in the Press. They are quoted to demonstrate the lack of understanding that occurred. On Sunday, 17th November 1940, the "Sunday Express" devoted the whole space allocated to the leading article to "A story of a Train Journey" from which extracts follow.

"Here is a simple story of a main line express train which made the journey from a provincial city to London a day or two ago" "The train pulled out of the station at 09.45, it was due in London at 13.50. At one point on the journey the train stood still for more than an hour. Then it went backwards for several miles. It eventually reached London at 20.00 – six hours late on a journey scheduled to last four hours. The train was packed. At many stations it stopped to pick up still more passengers. Although the news could have been telephoned all down the line that passengers, women and children, were already herded in the corridors like cattle, no attempt was made to fix additional coaches to the train" "There was a restaurant car on the train. Those who were rich enough to pay for the meal could get lunch in it. But after lunch the restaurant car went out of business" "When the train at last reached London most of the passengers had spent 10 hours without food or drink of any kind. The train arrived in town when the night raid was in full blast. No arrangement of any sort had been made to convey the passengers to their several destinations". This kind of resolute and calculated indifference to the comfort or convenience of their customers prevails over the whole of the British Railways. It exists on the branch lines and suburban lines as well on the main roads of railway traffic". "Goods traffic is in a chaotic condition". "The railways must realise that the public expects them to not only maintain a peace time efficiency, but to improve upon it". "Let this also be said, the railways not only let down the nation by their present parrot-cry of "Don't you know there is a war on?" as an excuse for 10,000 instances of avoidable inefficiency, but also lose the goodwill of the public". "The busmen who drive their vehicles to schedule through the bombardment, the firemen, the factory and munition workers, are all laying up for themselves an immense store of public sympathy by

the way they carry on their duties". "Only the railwaymen.............................are a disgrace. They may come to be regarded as people who, having failed the nation in its danger hour, have no claim upon the nation's bounty when the danger is past".

This scurrilous diatribe thus received particular prominence in a Sunday paper with a large circulation with the last paragraph causing a great deal of resentment from railway workers who carried on throughout the blitz. They together with other transport workers stuck to their jobs probably to a greater extent than any other class of worker, although they were working, either completely in the open or with little protection. What a contrast to the writer of the article, who at least would be ensconced in a substantial building or in protected accommodation below ground.

So what were the facts concerning the train in question? There is little doubt that the article referred to the 09.45 from Manchester (London Road) to Euston on Friday 15th November 1940. Owing to two unexploded bombs having been located on the lines between Nuneaton and Rugby, all traffic over that section of the main line was stopped. Normally the most suitable alternative route to bye-pass this section would have been via Coventry, but the date in question was that of the "Coventration" of that city. No members of the public in Manchester on the following day could be aware of this, and in fact, it was not until some days later that the public were made aware of the disastrous nature of this vicious raid. As might be expected on such an occasion, the railway lines and installations in the area were very severely damaged, and all lines were blocked over the alternative route from Nuneaton to Coventry and from Coventry to Rugby. Before the train left Manchester, arrangements had been made to divert it at Nuneaton to the line via Wigston (Leicester), thence by the Midland route, returning to the WCML at Rugby. It was realised that this diversion would add some time to the journey, but this, it will be appreciated, was absolutely unavoidable, and it was not anticipated that the delay would be much greater than an hour or so.

The train left Manchester with eleven vehicles and at Stockport three additional vehicles were added from Colne, making a total of fourteen coaches. When the train left Stockport, it was full, but there was no overcrowding and there was no necessity to advise the next stopping place that there was a shortage of seats. At Stoke a number of passengers joined the train and it was considered they would be able to find seats without due over crowding. As Stoke was the last booked stop it was not necessary to legislate for further passengers joining the train. Thus all went well until after the train left Stoke, which it did eleven minutes late, but almost immediately after its departure at 11.09 it became known that the line between Wigston had been closed owing to the discovery of two unexploded parachute mines that had been dropped so close to the railway that the authorities insisted that the railway stopped all traffic until Naval experts could be brought to the scene and render the mines harmless. Consequently the train had to be stopped at Stone at 11.20 and drawn back to Stoke. Some delay in an operation such as this is inevitable as the engine had to be transferred to the opposite end of the train and the required safety precautions complied with. The train again left Stoke at 12.42 (105 minutes late) being diverted via a much more circuitous route, travelling via Uttoxeter, Tutbury, Burton, Coalville and Leicester. As the line between Burton and Leicester was not constructed to admit the passage of main line engines, changes of engines and crew were necessary.. The train then followed the former Midland main line from Leicester to Market Harborough, whence it travelled via Northampton. In the later stages of the journey the troubles were not over, as when the train was running between Tring and Watford at 18.22 it had to be stopped and warned that an air raid was in operation and the driver instructed to proceed at 15mph, the warning being applicable through to Euston. Further, between Willesden and Euston all the steam trains normally worked over four lines, but were being passed over two lines in consequence of the lines through Kensal Green Tunnel having been put out of use by a bomb. The train reached Euston Station at 19.55 and the length of time taken on the journey was not surprising having regard to all that had happened en route. It was also understood that the restaurant car ran out of food, and in war-time additional supplies could not be readily obtained, especially in this case, when the route of the train had to be changed after it had commenced on its journey. In a case like this the Station Master at the originating end was not aware of the route that would ultimately be taken by the train that was settled by Control en route to meet the circumstances that arose. He was not, therefore able to map out or take precautions ahead to any extent, nor could he forecast how late the train was likely to be.

A further example was the publication in a prominent position in the "Daily Express" of 18th November 1940 of "An open letter to Lord Stamp, the LMS Chairman" that read as follows.

"Sunday Night.

"My Lord,

We were promised 25mph trains during daylight alerts. May I tell you of a train tonight that averaged 18mph over a ten-hour journey without an alert, and ended with a burst of 1½ mph for two hours? That was one of your crack express trains scheduled to do the journey in three-and-a quarter hours in peacetime and an hour longer in times of war. In the timetable it is marked 10.00 R., and the "R" - for restaurant car – only existed in the timetable. The dining car crew joined the train, but neither they nor the passengers could find the diner. Railway people hoped it would be connected at Crewe, but it wasn't. That meant ten hours without food or drink in a train so crowded that many people could not find room even to sit on their cases in the corridors. At only one station was there any sign of tea.

That was at noon and being provided by the WVS for soldiers only. The Guard told us that we should be in London soon after 14.30. At 16.40 he said "we are only ten miles away now". At18.30 he admitted London was still seven miles away. That meant one and a half miles an hour for two hours, and there was no alert until some time after that. Still the train did cover more than the last seven miles in one hour 20 minutes, for it spent some of the time going backwards.

I would like to ask three questions:-

Why were the passengers not warned before they joined the train that the advertised dining car was missing so that they could raid the refreshment room for sandwiches?.

Why, if a buffet car could not be substituted, were there no tea trolleys at some of the larger stations?

And why, oh why, when we got ten miles from London, were we not given the chance of alighting to complete the journey by electric train, bus or by walking it? Three hours and 20 minutes is fair walking time.

I have the honour to be, My Lord,

Your Lordship's obedient
And humble servant,
DAILY EXPRESS STAFF REPORTER!.

As noted earlier, It was on April 16th 1941 that the President of the LMS Railway - Josiah Stamp, First Baron Stamp of Shortlands, together with his wife, Olive Jessie and their eldest son Wilfred Carlyle Stamp were killed in their home near London by enemy action.

The circumstances connected with the running of the 10.00 Manchester (London Road) to Euston on Sunday 17th November 1940, were that it was scheduled to be formed of the coaches of the 17.30 train from Euston the previous night, but the latter train suffered exceptional delay. It was travelling northwards on Saturday when it was stopped short of an obstruction at Berkhamsted, where the 10.00 express Glasgow to Euston had just previously run into the debris of an over bridge that had been bombed and dropped on to the lines as the train was approaching. All four lines were blocked and the 17.30 from Euston had to be taken back to Willesden, where it was diverted on to the Midland line, and owing to the general upset to the working being experienced as a result of other diversions and reactions from air raids (at this time the raids were occurring every day and the Coventry attack had taken place the previous Friday night), the train did not reach London Road Station, Manchester, until 09.35 on the Sunday morning. The coaches were therefore too late to form the 10.00 return working, and consequently a fresh train had been made up from the sidings for the latter, but no restaurant car was available. Owing to the blockage at Berkhamsted the train had to be diverted at Nuneaton to travel via Wigston (Leicester) and then over the Midland line to Cricklewood, where it was again diverted over the Acton branch to Acton Wells Junction – the train being reversed there and a fresh engine provided – and run into Euston via Willesden. When diversions have to be carried out on a large scale as was necessary by the

Berkhamsted incident – which was of a major character – serious delays are inevitable, not only on account of the circuitous routes by which trains have to travel, but owing to the fact that it is necessary to ensure that the right type of engine is on the train to enable it to run over the alternative route – a procedure liable to cause delay on week days, but more so on Sundays when it involves calling out men from their homes. In addition the Midland line was much occupied with a heavy Sunday programme of freight and mineral traffic. As to the remarks respecting the provision of food, the difficulties obtaining and serving food to a trainload of passengers on a Sunday in wartime at almost a moment's notice are too apparent to need further comment. Had it been possible the train would have run into St. Pancras and so avoided returning it to the WCML near London, but the long platforms at St. Pancras were out of use through bombing, and difficulties were already being experienced in dealing with the normal Sunday traffic at this station.

The report went on to say – These two attacks on the LMS Company have been dealt with in detail to demonstrate their gross unfairness and because it is seldom that criticisms in the press are of a specific nature. They usually take the form of indefinite allegations that are difficult to refute. It would have been quite understandable in these two instances if the LMS had announced there would be no trains from Manchester to London on the two days under notice. Instead, the obstacles were surmounted, and there was not a single passenger who was not got through, but the efforts of the railway at improvisation received not reward but criticism. It was apparently forgotten that there are two sides to every question. The Company was not asked in confidence whether there were substantial reasons for the delays to the trains before the articles were printed, and no announcement by the railway was practical by the railway afterwards as information valuable to the enemy was involved. Outbursts of this nature by the newspapers were more difficult to understand when they themselves were suffering from the effects of enemy activity and were not keeping to their timetables of production. Morning after morning, week after week, the London papers – and the "Daily Express" was no exception – were not available for several hours after the usual time. At first the newspapers tried to saddle the railways with the blame for late delivery of newspapers, but this contention could not be upheld because it was quite a regular occurrence for the trains which run during the night almost solely for the conveyance of newspapers to be held up for hours until the arrival of the packages. The newspapers were not alone in their attempts to evade responsibility for delays and throw the onus on to the railways. During the blitz, letters and postal packages were generally taking three, four and more days in transit,

even though they may only be passing from one side of London to the other. Information was spread abroad in various ways, and statements were made in Parliament, that the railways were to blame. Such statements were a gross distortion of the truth and an attempt to shift the responsibility savoured of "passing the buck". It can be stated without fear of contradiction that between every town there was at least one train, and in most cases several trains, during the course of a day, with the exception of rare instances when communications of all types broke down, as in the case of the attack on Coventry. It is admitted that the trains frequently ran late in those trying times and to that extent delays occurred to the mails whilst actually in transit on the railway, but the delays were measured by hours only, and not by days.

It was also clear from reports that appeared in the press from time to time that difficulties experienced in regard to the country's war production were being ascribed by Works Executives and others to transport delays, whereas output was restricted by enemy air activity and through other causes that it was not convenient or political to divulge. No matter how grievously it was injured, at no time did the railway "put up the shutters", but manfully carried on its job of transporting the passengers and goods requiring to be conveyed, achieving a measure of success that was probably unparalleled in any other industry. It speaks volumes for the instructions issued for securing safety during traffic working and the efficient manner in which they were carried out by the staff, and of the millions conveyed, only 16 passengers or intending passengers were killed and 38 injured during air raids. All these fatal casualties and nearly all of the non-fatal injuries occurred at stations, and the life of not a single passenger was lost in an accident to a moving train out of enemy action.

During the whole of this period a more than usually heavy burden was that upon Mr. T. W. Royle, the Chief Operating Manager, his Headquarters' Assistants, Divisional Superintendents, District Controllers and District Locomotive Superintendents; the District Goods Managers and District Goods and Passenger Managers, and the respective staffs of each. All were affected to a greater or lesser degree, because, although some districts escaped physical damage, none was entirely divorced from the upset to railway working which resulted from air raids. The operating officers and staff were aided in their successful endeavours to keep the wheels turning by the untiring and unstinting efforts of Mr. W. K. Wallace, the Chief Civil Engineer, and Mr. A. F. Bound, the Signal and Telegraph Engineer, and their staff, who restored lines and communications with unexampled expedition. Reference to the above staff leads nicely to the final chapter.

18
MANAGEMENT AND STAFF

When the war commenced there were 563,264 men and boys and 25,253 women and girls working on the railways. LMS board minute 4845 on 25th October 1944 stated that 38,403 LMS staff were serving in the forces of which 1,049 were commissioned officers. .According to G. C. Nash, in the book 'LMS at War', the LMS contributed 44,375 serving personnel of which over 1,500 never returned and more than 1,000 were taken prisoner. A clerk rose to the rank of Lieutenant Commander, an apprentice to Wing Commander and a draughtsman to Lieutenant Colonel In the course of their service they received over 150 decorations and were mentioned in despatches on 88 occasions. The King made 54 awards for gallantry during the "blitz" to LMS railwaymen, one of which is particularly interesting. John Bridge of Coatbridge, a ganger with 54 years service, was employed on the up main line at Whifflet, and, having been warned by the look-out man that a train was approaching, all stood clear. One of the women labourers moved back too far and onto the adjacent loop line where an engine was propelling some empty wagons. Knocked down and sustaining severe injuries to her feet, she immediately tried to crawl out from behind the moving train and it was on hearing her screams that John first saw her. In a miraculous way John was able to dive between two of the moving wagons and drop onto the track and thus crawl back below the advancing wagons until he reached her, to then hold her down until the train stopped. Unfortunately both her feet were subsequently amputated but John's action most certainly saved her from more serious injury and maybe her life. As the war progressed the intensified industrial output together with the influx of Allied forces made tremendous demands on the LMS as a whole, and to meet these needs it was necessary to retain men due for retirement, to bring back those that had already retired and to employ women. By the end of November 1944 it was estimated that between 35 and 40% of the Operating departments staff of 137,000 were employed in a temporary capacity. Collecting salvage was also important for the war effort, and it was the job of all staff to do their bit. Station staff vied with each other to swell the collections with the lines and even canals being fished with shunting poles to retrieve anything of use. A station porter at Wigan, working in his spare time collected over 200 tons of various materials. Women were in the WVS (Women's Voluntary Service) and the 8,500 members of the LMS Horticultural Society used suitable line-side areas for allotments. Even the LMS Fur and Feather Society contributed to the nation's food rearing rabbits and chickens. There were over 1,000 groups making contributions to the war Savings Movement, as, for example, the workshops alone invested £489,389. In addition £171,000 was raised for the Red Cross and over 120,000 members helped to finance the Comfort Fund for LMS Prisoners of war, the final sum being £55,000. And so we finish with a woman working a 4 ton drop hammer, the stationmaster at Crewe, on being questioned about his heavy war responsibilities, simply replied "Well I just tried to keep things going", and of the signalman, who, having had the roof blown off his signal box, requested that it be replaced as soon as possible before he caught his death of cold. Then there was the enquiry office attendant who answered 489 calls in seven hours, not forgetting the 80 year old claims clerk and the signalwoman employed in the box where her husband started work 30 years previously. It was all down to one great team – The London Midland and Scottish Railway that served this Country so well.

If a similar crisis were to occur today, the current railways would have no chance of coping as there is insufficient rolling stock of all categories, no alternative routes and the Divisional Civil Engineers Depots have long since gone.. .

Labour relations and strikes.

As far as wages were concerned, on 28th July 1939, a minimum wage was agreed for all adult male staff in the conciliation grades of £2–5-0d (£2.25) from the lowest base rate of £2-1-0d (£2.05). This affected 16,000 men in Great Britain and it was further agreed that a reduction in the cost-of-living would no longer result in a reduction of pay. However all was not well on the labour front as towards the end of the war, in the middle of 1944, the shortage of staff became a very serious matter and the re-introduction of the "Special Procedure" was requested whereby the Government gave persons called up for military service the option of joining the railway. The regional offices of the Ministry of Labour did everything possible but it did not have the desired effect. There was only one instance of the "Special Procedure" being re-introduced in respect of 52 Goods Shunters urgently required in the Toton and Nottingham areas. Trains were having to be cancelled and the staff, particularly trainmen and shunters were having to work excessive hours and were becoming restive under the strain. The problem was not solved and a meeting with the Minister of Transport took place on 12th July 1945. Interestingly the Railways were not allowed to advertise adult vacancies but only those for boys and girls under 18 years of age and men over 51 and women over 40, all work vacancies were, at this time, dealt by the Employment exchanges. At the end of December 1945 there was still an acute shortage of experienced staff that affected all phases of the Operating Department. At that time there were still 19,808 members of

*Loco-men in their
canteen at Willesden
Junction shed.*
British Rail

staff still serving in the forces and only 1,380 had at that time returned to railway service although a considerable number were due for demobilisation in 1946. One solution to the staff shortage problem in 1944 was the use of Italian prisoners of war in mainly goods and MPDs, and to this end approximately 135,000 man-days were gained. Their use would have been extended but for the fact that staff in the larger goods depots in London, Birmingham, Crewe and Manchester raised objections.

There were no strikes until after "VE" Day, when, the Company decided to revert to single shift working in the traffic yards at Edge Hill, Liverpool from 8th July 1945. This was due to the decline in the amount of traffic. The men stated that if two-shift working was not reinstated they would not work on Sundays and also 'Work to Rule', but this request was rejected by the Company, and the strike spread to locomotive and traffic grades, the emphasis then moving to demands for increased pay. Many of the depots in Lancashire, Cheshire, including Crewe, North Wales and certain Central Division depots, as well as motive power men in Birmingham joined the strike, either refusing Sunday duty or overtime, or in some cases 'Working to Rule'. The settlement was with a wage increase although the men at the motive power depots at Crewe and Edge Hill continued to refuse to work on Sundays as they were not satisfied with certain aspects of the agreement negotiated by the Unions and the Railway Companies. The strike terminated at Edge Hill and Crewe on 14th October and in Birmingham on 28th October 1945. October also saw strikes in the docks with London, Hull, Leith, the Clyde and Mersey all affected with troops drafted in to deal with essential military traffic. The arrangement was extended after a fortnight to deal with

civilian traffic also. In all 14,000 troops were used requiring 40 special trains that ran between 10th October and 5th November.

Female Staff.

Right from the earliest times railwaymen resented women working on the railways as it was considered men's work. Those that were employed received less pay than a man doing the same work and whilst the Unions passed resolutions to this effect they were rarely persued and women were dismissed on marriage No woman was ever allowed on the footplate although they did become engine cleaners. When the war ended, women could be found within the wages staff, married or otherwise, employed as guards, signalwomen and in almost every class of railway employment, with clerical grades no exception. By the end of 1944 there were 377 women guards and 623 signalwomen. Women were eventually able to relieve the railway employment situation and could be found in just under 250 different railway grades including such things as concrete workers, fitters, electricians, boiler cleaners, painters, lock-keepers, weighbridge operators, blacksmiths, the total eventually reaching 39,000, or 17% of the whole staff. In 1939 there were 6,839 women who were members of the Railway Clerks Association that rose to 21,865 in 1945. At the end of the war many women felt duty bound to resign as men returned following their demobilisation, and many were pleased to do so, finding work with more sociable hours. No women were ever LMS Directors and a quick search through the LMS Board Minutes revealed only six women sufficiently senior to be mentioned, all were unmarried and all were Lady Welfare Officers. From the Civil Engineer's viewpoint what follows is a list of the duties of a Length-women employed in the maintenance of the permanent way – screening ballast, cleaning water courses, stripping chairs from sleepers, opening out ballast in preparation for changing sleepers, assisting men in changing timbers in sidings, tightening screws, assisting in the fixing of post and wire fencing, unloading ballast, ashes etc., loading ashes, picking, hoeing, and hand weeding running lines and sidings, salvaging coal and slack, sorting and stacking small materials. There were 98 women classified as Length-women, and over 400 more as labourers. One was a fitters mate, some helped with plumbing, glazing and gas fitting and much of the manufacture of reinforced concrete units including welding of the reinforcing rods at Newton Heath and Mossend, Glasgow was undertaken by women. At the former depot the crane driver was a woman. They were also extensively employed on painting work, and on refuse tips. They emptied wagons and helped to slue the sidings as required. They acted as incandescent burner attendants, as metal machinists, as flagmen and as point oilers, etc. etc.

Male Staff.

The inevitable effect of the loss of the younger men and the re-engagement of retired staff was to raise the average age. This may well have resulted in a loss of efficiency but there was no doubt that the restriction of the supply from which labour could be recruited from outside gave difficulties in this regard, with contractors hired by the Company being even more hampered by the shortage of trained and experienced staff. Because of the difficulties that beset contractors in the engagement of suitable men, and in obtaining materials, the system of carrying out work by direct labour supervised by Engineers within the Department was widely extended. Many wartime schemes were carried out by the Civil Works Section, such as the new bridge over the River Eden at Carlisle and the large siding scheme at Northampton. Outside of their normal jobs many men enrolled for the Home Guard, and although they were never called upon in battle, they nevertheless found time to do regular spells as guards and sentries, giving up their time to gain knowledge in weaponry and street fighting etc.

The Post-war Reinstatement of Railway Staff.

Under the Reinstatement of Civil Employment Act of 1944, that came in force on 1st August 1944, persons joining the forces for whole time service after 25th May 1939, had to be reinstated in their employment on application once their was service came to an end. The definition of 'former employer' was the firm who employed the man four weeks prior to their war service. The employee had four weeks to make his application and must have been ready to take up his employment by the ninth Monday. He must be given the job he had previously held, and be no worse off had he not performed war service and if that was not possible then work in the most favourable terms that were reasonable and practical. He had to be employed for a minimum of 26

weeks or 52 weeks if he had been employed for a year or more prior to his enlistment. There were also other conditions. The LMS divided staff serving in the armed services into two classes:-

1. Those who were recipients of the President's Circular No.1729, dated September 1939.
2. The others.

Staff in category 1, were, either members of the permanent staff or who had been previously employed for at least six months prior to the outbreak of the war and there were obligations to such staff with regard to their re-employment apart from the Act. With regard to category 2, re-instatement was obligatory. In the case of category 1 it was decided that something positive, sympathetic and appreciative about their return to railway employment and that they should not be allowed merely to drift back, but should be welcomed by a responsible officer of the Company. To this end a letter, as below was addressed to each person in the category by the President of the Executive:- *"I am writing to you to remind you of the undertaking given to you by the Company in regard to your reinstatement on demobilisation, and to let you know that we shall be pleased to welcome you back to your employment with the LMS Railway as soon as circumstances permit. It will facilitate arrangements in this direction if, when the time comes for your release from war service, you will communicate with ------"* *"Arrangements will then be made for you to be interviewed and for you to take up employment as soon as you are ready to do so. I should like to express, on behalf of the Company, their appreciation of the services you are performing and their best wishes for an early and safe return to them".* No such letter was apparently sent to the wages staff? It was, however arranged that all members of staff were interviewed and those with distinguished service or who had been commissioned be interviewed by Departmental Chief officer.

Fatalities.

The first fatality on the LMS Railway occurred at Shoeburyness during a heavy raid on the Thames Estuary on Sunday 18th August 1940 when, at 17.52, a bomb fell within a few yards of the signal box that was demolished, killing the signalman. During this same raid the homes of several members of the local staff sustained damage, but notwithstanding this fact, practically every member of the staff who was off duty reported at the station prepared to render any assistance possible in restoring traffic working. The indomitable courage and determination displayed on this occasion proved to be a forerunner of the splendid courage and resource shown by the staff throughout the raids, both in maintaining traffic movements whenever possible as well as attacking fires. There were instances where the permanent way staff commenced repairing damaged main lines with the aid of light from screened hand lamps only, while enemy planes could still be heard.

LMS casualties taken from the LMS Operational Manager's War Report dated March 1946 (TNA ref, Rail 418/200).

	1939		1940		1941		1942		1943		1944		1945		Total	
	K.	I.	K.	I.	K.	I.	K.	I.	K.	I.	K.	I.	K.	I.	K.	I.
Passengers	Nil		10	28	6	10	Nil		Nil		-	70	1	30	17	138
Rly. Staff on duty	Nil		27	281	21	125	-	13	Nil		1	122	2	26	51	567
Other Persons *	Nil		1	10	2	8	Nil		Nil		1	29	Nil		4	47
Total	**Nil**		**38**	**319**	**29**	**143**	**-**	**13**	**Nil**		**2**	**221**	**3**	**56**	**72**	**752**

Casualty figures vary dependant on the source both for civilians and railway staff as the listing below shows taken from B. W. L. Brooksbank's book – " Damage and Disruption on the railways of great Britain during World War Two" as below -

Analysis of Casualties due to Enemy Action on railway property, 1940-45 (By Category)														
	GWR		LMSR		LNER		SR		LPTB		Other		Totals	
	Killed	Injured	Killed	Injured	Killed	Injured	Killed	Injured	Killed	Injured	Killed	Injured	Killed	Injured
P'gers	32	108	17	130	10	240	39	464	20	123	-	5	118	1,070
Staff	52	241	48	533	115	702	130	796	40	111	7	27	392	2,410
Other Persons	42	157	4	7	45	133	131	412	165	177	-	3	387	899
Totals	126	506	69	680	170	1,075	300	1,672	225	411	7	35	897	4,397

(All Categories by Year)														
	GWR		LMSR		LNER		SR		LPTB		Other		Totals	
	Killed	Injured	Killed	Injured	Killed	Injured	Killed	Injured	Killed	Injured	Killed	Injured	Killed	Injured
1940	67	248	38	355	54	386	91	390	164	265	1	13	415	1,637
1941	40	199	28	132	71	261	89	192	60	112	5	21	293	917
1942	14	26	-	13	14	216	40	234	-	-	1	-	69	489
1943	3	5	-	-	11	39	17	89	-	-	-	-	31	1,080
1944	2	28	2	161	18	146	60	731	1	13	-	1	83	1,080
1945	-	-	1	39	2	27	3	36	-	21	-	-	6	123
Totals	126	506	69	680	170	1,075	300	1,672	225	411	7	35	897	4,379

The number of fatal accidents during the three years prior to the war averaged 30, but during the first five years of the war the average figure increased to 71, whilst in the sixth year of the war 50 fatalities were recorded, 27 of which occurred during the hours of darkness but were not entirely due to the limitation of lighting. Further analysis of the accidents during the sixth year of the war indicated that neither long hours of work or inexperience of duty contributed to fatal accidents to any serious extent.

Staff seconded to the Ministries.

As the LMS Railway possessed expertise in virtually every sphere of manufacturing it does not come a surprise that key LMS personnel were also requisitioned as 'consultants' for war-time production. These included Josiah Stamp (see chapter 5, E. J. H. Lemon (LMS Vice President, Operating and Commercial) who was seconded to the Air Ministry as

Director of Aircraft production for two years, following which he remained on a special body formed for production purposes. Willliam Stanier (CME) was lent to the Ministry of Production for special services that required a cessation of his work for the LMS. As Stanier was by this time 66 years old, it effectively retired him from the LMS service with the result that C. E. Fairburn was appointed LMS CME although Stanier did retain his full status as LMS CME. On 31st March 1944 Stanier was placed on superannuation but retained as consultant with a retainer of £575 per quarter. R. A. Riddles is well known for his design of the War Department 2-8-0 and 2-10-0 locomotives. There is one further employee who, whilst he was not directly seconded to any Ministry, deserves mentioning as being the LMS Vice President for Scientific Research etc. namely Sir Harold Hartley.

Sir Ernest J. H. Lemon OBE, MIME, Minst,T., was educated at the Heriot Watt College in Edinburgh before receiving his practical training in all departments of the Hyde Park Works of the North British Locomotive Co. He then moved to Brown Bros, Hydraulic Engineers in Edinburgh followed by a years Running Shed experience on the Highland Railway at Inverness. This was followed with a spell at Hurst Nelson & Co. Ltd. In 1911 he joined the Midland Railway as Chief Wagon Inspector, and was promoted to Works Manager in 1917 and Divisional Carriage and Wagon (C&W) Superintendent in 1923. January 1925 found him as Divisional C&W Superintendent (Earlestown and Newton Heath) with a salary of £2000pa and when R. W. Reid was made a Vice President in 1927 Lemon succeeded him as the LMS C&W Superintendent on 1st January, his salary being £3000 and later £4000. . He received his OBE at the end of WW1 in recognition of his work for the Government done in the C&W department at Derby. He was made a Vice President for Railway Traffic Operating and Commercial on 26th November 1931 on £5000 pa, increased to £6000 on 1st July 1935. On 1st July 1938 he was seconded to the Air Ministry at Government request as Director General of Production, Air Ministry and a member of the Air Council.
Whilst on secondment Ashton Davies took over his Vice Presidency... On 29th May 1941 Lemon's salary was £8000 and on 31st January 1943 he retired, having been on sick leave. He worked for the Air Ministry for 4½ years and it was thought better to retire than remain on leave. He was granted a pension of £3200 for life plus a lump sum totalling £16,000 on 1st February 1943.

Sir Harold Hartley CBE, MC, FRS was born in 1878 and educated at Dulwich College before proceeding to Oxford where he obtained a First Class in Natural Science. In 1901 he became a Fellow and Tutor of Balliol College, and subsequently Bedford Lecturer on Physical Chemistry. During WW1 he was Chemical Adviser to the 3rd Army and later Assistant Director of Gas Services eventually reaching the rank of Brigadier General. On 1st February he was appointed by the LMS as Vice President for New Works and Ancillary Undertakings on £5,000pa for five years. On 30th January 1936 Sir Harold was again appointed for a further five years as Vice President on the Executive of the Company and Director of Scientific Research on £5,500pa. The appointment was again renewed on 1st February 1930 at the same salary that was increased to £7500 on 29th May 1941. Sir Harold was elected Chairman of Railway Air Serviced Ltd in 1934. He retired and was succeeded by R. A. Riddles in 1946, to become the first Chairman of British European Airways. During the time he was with the LMS he also served as a Director of the Gas Light and Coke Company.
LMS Magazine.

Staff who had been Prisoners of War.

At the board meeting on 26th April 1945 the President recommended that authority to be given to re-equip out of the Company's funds, or out of the LMS Prisoners of War Comfort Fund, staff who were released prisoners of war who had lost all their personal belongings.

The 21st Anniversary of the LMS Celebrations.'

On the 1st January 1944 the British Main Line Railways came of age and on 22nd December 1943 a celebration luncheon was arranged by the Railway Companies Association at which the principal guest was Lord Leathers, the Minister of Transport. Twelve other Cabinet Ministers attended as well as other distinguished guests. Many congratulatory messages were received including one from

Sir William Arthur Stanier FRS, MIME, was born in Swindon on 27th May 1876 and joined the Great Western Railway as an apprentice in January 1892. Five years later saw him in the drawing office and in 1900 was appointed Inspector of Purchased Material. The following year he became Technical Inspector in the Swindon Running Shed and in 1903 he was appointed Assistant Locomotive Superintendent of the Swindon Division, later transferred in a similar capacity to the London Division. Two years later he returned to Swindon as Assistant in the Management of the Locomotive Works and a few months later he was appointed Divisional Locomotive and Carriage Superintendent, Swindon. In 1913 Stanier succeeded to the post of Senior Assistant Manager of the Locomotive Works that he held until becoming Works Manager in 1920. In 1922 he was Works Assistant and in 1923 Principal Assistant to the CME. On 1st January 1932 he replaced Sir Ernest Lemon as CME of the LMS Railway with a salary of £3325. In 1936 he was elected President of the Institution of Locomotive Engineers and on 1st July 1941 his salary was £4850. In 1941 he was seconded to the Railway Executive Committee and Ministry of Production. He received his Knighthood in the 1943 New Years Honour's list on 9th February and was placed on superannuation on 31st March 1944.although retained by the LMS as a consultant with a fee of £575 per quarter. C. E. Fairburn succeeded Stanier as CME with effect from 1st April 1944 on £5000pa. He passed away in Watford on 27th September 1965 aged 89.

LMS Magazine.

Robert Arthur Riddles CBE, MIME, MILoco.E., was born in Worthing on 23rd May, 1892 and entered Crewe Works as a premium apprentice in 1909. Following war service, in 1919 he was appointed Assistant to the Works Manager at Crewe and became Progress Assistant in 1925. In 1928 he was promoted to Assistant Works Superintendent at Derby and in 1931 transferred to Crewe in a similar capacity. On 1st July 1933 he was appointed Locomotive Assistant to the CME at Euston with a salary of £1500pa and became Principal Assistant in 1935, his salary increased to £2000. When the Electrical Department was amalgamated with the CME's Department in 1937 he was transferred to Scotland as Principal Assistant to the CME. on £2150. In 1943 he became Chief Stores Superintendent with a salary of £3000 gradually increased to £3750. That same year he was received by the King and invested with the Insignia of a Commander of the most Excellent Order of the British Empire. On 1st May 1946 he was made a Vice President on £4750pa., increasing to £6000 on 1st November 1947. On Nationalisation he was appointed as a member of the Railway Executive and retired on 30th September 1953.

TNA Rail 418/24

MANAGEMENT AND STAFF

Following the untimely death of Lord Stamp on 16th April 1941, Sir Thomas Royden became chairman of the LMS. He was born on May 22nd 1871 in Liverpool and educated at Yarlet Hall Preparatory School, Winchester College and Magdelen College, Oxford. He then went into the shipbuilding and ship owning firm of Thomas Royden and Sons. His association with Railways commenced when he was elected to the Board of the Lancashire & Yorkshire Railway, later the London & North Western Railway and finally the LMS on the 1923 grouping. Sir Thomas was also Chairman of the Cunard Steamship Company, the Anchor line and the America –Levant Line. He was also a Director of the Commonwealth and Dominion, the Anchor Brocklebank, and Santa Clare Steamship Companies, the Midland Bank, the Phoenix and Union Marine Insurance and other companies. He was a Magistrate and Deputy-Lieutenant of Cheshire and High Sheriff in 1917. He represented Bootle as an MP from 1918 to 1922 when he retired due to pressure of business. He was a member of the Order of Companions of Honour, a Commander of the Legion of Honour (France), and of St. Maurice and St. Lazarus (Italy). He died in his 90s. In his book "Man of the Rail", A. J. Pearson summed Royden up as "being a remarkable person in a negative kind of way. He was utterly undemonstrative with little sense of humour, and his approach to business was ice cold. He tackled difficult staff problems at the top with no sign of emotion. Men like Towle and Lemon left during his period of office and although both were considerable personalities Royden was not disturbed. He was not afraid of anyone or anything and Pearson never saw anyone more economical of effort and nervous energy".

LMS Magazine

the Prime Minister, Winston S. Churchill that read –

"It is not given to many organisations to celebrate their 21st Anniversary after they have achieved their centenary. Yet, because Parliament placed the Railways Act of 1921 on the Statute Book, the four British Main Line Railway Companies have been able to accomplish this most remarkable feat. On this occasion I would like to take the opportunity of expressing to the Railway Managements and to every Railway Employee the Nation's thanks for the highly efficient manner in which they met every demand made on them during the last four years of our desperate struggle with Nazi Germany. Throughout the period of the heavy German air raids on this country, the arteries of the nation, the Railways, with their extensive dock undertakings were subjected to intensive attacks. Yet the grim determination, unwavering courage and constant resourcefulness of the railwaymen of all ranks has enabled the results of the damage to be overcome very speedily and communications restored without delay. Thus, in spite of every enemy attack, the traffic has been kept moving and the great flow of munitions proceeds". "Results such as the Railways have achieved are only won by blood and sweat, and on behalf of the Nation I express gratitude to every railwayman who has participated in this great transport effort, which is contributing so largely towards final victory".

Winston S. Churchill.

The War is over.

The War ended in Europe on 8th.May 1945 and the first

Board meeting following victory was held on 24th.May when an address was sent to Their Majesties as follows – Board Minute 4937 with Sir Robert Burrows in the Chair, in the absence of The Hon. Lord Royden, C.H.

"May it please Your Majesty,

The Directors of the LMS present their humble duty and ask permission to express to you on behalf of the stockholders and servants of the LMS Railway their sincere and respectful congratulations on the unconditional surrender of the common enemy on the Continent.

It is a matter of pride to all associated with the LMS Railway that under Your Majesty's Ministries, the Company has played no small part in helping to bring about a victorious end of the war.

Vast numbers of troops, ammunition and stores have been conveyed under conditions of exceptional difficulty; workshops created for the manufacture of rolling stock have been adapted to the construction of aeroplanes and the accoutrements of war; a large number of staff has been called to the colours and many others have been rostered for duty where their technical qualifications have been needed for the prosecution of the war.

In all their arduous efforts the spirits of all ranks have been heartened by the presence among them of Your Majesty and The Queen on the many occasions on which you have travelled over the LMS Railway, and it is the sincere and devout wish of all that you may be long spared to rule over an empire of peace".

An appropriate military picture showing the last Chairman of the LMS Railway, Sir Robert Burrows, accepting plaques for Royal Scot 6135 "The East Lancashire Regiment" from the Colonel of the Regiment, Brigadier J. W. Pendlebury at Preston Station. The driver, Francis Fox and fireman Albert Cartmell were presented with silver tankards, both were from Preston MPD and both served with the Regiment in the 1914/18 war. Picture from August 1947 edition of "Carry On".

On the cessation of Hostilities, Lord Royden, Chairman and Sir William Wood, President, sent the following message to all LMS staff both at home and in the services ;-

"The complete surrender of Germany has brought to a glorious conclusion the resistance of the Allied nations to the attempts to bring under Nazi Fascist domination our liberty loving country. To that great effort and in preparation for it the whole LMSR organisation has played a really great part during the past six years. Alike in the movement of traffic on the line, at stations and offices, in the workshops, on the permanent way, in the special tasks of the steamship fleet, in the Home Guard, in resisting air attacks and overcoming their effects, and above all in direct service in the armed forces, we have every reason to be proud of the National Services of the LMSR staff. All difficulties have been successfully overcome, and every demand made upon us by the Government, whether for transport purposes or for the many direct war services, has been met in full. To you all, at home and overseas, we send you the thanks and best wishes of the Board and executive of the Company".

The war against Japan ended on 14th August 1945, but with no Board meeting until 27th September, this event surprisingly received no mention".

The Chief Operating Manager, Mr S. H. Fisher, had this to say as his concluding remarks in March 1946.

"After six years of conflict, victory came suddenly in 1945 and that year will remain memorable in that a mighty task was finished and a fresh venture commenced. When the year opened rockets were falling daily in London and the Southern Counties and the enemy was threatening to break through the Allied lines in the Ardennes. Five months later, Victory in Europe was complete, and during the process of transferring the whole weight of Allied power to the Far East, the use of the atomic bomb at Hiroshima on 6th August precipitated the end on the 14th August when the surrender of Japan marked the beginning of a new epoch in history. During the long period of the struggle the vicissitudes of War called for an unprecedented contribution to the common cause from all ranks of the railway staff, whose energy, courage and resource in meeting all demands for the transport with the traditional pride of LMS service, is

detailed in this and the previous volumes of the story of the Operating Department in the Second World War In looking back and reviewing the problems which had to be surmounted, confidence is gained that the same good spirit will solve the perplexing and urgent tasks of the post war world. The aftermath of war still imposes considerable strain upon LMS resources, whilst the travelling public, wearied by years of war work and irritated by the austerities of war-time, press for the standard of pre-war service to be re-established. The restoration of these facilities presents a formidable task and must of necessity be a gradual process coinciding with the liberation of experienced staff from the Forces and the availability of materials, to revitalise and recondition an undertaking after its long travail in the conflict. The need now is that the spirit displayed during the war years shall be introduced in the enterprise of Peace, that we may by arduous labour repair the ravages of war as quickly as possible and restore the operation of the LMS Railway to the high level it attained before War intervened. I know I can rely upon the energy and support of every member of my staff in this great effort and I, therefore, look forward to the future with confidence and high hopes".

S. H. Fisher

Chief Operating Manager

Victory Holidays and Staff Conditions.

At the end of the war the staff were given holidays as follows:-
8th May 1945, VE day (Victory in Europe) - one day.
9th May 1945, VE + 1 Day – one day.
A third days holiday was given at a later date.
15th August, VJ Day (Victory over Japan) – one day.
16th August, VJ + 1 Day – one day.
From 30th July 1945, agreement was reached with the Unions for improvements in the rates of pay for both salaried and conciliation staff with new composite rates, but the most outstanding improvement was the granting to Conciliation staff of two weeks' (12 days) holiday with pay (plus two public holidays) in lieu of the six days as previous.

The Post War Future.

One of the first casualties of the War was the cessation of

building work on the Rugby Locomotive Testing Station that was a joint LMS/LNER venture. The initiative originally came from Sir Nigel Gresley duly supported by Sir Harold Hartley, the LMS Vice President for Research and Development. The building and its foundations were designed in the LMS Civil Engineers Department with R. C. Bond being in charge of the project and the testing gear to be supplied by Heenan and Froude of Worcester. The Rugby test plant was eventually completed and opened by the Minister of Transport, Alfred Barnes on 29th October 1948.

As the war was nearing its end, attention turned to what was to happen next and to this end, at the Board meeting on 28th June 1945, a committee was formed who's remit was "to consider the future policy of the LMS Railway". This Committee consisted of Sir Robert Burrows, Sir Samuel Beale, Lt. Col. Francis M. G. Glyn and Sir Robert Greig. As stated, the pre-war depression had curtailed the maintenance of goods sheds, warehouses, loco sheds and other structures. It was calculated that about £30,000,000 would be required for renewals and repairs to return to the pre-war standard. A figure that did not take into account the damage due to enemy air attacks. In addition much war damage had only been temporarily repaired and only the minimum of painting carried out. All this added up to a massive backlog of work for the Railway. Running lines, bridges, sidings were indispensable to the working of the railway and were restored at the earliest possible moment. However in the case of the destruction of, or serious damage to passenger or goods station buildings, offices and warehouses, many could not be restored within a short period, or in many instances until after the war, in which case consideration had to be given having regard to the wider issues of the future. It was not sufficient to merely reproduce structures in their former positions or to the original design. Accordingly a War Damage Committee was appointed composed of representatives of the appropriate sections of the Operating, Commercial and Engineering departments, whose duty it was to recommend the extent to which damaged property should be restored, what alterations should be incorporated, and to determine the priority of restoration. In addition it was necessary to replace lost steamers and to refit others, all of which would take time. Carriages and wagons required replacing, all at a time when materials would still be difficult to obtain in the quantities required. It was considered that some £120,000,000 would be required over the five years from

This April 1947 edition No. 78 is printed on poor quality wartime paper and shows the diesel electric locomotives pioneered by the LMS and built at Derby. The first No.10000 was completed in December 1947 and ran as an LMS engine, whilst 10001 entered service in BR days. As stated in the text, had C. E. Fairburn not died prematurely diesel traction would surely have been more actively pursued. As it was steam construction continued by British railways for a further fourteen years with diesel traction being hastily introduced from the mid 50s onwards.

1945 to 1950 to return everything back to normal. All this against a background of what would be the post-war transport position, and what part would the railways play?. Nationalisation had always been associated with railways since WW1 and duly came about on 1st January 1948, but that's another story. One post-war opportunity that was missed was the pursuit of a standard steam locomotive fleet for British Railways instead of actively taking the LMS introduction of main line diesel electric locomotives to a conclusion, which is surprising as LMS engineers Bond and Riddles both become BR CME's. One thing that could be said with confidence was, that there would be no shortage of work for any of the Departments.

The LMS Staff Newspaper.

Carry On" issue No.1, October 1939 with the introduction by Lord Stamp.   *Courtesy Nelson Twells.*

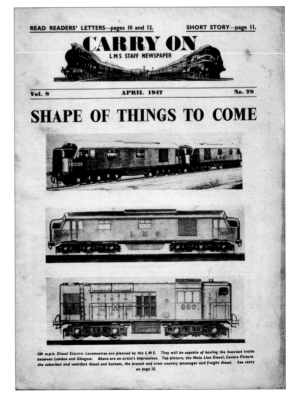

YOU—AND YOUR PAPER

"Carry On's" success has now become almost embarrassing, for the demand exceeds the number which can be printed. As soon as the paper position becomes easier, however, increased quantities will be available.

Meantime, will you please lend this copy to a friend?

Why is "Carry On" so popular among L M S men and women?

1. Because it is a staff newspaper — your newspaper.
2. Because it believes in good workmanship and good sportsmanship and is quick to record both.
3. Because it is keenly interested in you, whatever your job on the L M S, and whatever your interests outside working hours.

Like you "Carry On" is always striving to do its best, to improve its work and to give increasing "Service with a Smile." Therefore letters of criticism and of approval are equally welcome.

"Carry On" wants to hear from you. It wants to print your railway stories and interesting news about your work, your hobbies and your sports. As you read through this copy you surely will be reminded of something you know which would be of interest to L M S men and women far away up the line.

And so, whenever you have anything to say, please write. A swollen postbag will not give "Carry On" a swollen head. More and more letters will simply mean more and more "Carry On" items of interest for everybody on the L M S.

The Editor.

ROOM 400, EUSTON HOUSE, L.

Left - Quite clearly "Carry On" was a great success as paper rationing did not allow enough copies to be printed for all the staff, and this almost two years after the war was won.

Bottom right - With effect from the July or August, the "Carry On" magazine reverted to a coloured cover (this one was in blue) and slightly better paper.

Bottom left - Let the ladies have the last word seen here transferring petrol jerry cans from lorry to railway wagon.

British Rail

From 1924 the Company issued a monthly staff publication "LMS Magazine" that continued until September 1939, when, with the October issue it was renamed "Carry On". This continued into the British Railways era, terminating with issue 110 in December 1949. With 123 months covering the time from September 1939 to December 1949, thirteen months must have gone by with no issue.

The LMS also issued other staff publications – "Quota News" published by the Chief Commercial Manager and "On Time" published by the Chief Operating Manager both of which were discontinued.

CARRY ON
LMS STAFF NEWS MAGAZINE

Vol. 8   AUGUST 1947   No 82

Mr. T. H. Moffat, recently appointed Acting Chief Officer for Scotland on the retirement of Major Malcolm Spier, received his early training in the Accountants Department of the former Caledonian Railway.

Mr. Moffat's appointment is a source of gratification to L.M.S. Scottish staff and Chiefs of Industry and Traders throughout Scotland. He is an ardent follower of Ambulance work—see page 3.

And finally – the LMS produced its very own WW2 publication "The LMS at War" detailing its many achievements.

April, 1947   "CARRY ON"

WHAT <u>YOU</u> DID

SEND FOR THIS BOOK NOW— OR YOU'LL BE TOO LATE

A 5/- HISTORY FOR 3/6

Afar off, beyond the fields of ripening corn, an express train stole swiftly across the horizen, wearing, against a sky of peerless blue, a head-dress of billowing smoke as gay as the white plumes of Navarre.

No sound disturbed that hushed and sunny forenoon of September 3rd, 1939. Yet that distant train, like hundreds of others at that moment, was loaded with people whose hearts were heavy with foreboding. Then, suddenly, the breathless air was rent by the siren's wail of woe — and Britain was at war.

Everyone knew now that bitter years of struggle lay ahead. Everyone knew, too, that Britain had at least one ready-to-hand mechanical advantage over all — the finest railways in the world manned by staff highly skilled in the business of transport.

That white-plumed train, speeding along so confidently was indeed re-assuring — but would the railwaymen and women of Britain prevail against the unknown trials and dangers which were to come ?

The next six years told a story of L M S transport which far transcended, in terms of human effort and mechanical skill, any that had gone before. That story has been recorded by the well-known author, George C. Nash in a book "The L M S at War." It is a record of the ordeals and sacrifices which you had to face and of the way a traffic system, designed for peace, was swiftly turned to the grimmer purpose of war.

This gripping 88 page story published at 5/- is available to all L M S staff at the reduced price of 3/6d, provided the coupon on this page accompanies your remittance.

Already over 3,000 L M S men and women have received this book at the reduced price by sending in the application form which appeared in a previous issue of " Carry On." If you were not one of those fortunates, here is your chance, while copies are still available. Complete the order form below, now.

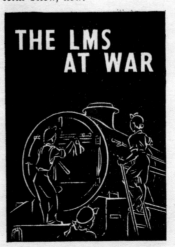

Dust cover of Book.

ORDER FORM
A 5/- BOOK FOR 3/6

Please send me, post free, ...
copy/copies
of the book, " The L M S at War " for
which I enclose P.O. No. ....

value...... ... .
Name (in caps)

....

Address

....

....

To Editor " Carry On," Room 400,
Euston House, I.
(P.O. to be made payable to LMS Railway and crossed)

Acknowledgements and Bibliography

The importance of attending shows such as the Warley Model Railway Exhibition at the NEC is made all the more worth while when it leads to a member of the public providing information that leads to something important. In this case to a report written by the LMS Assistant Chief Civil Engineer, F. E. W. Cox, dealing with the Civil Engineer's preparation for WW2, which as far as can be ascertained is not in the National Archive. This report reminded me that I also had similar reports prepared by the LMS Operating Department and also the Signal and Telegraph Engineer. It was therefore obvious that to put all three together would give an official commentary on the LMS Railway in wartime. My thanks go to Kevin Robertson of Noodle Books for allowing reference to B. W. L. Brooksbank's unpublished work "Damage and Disruption on the Railways of Great Britain during World War Two" and for supplying many of the photographs used in this work.

Other books referred to were:-

The LMS Operating Manager's War Reports, 1939 to 1945, TNA Rail 418/197 to 201.
The LMS Civil Engineer's War Report, 1939 to 1945.
The LMS Signal and Telegraph Engineer's Report to 1944.
Damage & Disruption on the Railways of Great Britain during World War Two, by B. W. L. Brooksbank.
Railwaywomen, by Helena Wojtczakand.
War Department Locomotives, by R. Tourret.
Middle East Railways, by the Continental Railway Circle.
LMS at War, by C. G. Nash.
Locomotive Profile series by Wild Swan,

The LMS Board Minutes, TNA Rail 418 series.
Signal Failure, by David Wragg.
The Railway Gazette.
Man of the Rail, by A. J. Pearson.

Alan Fozard and Juan Houston for providing the LMS Chief Civil Engineer's Report.

In addition many others have provided information, including the late W. J. Sadler and Roy Anderson,

Vic. Phillips, Mike King, Tony Graham,

Reg. Instone and Mike Addison of the Signalling Record Society.

LMS Society colleagues –David Hunt, John Jennison, Peter Tatlow, Nelson Twells.

Michael Byng with particular regard to financial matters in Chapter 5.

Also Trevor Moseley and Bob Essery for constantly checking the manuscript.

Sandra Warburton and David Butcher for their painstaking proof reading.

And finally thanks must also go to "my best friend" Pam for the endless supply of cocoa, and not the least checking the vast amount of dates and

Appendices

Appendix A - Lines blocked by enemy action in the London area from August to November 1940 as extracted from TNA Rail 418/197.

Wembley to Euston				
1940 September	Location	Lines Blocked	Days	Hours
9th	Euston	Up & down fast Up & down slow		2 2
12th	Camden	Up & down fast	1	12
12th	Willesden	Up & down fast		3
14th	Chalk Farm	Up & down electric		8
22nd	Camden	Up & down fast Up & down slow		3 3
26th	Camden	Up & down fast Up & down slow		2.5 2.5
27th	Chalk Farm	Up fast Down fast Up slow Down slow		11 6.5 11.5 6.5
29th	Harlesden	Up & down electric	7	17
29th	Willesden	Up & down fast		4
October				
2nd	Willesden (New)	Up and down electric		5
8th	Kilburn (High Road)	Up & down fast Up & down slow		21 15.5
12th	Kensal Green	Up electric	14	15
15th	Queen's park	Up & down fast Down slow	4	21 18
15th	Queen's Park	Up electric Down electric	5 1	8.5 15
November				
8th	Queen's Park	Up electric	3	14.5
7th	Kensal Green	Up & down slow	14	1
16th	Wembley	Up slow Down slow		10 11
18th	Wembley	Up & down fast Up & down slow		8.5 2
23rd	Willesden	Up fast Down fast Up slow Down slow		9.5 1 1 10

North London Section
Willesden to Broad Street via Hampstead Heath,
including the short section from Chalk Farm to Camden Town

1940 September	Location	Lines Blocked	Days	Hours
8th	Between Dalston Junc. and Haggerton	No.1 up & down No.2 ditto		15 3.5
9th	Broad St.	No.1 up & down No.2 ditto		8 8
13th	Canonbury	Up & down		3
18th	Dalston Junc,	Up & down		11
18th	Broad Street	No.1 up & down No.2 ditto		9.5 9.5
19th	Between Camden Town And Chalk Farm	Up & down		3
21st	Dalston	No. 1 up & down No.2 ditto		5.5 5.5
22nd	Haggerston	No. 1 up & Down No.2 ditto		15 11
24th	Camden Town	Up & down		4.5
26th	Camden Town	Up Down		13 16.5
26th	Chalk Farm	Up Down		14.5 17.5
27th	Camden Town	Up & down		10.5
27th	Broad Street	No.1 up & down No.2 up No.2 down		2 9.5 15.5
27th	Brondesbury	Up & down		1.5
October				
1st	Finchley Road	Up Down	103 3	8 22
2nd	Between Dalston and Canonbury	No. 1 up & down No.2 ditto		0.5 14.5
9th	Willesden	Up goods Down goods	1 1	5.5 11
10th	Willesden	Up goods	8	14
13th	Dalston Junc.	No.1 up & down No.2 up & down	1 7	3 22
13th	Shoreditch	No. 1 up & down No.2 up No.2 down	488 12 1	18 7 3
13th	Hampstead Heath	Up Down	20 3	20 19.5
14th	Highbury	No.2 up & down		13.5
14th	Broad Street	No.1 up & down No.2 ditto	487 27	10 18
15th	Camden Town	No.1 up & down		10.5 10.5
15th	Camden Town	Up and down		4.5
15th	Chalk Farm	Up Down	4 2	21.5 14.5
19th	Canonbury	No.1 up No.1 down No.2 up & down	11 5	12.5 20.5 20.5
19th	Hampstead Heath	Down		18

23rd	Camden Town	No.1 up	7	14.5
		No.1 down		20.5
		No.2 up		20.5
		No.2 down	1	20.5
25th	Haggerston	No.1 up & down	476	10
		No.2 up	7	12
		No.2 down	8	`12
November				
7th	Camden Town	Down	7	1
8th	Dalston Junc	No.1 up & down	5	19
		No.2 up & down		1.5
15th	West End Lane	Up		17.5
16th	Willesden	Up & down High Level goods.		15.5
		Up & down City Goods		12.5
16th	Kensal Rise	Up & down		15.5
16th	Gospel Oak	Up & down		12

North London Section - Dalston to Poplar				
1940 September	**Location**	**Lines Blocked**	**Days**	**Hours**
7th	Bow (Devons Road)	Up & down	1	2
9th	Homerton	Up & down		3.5
16th	Victoria Park	Up & down		13
18th	Bow	Up & down	3	5.5
20th	Old Ford	Up		11.5
		Down		10.5
23rd	Bow	Up & down		11
October				
13th	Dalston Junc.	Up & down	1	21
25th	Bow	Up & down	1	1.5
31st	Dalston Junc.	Up & down		15

Hendon to St. Pancras.				
1940 September	**Location**	**Lines Blocked**	**Days**	**Hours**
8th	St. Pancras	Up & down fast		21
		Up & down slow		21
		Up goods		9
		Down goods		6
20th	Hendon	Up & down slow		23.5
21st	Hendon	Up & down goods		8
26th	Cricklewood	Up & down fast		2
		Up & down slow		2.5
		Up & down goods		2.5
		No.2 up goods		9
27th	Cricklewood	Up fast	4	17
		Down fast	2	17.5
		Up slow	1	12.5
		Down slow	4	16
		Up goods	1	12.5
27th	Kentish Town	Up & down goods		19
28th	Kentish Town	Up & down fast		2.5
		Up & down slow		2.5
		Up & down goods		2.5
October				
2nd	Kentish Town	Up goods		3
		Down goods		2
3rd	Cricklewood	Down fast		1.5
5th	Hendon	Up fast		2.5
		Down fast		2
		Up & down goods		2

			Days	Hours
10th	Hendon	Up fast		13.5
		Down fast		17.5
10th	Kentish Town	Up & down slow		10.5
		Up goods		17.5
		Down goods		14
15th	Kentish Town (Kings Cross Tunnel)	Up & down	4	15.5
15th	Kentish Town	Up main		5.5
		Down main		1.5
15th	Kentish Town	Up main		14
		Down main		11.5
15th	Cricklewood	Up fast		13
		Down fast		14.5
		Up slow		15.5
		Down slow		16.5
		No.2 up goods		9.5
23rd	Kentish Town	Up & down fast		22
November				
7th	St. Pancras Station	Nos 1,2,& 3 Platform lines	3	9

Kentish Town to Leyton				
1940 September	**Location**	**Lines Blocked**	**Days**	**Hours**
10th	Junction Road	Up		12
		Down		15
14th	Kentish Town	Up & down		19
19th	Leyton	Up		14
		Down	39	15.5
19th	Leyton	Up		8
16th	Kentish Town	Up	1	17.5
28th	Upper Holloway	Up & down		18
October				
2nd	Crouch Hill	Up & down		7
5th	Upper Holloway	Down		12.5
10th	Kentish Town	Up & down		10.5
10th	St. Anne's Road	Up & down		10.5
12th	Kentish Town	Up & down goods	21	15
19th	Upper Holloway	Up	2	16.5
		Down	5	14
22nd	Junction Road	Up & down	1	2.5
21st	Harringay Park	Up	2	16.5
		Down		12

Acton Branch (Cricklewood to Acton).				
1940 September	**Place**	**Lines Blocked**	**Days**	**Hours**
16th	Harlesden	Up & down	2	15.5
25th	Near Acton Wells Junc.	Up & down		4
27th	Acton Branch	Up	2	16
		Down	2	6.5
October				
4th	Acton Branch	Up & down		10
10th	Dudding Hill	Up	16	22.5
		Down		22

Appendix B – Lines blocked by enemy action – Birmingham, Coventry and Wolverhampton Area from August to November 1940.

Main line – Rugby to Wolverhampton				
1940 September	Location	Lines Blocked	Days	Hours
12th	Coventry	Up & down		3
15th	Coventry	Down		6
16th	Birmingham (New St.)	Up & down		12
24th	Ditto	Up & down		18
25th	Birmingham (Curzon St.)	Up & down		1
26th	Monument Lane	Up & down		11
26th	Birmingham (New St.)	Up & down		19.5
28th	Ditto	Up & down		3.5
November				
1st	Ditto	Up & down		3
14th	Coventry	Up	1	11.5
		Down	1	20
14th	Brandon & Wolston	Up & down		13
14th	Coventry	Down	1	20
19th	Adderley Park	Up & down		21.5
19th	Birmingham (New St.)	Up & down		19.5
19th	Spon Lane	Up	241	21
		Down	39	12
19th	Winson Green	Up fast		17
		Down fast		7.5
		Up slow		11
		Down slow		18
22nd	Stechford	Up & down main		15.5
23rd	Marston Green	Up & down		2.5
23rd	Birmingham (New St.)	Up & down	8	23
23rd	Winson Green	Up & down		1

Birmingham To Wolverhampton via Aston or Soho Road and Bescot.				
1940 September	Location	Lines Blocked	Days	Hours
17th	Aston	Up & down		4
19th	Birmingham (New St.)	Up		3.5
		Down		1.5
19th	Aston	Up & down		1
21st	Wittton	Up & down	1	17
November				
1st	Vauxhall	Up main		10.5
		Down main		14
		Up & down goods		3
19th	Vauxhall	Up & down main		16
		Up goods	11	19.5
		Down goods	18	19.5
20th	Aston	Up		16.5
		Down		13.5
21st	Vauxhall	Up & down fast	20	12.5
22nd	Stechford	Up & down Aston		15.5
23rd	Vauxhall	Up & down fast	2	9
		Up & down slow	2	9

Other Sections of Line				
1940 **August**	**Location**	**Lines Blocked**	**Days**	**Hours**
26th	Aston (Windsor St. Branch)	Down goods		4
27th	Cosford Green	Up goods Down goods		12.5 19
27th	Between Foleshill and Coundon Road	Up Down		4 5.5
October				
12th	Coventry (Leamington Branch)	Single		5
12th	Foleshill	Up & down	2	13
12th	Coventry	Up & down branch		3
15th	Wylde Green	Up Down		17 18.5
21st	Bell green	Up goods Down goods		12 15.5
25th	Wednesbury	Down Princes End Branch		1.5 1.5
25th	Gravelly Hill	Up & down		2
29th	Foleshill	Up & down		1.5
November				
14th	Foleshill (south of station)	Up & down	10	6.5
14th	Foleshill (north of station)	Up & down	3	10
14th	Coundon Road	Up & down	12	17.5
14th	Coventry	Up Leamington Down Leamington	1 2	19 11
14th	Bell Green	Up & down goods	7	10.5
20th	Gravelly Hill	Up & down		13.5

Main Line - Derby to Gloucester				
1940 **August**	**Location**	**Lines Blocked**	**Days**	**Hours**
24th	Castle Bromwich	Up goods Down goods		6 5.5
25th	Castle Bromwich	Up & down main		1
October				
16th	Birmingham	Up & down		12
17th	Saltley	Up main Down main	4 5	16.5 17
24th	Birmingham (New St.)	Up & down		5
25th	Ditto	Up & down		1
26th	Ditto	Up & down		5.5
26th	Somerset Road	Up & down		1.5
28th	Birmingham (New St.)	Up & down		6
November				
1st	Ditto	Up & down		3
19th	Ditto	Up & down		18.5
23rd	Ditto	Up & down		16
23rd	Saltley	Up main		13.5
23rd	Coleshill	Up & down		7.5
22nd	Birmingham (New St.)	Up & down		15.5
23rd	Selly Oak	Up & down		10.5

Birmingham Avoiding Line via Kings Heath.				
1940 **August**	**Place**	**Lines Blocked**	**Days**	**Hours**
27th	Camp Hill	Up Down		10.5 12
October				
15th	Brighton Road	Up Down		9 16
17th	Saltley	Up Camp Hill	9	18
18th	Camp Hill	Up & down		2.5
27th	Kings Heath	Up & down		0.5
November				
23rd	Saltley	Up & Down Camp Hill		13.5
23rd	Kings heath	Up Camp Hill Down Camphill	1	13.5 15

Line Blockages by Enemy Action 1939 to 1945.								
	1939	1940	1941	1942	1943	1944	1945	Total
No. of occasions damage was caused	Nil	1,140	576	70	24	224	29	2,063
No. of occasions running lines were obstructed	Nil	447	204	26	5	35	8	725
No. of hours lines were blocked	Nil	43,999	92,133	6,497	99	638	98	143,464

Appendix C - Air Raid Warnings – Central London Area 1939 to 1945.

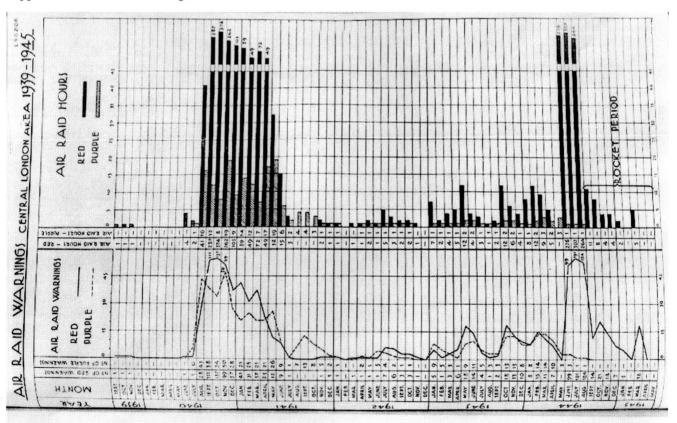

Wartime LMS Index

INDEX